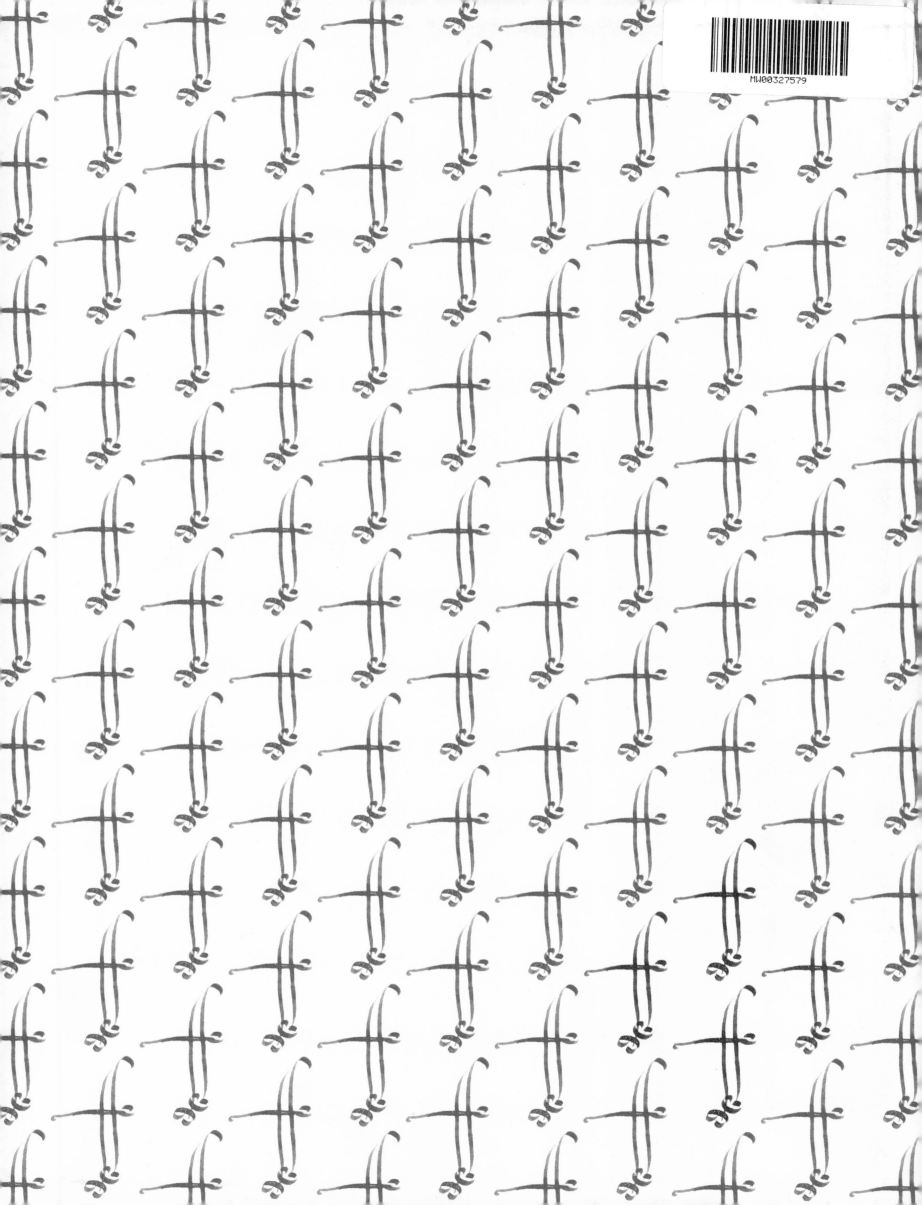

Published in partnership
with the

**LIBRARY OF
CONGRESS**

"…by divine will, I have put another
world under the sovereignty
of the king and queen, our lords.
Consequently, Spain, once considered poor,
is now the richest."

– CHRISTOPHER COLUMBUS

CHRISTOPHER COLUMBUS
Book of Privileges

CHRISTOPHER COLUMBUS
Book of Privileges

1502

The claiming of a New World

LIBRARY OF CONGRESS

John W. Hessler

Daniel De Simone   Chet Van Duzer

Published by Levenger Press
420 South Congress Avenue
Delray Beach, Florida 33445 USA
www.levengerpress.com

in association with the
Library of Congress
Washington, D.C. 20540-4980

First Edition 2014

The facsimile of this version of Christopher Columbus's *Book of Privileges* (the Washington Codex) is from the original housed in the Library of Congress.

Illustrations

Van Duzer essay, pages 1-26

Fig. 1. The moment of contact between Columbus and natives of the New World. Rare Book and Special Collections Division, Library of Congress.

Fig. 2. An anonymous manuscript map of Hispaniola made in about 1516. In Pietro Martire d'Anghiera, *De orbe novo decades* (Alcalá: Arnaldi Guillemi, 1516). Courtesy of Biblioteca Universitaria, Raro D.26, Bologna.

Fig. 3. The Terrestrial Paradise on the world map in the *Rudimentum novitiorum*. Reproduction by permission of the Buffalo & Erie County Public Library, Buffalo, New York.

Fig. 4. A statue of Columbus being taken back to Spain in chains after his Third Voyage. From William E. Curtis's *Columbus and the Discovery of America*, 1893?, Library of Congress.

Fig. 5. World map by Henricus Martellus, made in about 1491. Beinecke Rare Book and Manuscript Library, Yale. Art Store 1980.157.

Fig. 6. Detail of Martin Waldseemüller's *Carta marina* of 1516. Jay I. Kislak Collection, Geography and Map Division, Library of Congress.

Fig. 7. Map of the northern coast of Hispaniola, early 1493. Courtesy of the Fundación Casa de Alba, Palacio de Liria, Madrid.

Fig. 8. A map-like image of the islands of the Caribbean, with Columbus sailing before them. From *De insulis nuper in Mari Indico repertis* (Basel, 1494). Thacher Collection, Rare Book and Special Collections Division, Library of Congress.

Fig. 9. Construction of the settlement of La Navidad on Hispaniola. From *De insulis nuper in Mari Indico repertis* (Basel, 1494). Thacher Collection, Rare Book and Special Collections Division, Library of Congress.

Figs. 10 and 11. Manuscript nautical chart by Juan de la Cosa, 1500. Courtesy of the Museo Naval Madrid, shelfmark MN 257.

Figs. 12 and 13. Anonymous nautical chart, 1502. Courtesy of the Biblioteca Estense Universitaria Modena, shelfmark C. G. A. 2.

Fig. 14. Sketch map made by Alessandro Zorzi in the first quarter of the sixteenth century. Courtesy of Biblioteca Nazionale Centrale, Florence, Banco Rari 234, f. 60v, F.

Fig. 15. World map of 1507 by Martin Waldseemüller. Geography and Map Division, Library of Congress.

Fig. 16. Hand-colored exemplar of the world map by Johannes Ruysch from the 1508 Rome edition of Ptolemy's *Geography*. Geography and Map Division, Library of Congress.

Fig. 17. Hand-painted exemplar of the world map by Francesco Rosselli, c. 1508. Courtesy of the Ratsschulbibliothek , Zwickau, Germany.

Fig. 18. Martin Waldseemüller's *Carta marina* of 1516. Jay I. Kislak Collection, Geography and Map Division, Library of Congress.

Illustration credits continued on page 173

Library of Congress Cataloging-in-Publication Data

Hessler, John W.
  Christopher Columbus Book of privileges : 1502, the claiming of a new world / John W. Hessler, Daniel De Simone, Chet Van Duzer. -- First edition.
      pages cm
  Summary: "An interpretive examination of the legal documents that granted Columbus rights in and to the New World, with a facsimile of the original copy of the Book of Privileges that is housed in the Library of Congress"--Provided by publisher.
   ISBN 978-1-929154-53-1
  1. Columbus, Christopher. Codex diplomaticus. 2. America--Discovery and exploration--Spanish--Sources. 3. Spain--History--Ferdinand and Isabella, 1479-1516--Sources. 4. Spain--Charters, grants, privileges. I. De Simone, Daniel. II. Van Duzer, Chet A., 1966- III. Columbus, Christopher. Codex diplomaticus. IV. Title.
   E114.H47 2014
   970.01'5092--dc23
                                    2014014950

Printed on paper from a renewable and sustainable source, using soy-blended inks. Manufactured by Worzalla, an environmentally responsible printer.

Cover and book design by Danielle Furci
Mim Harrison, Editor

Printed in the USA

Contents

PROLOGUE

An Audacious Blessing

his is a story of exploration, of bravery, of greed, of law, of the possibility of vast riches, of a high-stakes gambit played out in newly discovered worlds for historical immortality. It is the story of a business contract between a visionary explorer and the colonial power of one of the most influential husband and wife monarchs ever to rule, and who, during the late fifteenth and early sixteenth centuries, exerted their reign over a substantial portion of the known world. It is a story that will be told not through the narrative of an adventure on the high seas, nor with firsthand reflections on the events that took place on some distant and bloody battlefield, but rather, on the pages of a simple collection of legal documents.

This is the story contained in one of the great treasures housed in the Library of Congress, a manuscript book of charters and privileges granted to Christopher Columbus by Ferdinand and Isabella of Spain during his voyages of discovery. These documents, which were some of Columbus's most valuable possessions, were at some time handed over by him to a scribe or legal notary, copied for safekeeping, and through that act preserved for history.

These charters and privileges have all the trappings of a set of dry legal documents written in the language of a Renaissance Spanish court. But they would inexorably change the history of Europe and of the Americas, eventually altering the lives of those peoples who had lived in Columbus's New World for many centuries before his coming. This single set of charters granted Columbus permission to sail, to conduct trade, and to colonize for Spain, and also included privileges from Pope Alexander VI. These not only allowed the Spanish Crown to claim the territory Columbus would discover, but also gave Spain the blessing of the Vatican to colonize any that might be purposefully, or accidentally, stumbled upon in the near future.

Columbus's *Book of Privileges* is composed of formal legal documents, not unlike those each of us today has had notarized and then squirreled away in some important place. But this collection of fewer than one hundred pages is different, for what it granted and contracted for would transform the face of the earth, and alter the fates, destinies, and futures of both the peoples of Europe and the great indigenous civilizations of the Aztecs, the Maya and the Inca. Here in Columbus's cartulary we have the blessings of popes, the laws of colonization, the contracts for profits won and losses to be borne, and the privileges granted to one man and to one country that would change the course of empires.

An illustration from the Genoa Codex of Columbus's **Book of Privileges,** *believed to depict a Native American on the left and Columbus on the right. It would make this the only known portrait of Columbus created during his lifetime.*

Geography

Chet Van Duzer

Columbus and the Nature of a New World

hen we think of Christopher Columbus early in the twenty-first century, two things likely come to mind. First, we inevitably imagine the thrill of the moment of discovery, the epoch-making sighting of land early on the morning of October 12, 1492. After two long months of sailing westward across the Atlantic, Columbus's men had spied birds on October 3 and 4, suggesting the proximity of land; but then, perhaps because of hopes inspired by the birds, there followed repeated false sightings of land. On October 10 Columbus averted an incipient mutiny on his flagship, the *Santa María*, by members of the crew who insisted that the ships should turn back before they went so far west as to render a return voyage impossible. Columbus mollified them by promising that if they did not find land within three days, they would indeed bear eastward back to Spain.

But on October 11, the sea offered many clear signs that land was close, for the crew of the *Niña* found a green branch with a flower, and the crew of the *Pinta* a terrestrial plant and wood that had been carved. That night Columbus ordered the ships to continue sailing west, rather than heaving-to for safety. At 10 pm, Columbus saw a mysterious light in the distance, like a candle rising and falling, and was convinced he had seen land, though in fact the ships were still far from shore.

At two o'clock on the morning of October 12, Rodrigo de Triana, a lookout on the *Pinta*, sees by the light of the moon two white cliffs and the dark outline of land between them, and cries out "*Tierra! Tierra!*" Daylight reveals the island that Columbus named San Salvador, in the Bahamas, and that afternoon the Admiral and men from his ships step ashore on the island, claim possession of it for the Spanish Crown, and interact peacefully with the Lucayan people who live there (fig. 1).[1]

If the moment of discovery is the first thing that comes to mind, the second is the horrific consequences that the arrival of Europeans wrought on the Native peoples of the Americas, the blame for which is often placed on the shoulders of Columbus. Whole peoples and cultures were wiped out by European diseases and campaigns of conquest.[2] Of the Taíno people, who lived on the Bahamas and the Antilles, including the island of Hispaniola, on which Columbus established a colony during the first two years of his Second Voyage, nothing remains today except a brief and incomplete account of their religion, written

Figure 1. The moment of contact between Columbus and peoples of the New World, depicted here on the island of Hispaniola, from the Basel 1494 edition of Columbus's account of his First Voyage, *De insulis in Mari Indico nuper inuentis* (*On the Recently Discovered Islands in the Indian Ocean*).

between 1495 and 1500, along with some archaeological artifacts.[3] Many other similar examples could be adduced. Across two continents, European powers killed Native leaders, destroyed cities, seized political control, suppressed

Native religions and cultures, and exploited Native labor. Europeans justified many of these deeds through depictions of Native peoples as barbarous heathens, cannibals, and monsters.[4]

This history is a thousand iterations, in different forms, of the Trail of Tears. Yet to heap the blame for these many misdeeds solely on Columbus,[5] to demonize him and therefore ignore his career, would be to lose out on the lessons that Columbus's experiences have to offer—not only about legal history, as John Hessler shows in his essay, but also about exploration and the difficulty of adapting one's world view to accommodate new information.

Columbus's arrival in the New World was one of the great turning points in the history of Western civilization. To understand the relationship of Columbus's *Book of Privileges* to his career as an explorer, we will visit a much less examined but nonetheless important part of his life. Accounts of Columbus's career tend to focus on his four voyages to the newly discovered lands to the west, but to appreciate the *Book of Privileges* and the light it can shed on Columbus's conception of the lands he had discovered, we must look at the time between two of his voyages, specifically the period from October 1500 to May 1502, between his Third and Fourth Voyages. But first, some background.

Columbus's Second Voyage,[6] which lasted from September 1493 to June 1496, was very different from his first. Instead of three ships, he commanded seventeen, and brought more than one thousand colonists to settle on the island of Hispaniola, which is today divided between the Dominican Republic and Haiti (fig. 2). Establishing and organizing a

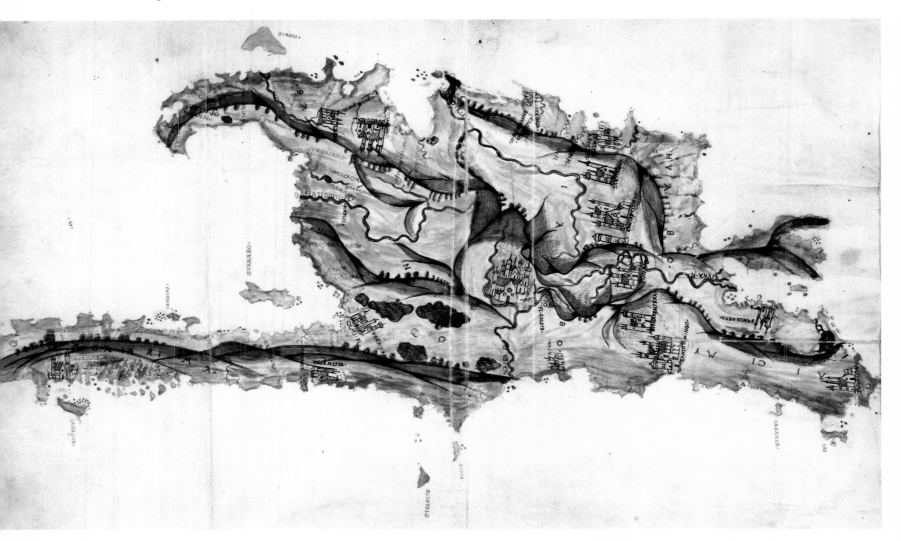

Figure 2. An anonymous manuscript map of Hispaniola, probably made between 1508 and 1516, shows the increasing colonization of the island at a later period.

settlement on the island was laborious, and some of the colonists instigated a rebellion, which Columbus crushed. Leaving the settlement under the command of his brother Diego, Columbus went exploring, eager to find the rich civilizations of mainland Asia. He tried to convince himself that Cuba was that mainland,[7] and returned to Hispaniola in September 1494 to take up his duties as governor. Columbus was a poor administrator, and the anger of the Spanish settlers toward him grew increasingly pronounced. To compound the problem, a *cacique*, or Native leader, named Guatiguaná organized a rebellion against the colonizers. Reports of the unrest on Hispaniola filtered back to King Ferdinand and Queen Isabella in Spain; when they sent a man to investigate, Columbus realized that he needed to return to Spain to tell his own version of events. The Second Voyage was far from successful: the colony was torn by strife and was generating little in the way of profit, Columbus still had not found the rich Asian civilizations that he was hoping to encounter and trade with, and his reputation at court was tarnished.

The Third Voyage,[8] which lasted from May 1498 to October 1500, had one bright spot, but was otherwise a grim affair. Six ships departed from Spain, three carrying supplies for the colonists on Hispaniola, while three others, under the command of Columbus, sought contact with the famous cities of Asia. Columbus took those three ships farther south than he had on his previous voyages and made landfall on an island he named Trinidad. Unbeknown to him, it was located just off the coast of South America. From the southwestern tip of Trinidad he headed north until he encountered land, which he assumed was an island, thus calling it Isla de Gracia. It was actually a peninsula in what is now northern Venezuela, and part of the continent of South America. On the morning of August 4, 1498, the thundering wave of a powerful tidal bore caught the ships near the strait between Trinidad and "Isla de Gracia," lifting them high and then dropping them again—something Columbus feared could have capsized the ships. On August 5, his men landed in a cove along the southern coast of this peninsula, the first time that a European had set foot on the Americas since the Vikings reached Newfoundland around the year 1000.

Sailing west in the hope of finding a way around the supposed island to the sea, the crew found the water first brackish and then fresh, and they spied four river mouths, those of the Rio Grande, spilling water into the gulf. So they turned back first to the east, then sailed north through the strait between Trinidad and "Isla de Gracia," again experiencing a powerful tidal bore, then west. The sight of the long coast of what is now northern Venezuela provided the last bit of evidence that sparked Columbus's realization that the land before him was not an island, but a continent. In a passage preserved by the sixteenth-century Spanish historian Bartolomé de las Casas, Columbus wrote to the king and queen:[9]

> I am convinced that this is a very large mainland, which has not been known until today, and I am led to this conclusion by the existence of the very large river and the freshwater sea....And if this is mainland, it is a wonderful thing and will be seen as such by all learned men, for such a large river empties here that it makes a freshwater sea which extends for forty-eight leagues.

Columbus then deduced from the beauty of the continent, and from the tremendous volume of fresh water flowing from it, that the Terrestrial Paradise must be located within it. This apparently strange theory made some sense in the context of late medieval geographical thought. Columbus thought he was in the eastern reaches of Asia, and the Terrestrial Paradise, or Garden of Eden, was believed to be in that same area.[10] Moreover, the fountain in the Garden of Eden was thought to be the source of the world's four largest rivers (Genesis 2:10-14), and Columbus had seen a large gulf of the sea filled with river water (fig. 3). The tidal bores had made a strong impression on him, for they persuaded him to believe not only that the largest source of fresh water in the world was nearby, but also that it was raised up on a stupendously large and broad mountain, down whose sides the water coursed.[11]

For Columbus, all of the signs indicated that after so many years of planning, seeking support, and sailing, he had finally found the mainland he had been searching for. The idea that he was near the Terrestrial Paradise must have been enormously exciting. But rather than stay and search out the Asian civilizations with which he hoped to trade, or learn

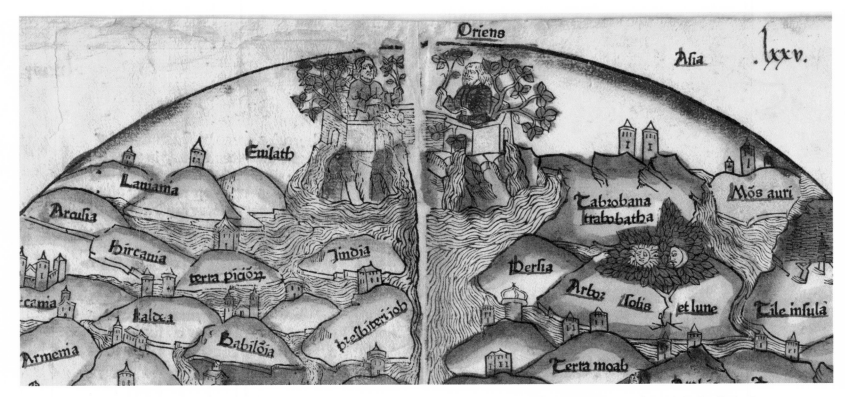

Figure 3. The Terrestrial Paradise on the world map in the *Rudimentum novitiorum* (*Handbook for Beginners*), published in Lübeck in 1475. Paradise is situated on a mountain at the extreme eastern edge of the world, and the four rivers of Paradise flow down into the water systems of the world. Within the walls of Paradise, Enoch and Elijah await the Second Coming of Christ.

more about the interior of the continent, or at least spend a few days collecting some of the pearls in the area, he set sail for Hispaniola, conscious of the need to bring the supplies in his ships' holds to the colonists there.

What would otherwise have been the transcendent exultation of finding the mainland was tempered by an illness that had struck Columbus, apparently a type of arthritis accompanied by an inflammation of his eyes.[12] And things only got worse. Christopher's brother Bartholomew had been left in charge of the colony on Hispaniola,[13] replacing Diego, and his administration had been brutal and disastrous. Francisco Roldán, a local administrator, had revolted against Bartholomew, and had drawn almost half of the colonists to his rival regime in the western part of the island. Columbus reached Hispaniola at the end of August 1498. After protracted negotiation, he was able to make peace with Roldán and bring him and his followers back to Santo Domingo. Before that had occurred, however, complaints about Bartholomew's administration, together with Columbus's own report of Roldán's revolt, reached the Spanish Crown, which sent Francisco de Bobadilla to investigate.[14]

The degree of harshness of the Columbus brothers' rule in Santo Domingo is unclear, as there are conflicting testimonies, but harsh it was, and demonstrated that they were ill-suited for governing.[15] When Bobadilla arrived in Santo Domingo on August 23, 1500, he quickly sized up the situation, took charge, and threw the Columbus brothers in jail one by one: Diego, Bartholomew, and Christopher. Within weeks, Christopher and Bartholomew, in chains, were set aboard a ship and sent back to Spain in disgrace (fig. 4).[16] Diego, also in chains, was sent on another ship soon thereafter. Thus ended Columbus's Third Voyage: in a return to Spain not as Admiral of the Ocean Sea and Viceroy and Governor of the Indies, but rather as a prisoner, and very far indeed from the Terrestrial Paradise.

The trip back to Spain was relatively quick, but even so offered Columbus a few weeks for reflection. When he and his brothers told their side of the story to the sovereigns, Ferdinand and Isabella promised justice and a restitution of the rights and offices that Columbus had negotiated with them, but months passed with no redress. Columbus realized that his political position needed reinforcement. It was during this period, after reflecting on the nature of his discoveries, that he compiled his *Book of Privileges*, and also his *Book of Prophecies*.

Earlier experiences had taught Columbus the importance of safeguarding documents. During his return from his First Voyage in 1493, just a few days before he reached the Azores, on February 13 and 14 his ships were overtaken by a violent storm. All of the men feared death, and vows were made to perform pilgrimages if they were delivered from the storm. Columbus was horrified by the thought that he might perish without having brought the news of his discoveries to Ferdinand and Isabella, so he took a piece of parchment, wrote on it the basic facts of his voyage and what he had found, with a note asking whoever found it to bear it to the king and queen of Spain, wrapped it in a wax cloth, placed it in a barrel, and threw it overboard.[17]

Columbus had been in the habit of carrying with him on his voyages his "privileges," copies of the agreements that he had negotiated with the Spanish Crown that guaranteed him the title Admiral of the Ocean Sea and Viceroy of the Indies, a share of the profits from any lands he discovered, and so forth. In addition to the storm on his First Voyage, other experiences made him realize that these documents needed safeguarding. During his Second Voyage, in June 1495, a hurricane destroyed three of his four ships while they were at harbor at Hispaniola. In December of that year, Columbus had Rodrigo Pérez, the clerk of the struggling colony of La Isabella on Hispaniola, make a copy of the agreement he had signed with the Spanish Crown in April 1492. Columbus made the request, Pérez explained, because "it might happen that the ship or ships

Figure 4. A statue of Columbus being taken back to Spain in chains at the end of his Third Voyage because of misdeeds in his administration of the colony on Hispaniola. The statue was made by the sculptor Venanci Vallmitjana y Barbany (1826-1919) and presented to the Real Sociedad Económica de la Havana (Cuba) in 1881.

on which these documents were traveling could be lost."[18] And on March 15, 1498, just before his Third Voyage, Columbus had copies of some of his privileges made by a notary, because (in Columbus's words, written by the notary):[19]

> ...he was worried that, if he had to carry them by sea to the Indies and elsewhere, they could be damaged by fire, water, other accidents, or just by being carried around, with the result that his rights would perish, and Their Highnesses would be ill served, because these privileges, writs, and decrees pertain to the service of Their Highnesses.

These privileges, these documents, represented and guaranteed all of the rewards that Columbus would obtain from his discoveries, and the rewards that his descendants would obtain as well. Following his Third Voyage, he realized that he had to be concerned not just about the documents' survival aboard ship, but also about their force in the political arena. And so before his Fourth Voyage, on which he departed on May 11, 1502, Columbus brought to a culmination his project of commissioning copies of his privileges, and had four bound copies of them created, which he called his *Libro de privilegios*, or *Book of Privileges*.[20] As Columbus obtained new documents from the Spanish Crown related to his Fourth Voyage, he had copies of them added to the book.

Following his Third Voyage, Columbus also wrote about the significance of what he had accomplished and still hoped to accomplish through his voyages in a manuscript titled the *Libro de las profecías*, or *Book of Prophecies*. Columbus had always thought of himself as a man of destiny, and in annotations he made in one of his books before his First Voyage, there are hints of the ideas contained in the *Book of Prophecies*.[21] But it is difficult to doubt that it was the combination of his discovery of the mainland and the humiliation of being shipped home in chains that caused him to write down his beliefs in greater detail following his Third Voyage. It is also difficult to think that these experiences did not radicalize Columbus's ideas about his mission. For example, one can hardly imagine Columbus saying before or even after his First Voyage—as he does in the *Book of Prophecies*—"I have already said that for the voyage to the Indies neither intelligence nor mathematics nor world maps were of any use to me; it was the fulfillment of Isaiah's prophecy."[22] It was during this same time, between his Third and Fourth Voyages, that Columbus started consistently adding a line to his unique and much-discussed sigil, or signature, that proclaimed himself *Christoferens*, or bearer of Christ (to the newly discovered lands), turning his name into a proclamation of what he saw as his destiny.[23]

> Columbus believed that he was playing a pivotal role in preparing the world for the Second Coming, and that the end of the world would come in just 155 years from 1501.

The *Book of Prophecies* was largely ignored by early scholars studying Columbus, who dismissed it as the work of a man caught up in a mania,[24] but in fact it is very revealing of his ideas about his mission and discoveries. In recent years it has received considerable scholarly scrutiny and has been translated into English repeatedly.[25] The unique manuscript that has come down to us was written by multiple hands, including those of Columbus himself, his son Ferdinand, Gaspar Corricio (a Carthusian monk who befriended Columbus), and an anonymous scribe.[26] It consists of a prefatory letter written by Columbus to Ferdinand and Isabella, followed by a large collection of quotations from the Bible, classical authors, and medieval works of theology and geography[27]—notes that were awaiting further development on the recovery of the Holy Land by Christians through a new crusade, the bringing of the Gospel to the most distant regions of the earth, and the chronology of the world, including the Apocalypse. According to many medieval theologians, before the Second Coming of Christ could take place, Jerusalem had to be in Christian hands, and the Gospel had to be carried to all parts of the earth.[28] Columbus believed that he was playing a pivotal role in preparing the world for the Second Coming: he believed that the income from his discoveries would help finance a new crusade to take Jerusalem; that he was bringing the Gospel to the last and most distant parts of the world that it had not yet reached—and that the end of the world would come in just 155 years from 1501.[29]

Two words that come to mind upon understanding Columbus's beliefs are "arrogance" and "megalomania," and there is some justice in ascribing both to him. It is worth bearing in mind, though, that it was exactly the same striking boldness and capacity for looking at things on a global scale that led him to conceive the idea of sailing across the Atlantic to reach Asia in the first place, and to discover new lands in the West.

The Meaning of Discovery, and the Nature of the New World

The idea of discovery is not as simple as it might seem at first brush, particularly in the case of the New World—a fact that becomes clear in examining some of the earliest documents relating to Columbus's voyages. On April 17, 1492, a few months before he set sail on his First Voyage, Columbus reached agreements with Ferdinand and Isabella that set ground rules regarding anything that Columbus found. The agreements were finalized in Santa Fe, Spain, and are therefore called the Santa Fe Capitulations, the word "capitulations" having nothing to do with surrender, but referring rather to an enumeration of terms agreed upon, along the lines of the modern word "recapitulation." A copy of this document is included in Columbus's *Book of Privileges*; part of the agreement states:[30]

> First, Your Highnesses, as the lords you are of the Ocean Seas, appoint Sir Christopher Columbus from now on as your admiral on all those islands and mainland discovered or acquired by his command and expertise in the Ocean Seas during his lifetime…. Also, Your Highnesses appoint Sir Christopher your viceroy and governor general in all those islands and any mainland and islands that he may discover and acquire in the seas.

Columbus was hoping to reach Japan and mainland Asia, which he had seen depicted on maps and read about in Marco Polo (fig. 5).[31] Why, then, are Ferdinand and Isabella talking about lands that Columbus would discover? Similar phrasing occurs in the Papal Bull *Dudum siquidem*, a copy of which is appended at the beginning of the Library of Congress manuscript of the *Book of Privileges*, but not in any of the other extant copies. Pope Alexander VI (1431-1503) issued this bull on September 26, 1493, following Columbus's First Voyage, to extend the provisions of an earlier bull that ceded ownership of lands that would be discovered by Columbus to the Spanish Crown:[32]

Figure 5. A large world map by Henricus Martellus, made in about 1491. This map, or another very similar to it made by Martellus, influenced Columbus's ideas about the world's geography, particularly regarding the location of Japan (at the right-hand edge of the map) and the configuration of eastern Asia.

> But since it may happen that your envoys and captains, or vassals, while voyaging toward the west or south, might bring their ships to land in eastern regions and there discover islands and mainlands that belonged or belong to India…we do in like manner amplify and extend our aforesaid gift, grant, assignment, and letters, with all and singular the clauses contained in the said letters, to all islands and mainlands whatsoever, found and to be found, discovered and to be discovered, that are or may be or may seem to be in the route of navigation or travel toward the west or south, whether they be in western parts, or in the regions of the south and east and of India.

This passage speaks of discovering lands that belong to India, and yet India had been described earlier by several medieval authors,[33] and had been depicted on many maps, including the 1478 edition of Ptolemy's *Geography*, a surviving copy of which bears Columbus's mark of ownership.[34] The question arises, then, of how one can be said to "discover" a land that has already been written about and mapped. But the historians Franco Machado and Samuel Eliot Morison have shown that in the fifteenth and sixteenth centuries, the Portuguese verb *descobrir*, "to discover," had two meanings. It could mean "to find for the first time a land that was not known to exist," which is the modern sense of the word, but it could also mean "to find a land about which one had previous knowledge, though perhaps that knowledge was vague or incomplete."[35] While a similar study of use of the Spanish word *descubrir* has not been made, it is clear that in the documents just cited, Ferdinand and Isabella and Pope Alexander are speaking of discovery in the second of these two senses. In reading contemporary statements about Columbus's voyages and discoveries, then, one must be careful not to interpret words expressing the idea of discovery in the purely modern sense.

There is another term that presents problems in understanding statements about Columbus's discoveries, and that is "another world" (*otro mundo*) or "New World" (*nuevo mundo*, *mundus novus*). Today, if we read that Columbus discovered another world or a new world, we would understand that he found a large land that was both unknown before and separate from any other known land. But the term was used more loosely in the late fifteenth and early sixteenth centuries. The nineteenth-century geographer Alexander von Humboldt demonstrated that during this period, the phrase "new world" was often used to designate previously unknown parts of known regions.[36] The phrase is first used with respect to Columbus's discoveries in a letter written by Peter Martyr d'Anghiera (1457-1526), an Italian historian who wrote extensively about the lands found in the west. The letter is dated November 1, 1493, shortly after Columbus's departure on his Second Voyage, and was addressed to Ascanio Sforza. In it Peter Martyr refers to *Colonus ille novi orbis repertor*, "Columbus, that discoverer of a new world,"[37] meaning that the islands among which Columbus had sailed were new and striking, but not that the newly discovered lands were a separate, newly discovered continent.

Columbus himself first refers to the lands he discovered as another world in a letter he wrote following his Third Voyage to Doña Juana de la Torre, a nurse in the Spanish royal household whom Columbus relied upon to convey the letter to Ferdinand and Isabella. Columbus included a copy of this letter in his *Book of Privileges*,[38] thus indicating the importance he accorded it, and though the letter is also included in Bartolomé de las Casas' *Historia de las Indias*,[39] the text in the *Book of Privileges* is superior. Columbus writes:[40]

> ...por voluntad divina, he puesto so el señorío del Rey e de la Reyna, nuestros señores, otro mundo, y por donde la España, que hera dicha pobre, es la más rica.

> ...by divine will, I have put another world under the sovereignty of the king and queen, our lords. Consequently, Spain, once considered poor, is now the richest.

It is tempting to take the phrase *otro mundo* as reflecting Columbus's understanding that the mainland he had found on his Third Voyage was a previously unknown continent totally separate from Europe, Asia, and Africa—that is, that Columbus fully understood the nature of the lands that he had discovered—but the examples adduced by Alexander von Humboldt show that this conclusion is not justified.[41] Columbus believed that the Terrestrial Paradise was in the mainland he had discovered, and that the Terrestrial Paradise was in eastern Asia. Thus it would not make sense to conclude that Columbus believed that the mainland he discovered was totally distinct from Asia.

As if the question of the meaning of "new world" or "other world" was not already complicated enough, Columbus confused it further by referring to the lands he had found as being the "new heaven and earth" spoken of in the Revelation. In the same letter to Doña Juana de la Torre that appears in the Genoa and Paris manuscripts of the *Book of Privileges*, he writes:[42]

Del Nuevo çielo e tierra que hazía Nuestro Señor, escribiendo sant Juan el *Apocalís*, después de dicho por boca de Ysaýas, me hyzo d'ello mensagero y amostró a quál parte.

Of the new heaven and earth that our Lord made, as Saint John writes in the Apocalypse, after having spoken through the mouth of Isaiah, I was made the messenger and showed the place.

The reference is to Revelation 21:1, "Then I saw 'a new heaven and a new earth,' for the first heaven and the first earth had passed away, and there was no longer any sea," but Columbus's meaning is obscure.[43] The passage in Revelation describes a change that will take place during the Apocalypse, but the Apocalypse obviously had not taken place when Columbus was writing. His use of the past tense ("that our Lord made") makes it seem that Columbus was not clear on this point, but as we saw, Columbus believed that the Apocalypse was still about 150 years in the future. In this case, Columbus's conviction of his central role in ushering in the Last Days has resulted in a forced and puzzling pronouncement.[44]

The fact that for Columbus, "new world" did not mean what it does to us, suggests we must be careful in interpreting some of the navigator's most striking statements about his accomplishments. One of the passages from classical authors that he copied in his *Book of Prophecies* is a quotation from the tragedy *Medea* by the Roman poet Seneca. The passage runs:[45]

During the last years of the world, the time will come in which Oceanus will loosen the bounds, and a huge landmass will appear; Tiphys will discover new worlds, and Thule will no longer be the most remote land.

Tiphys was Jason's pilot when he sailed with the Argonauts, and Thule is Iceland. Columbus then offers his own free translation of the Latin text into Spanish:[46]

Vernán los tardos años del mundo, ciertos tiempos en los quales el mar Occéano afloxerá los atamentos de las cosas e se abrirá una grande tierra; e um nuebo marinero como aquel que fue guýa de Jasón, que obe nombre Tiphi, descobrirá nuebo mundo e entonçes non será la isla Tille la postrera de las tierras.

During the last years of the world, the time will come in which the Ocean sea will loosen the bonds of things and a large land will appear. A new sailor like the one named Tiphys, who was the guide of Jason, will discover a new world, and then Thule will no longer be the most remote land.

Even in this dramatic passage, then, in which Columbus conceives himself as privy to the revelation of a large land by divine forces, we must avoid the conclusion that Columbus thought of his discoveries as a new world in the modern sense of that phrase.

An Ongoing Quest for Asia

But where did Columbus think he was during his voyages? Did he go to his grave believing that he had been in Asia, or did he understand that he had reached an entirely separate continental landmass that was essentially unknown in Europe before he sailed? We have seen that his references to the ideas of discovery or a new world do not shed light on this question. What evidence, then, is available?

Columbus's denomination of all of the lands he found as "Indies," right from the start and through the end of his career, implied that they were close to Asia.[47] He repeatedly sought to identify lands he discovered with parts of Asia. He became convinced, for example, that the island of Hispaniola was Ophir, a region thought to be in Asia, and described in the Bible from which gold and other riches were brought to King Solomon.[48] He mentioned this belief in his letter on his Third Voyage, which he wrote to the sovereigns from Hispaniola on October 18, 1498,[49] and he reiterated it in two letters dated February 3, 1500, also during his Third Voyage, preserved in his *Libro copiador*, or

Figure 6. A detail of Martin Waldseemüller's *Carta marina* of 1516 showing the island of Hispaniola, which the text below identifies with Ophir, the region mentioned in the Bible from which King Solomon obtained gold, silver, sandalwood, and other treasures. Thus part of the New World, in accordance with Columbus's beliefs, is identified with part of Asia.

Letter Book.[50] In his *Book of Prophecies* there is a section devoted to biblical passages about Ophir,[51] and he identified Hispaniola with Ophir in a letter he wrote in February of 1502, a few months before he left on his Fourth Voyage.[52] On Martin Waldseemüller's *Carta marina* of 1516, the legend about Hispaniola mentions that some identify the island with Ophir (fig. 6).[53]

It seems that Columbus was not entirely sure of the nature of the mainland he discovered on his Third Voyage. On the one hand, as we have seen, he thought that the Terrestrial Paradise was in that mainland, and believed that the Terrestrial Paradise was in the farthest reaches of Asia. Eastern Asia was not entirely unknown, as it had been described and depicted on maps (fig. 5). On the other hand, in his letter describing his Third Voyage to Ferdinand and Isabella, Columbus twice states emphatically that the landmass he discovered on that voyage was previously unknown.[54] In propounding his theory that the Terrestrial Paradise was located on this mainland, and that it was on a mountain so high that the earth was not spherical there, he writes:[55]

> Mas este otro digo que es como sería la mitad de la pera bien redonda, la qual toviese el peçñ alto, como yo dixe, ó como una teta de muger en una pelota redonda. Así que d'esta media parte non ovo notiçia Ptolomeo, ni los otros que escrivieron del mundo, por ser muy ignoto.

> I declare that this other hemisphere is as the half of a very round pear, which has a raised stalk, as I have said, or like a woman's nipple on a round ball. Of this half, neither Ptolemy nor the others who wrote of the world had knowledge, as it was then utterly unknown.

In another passage in the same letter, he is less certain that the land was unknown: he says that the flow of water from the landmass was so great that it must come either from the Terrestrial Paradise, or from a vast previously unknown land in the south:[56]

> Y digo que si no procede del paraýso terrenal, qua viene este rio y proçede de tierra infinita, pues al austro, de la qual fasta agora no se a avido notiçia.

> And I say that if it be not from the earthly paradise that this river comes, it originates from a vast land, lying to the south, of which hitherto no knowledge has been obtained.

During his Fourth Voyage (May 1502 to November 1504), on which he again reached the mainland, this time in what is now Central America, he returns to his belief that he was in Asia. In his letter about the Fourth Voyage, he says that he understood from the Native peoples that there was a wealthy region called Ciguare nine days inland from the coast, where there was infinite gold and also spices, and that a ten days' voyage east of Ciguare was the River Ganges.[57] Later in the letter he says that on May 13, 1503, he reached the region of Mago or Mango, part of Cuba that he believed was close to Cathay (China).[58] Columbus clearly thought himself on the outskirts of Asia.

In a remarkable passage in the same letter, Columbus rather allusively claims to have found a wealthy Asian people, the Massageteans, mentioned by Pope Pius II in his *Cosmographia*, but Columbus has convinced himself that he is not seeing their wealth because they have relegated the coasts to simple fisherfolk:[59]

> La gente de que escrive papa Pio segundo el sitio y señas, se a hallado, más no los cavallos, pretales, i frenos de oro. Ni es maravilla; porque allí las tierras de la costa do la mar no requieren salvo pescadores, ni io me detuve, porque andava á prisa.

> The people of whom Pope Pius II writes, the country, and its characteristics have been found, but not the horses with saddles, breastplates, and bridles of gold. Nor is this strange, for there the coasts require only fisherfolk, nor did I stay there, since I went in haste.

There can be no doubt, then, that Columbus thought he was in Asia on his Fourth Voyage: he clearly believed that the wealthy Asian peoples he sought were, tantalizingly, just some distance inland.

There is one other important piece of evidence regarding Columbus's conception of the lands he discovered, and it comes from his *Book of Privileges*. It is found in an anonymous attorney's explanation of Columbus's rights under the Santa Fe Capitulations, an explanation that Columbus commissioned in 1501—between his Third and Fourth Voyages—as part of the same effort to confirm his rights that led him to create the *Book of Privileges*. This document does not appear in the Library of Congress manuscript of the Privileges, but it is in the Genoa, Paris, and Providence manuscripts. The relevant passage occurs in the discussion of the fourth article of the Santa Fe Capitulations, in the final paragraph of that section. In the Genoa manuscript the passage reads as follows; the key is the reference to the "West Indies":[60]

> Y aun de la persona del dicho almirante proçede ser justa la dicha provisión, porque segund la calidad de las dichas Yndias oçidentales a todo el mundo ynnotas, de neçesydad se avía de poner acá jues de çierta yspirençia para dar justa sentencia; pues ¿Quién las avría más experimentado, nin ternía más çierto conosçimiento de la calidad de los pleitos d'ellas, qu'el tal almirante que continuamente en ellas ha residido y milagrosamente con su mucha sotileza y çiençia de la mar, corriendo mucho peligro, del mismo mar las sacó?

> Also from the character of the admiral does this appointment proceed justly, because the quality of these West Indies being unknown to everyone, of necessity there had to be appointed here a judge of sure experience in order to give just judgment. Well, who could have experienced them (the Indies) more, or possessed more accurate knowledge of the quality of their lawsuits, than the admiral who has lived on them continuously, and who, with his great acumen and knowledge of the sea, running great risks, miraculously found them in the midst of the sea?

The corresponding passages in the Paris[61] and Providence[62] manuscripts are similar. The nineteenth-century historian John Boyd Thacher first drew attention to the importance of the use of the expression "West Indies" here.[63] Thacher insists that the designation "West Indies" comes from Columbus himself, and not from the attorney drafting the document, and that it indicates that Columbus understood that the lands he had found were something different from Asia. Columbus's son Ferdinand confirms that his father used the phrase "West Indies."[64] Thacher's point has not received sufficient attention in discussions of where Columbus thought he was during his voyages,[65] but needs to be considered in context. As we have seen, during his Fourth Voyage, Columbus certainly thought he was on the coast of Asia. In his letter describing his Third Voyage, Columbus repeatedly mentions the "end of the East,"[66] by which he means the farthest reaches of the east, and where he believes the Terrestrial Paradise to be located. It is tempting to think that he applied the phrase "West Indies" to the lands west of that line. It seems reasonable to conclude that "West

Indies" was a phrase Columbus chose to apply to the westernmost lands he discovered, acknowledging that they did not contain the civilizations of Japan and China that he was hoping to encounter. But they were still the Indies, in his mind, still close to Asia. They were just outlying regions of what he sought. The evidence indicates that Columbus did go to his grave believing that he had been to Asia.

Mapping a New World

If we could see a map that Columbus made of the lands he found, it would be very helpful in clarifying his views of those lands. And we know that Columbus made maps. In his *Book of Prophecies*, he boasts of his skill in chart-making:[67]

> A este mi deseo fallé a nuestro Señor muy propicio, e ove d'él para ello espíritu de ynteligençia. En la marinería me fiso abondoso, de astrología me dió lo que abastava y asý de geometría y arismética e engenio en el ánima, y manos para debusar espera, y en ella las çibdades, rýos y montañas, yslas y puertos, todo en su propio sytio.

> For this my purpose I found Our Lord very favorable and he gave me the intellectual enlightenment for it. In seamanship he endowed me generously, in astrology he gave me what was necessary, and likewise in geometry and arithmetic, and the talent and hands to draw a sphere and upon it cities, rivers and mountains, islands and ports, all in their proper place.

In the journal of his First Voyage, Columbus had talked about making a map:[68]

> And also, noble princes, besides writing every night the events of the day and every day the course of the night I intend to draw a new nautical map in which I will place the whole sea and the lands of the Ocean Sea with notes of the different winds and moreover to write a book and put in it everything as it is, even with pictures, with equinoctial latitude and western longitude, and above all I must forgo sleep and study navigation in depth, for that is most important, even though all this will be a great labor.

And in a letter that Queen Isabella wrote to Columbus shortly before his Second Voyage, which is preserved in the *Book of Privileges*, she asks him to please send soon the map he had promised to make.[69] Many of the texts that refer to maps that Columbus made have been ably collected by the nineteenth-century bibliographer and historian Henry Harrisse,[70] but a particularly interesting one that Harrisse does not include, as its source was discovered after he wrote, describes a map that Columbus sent to Ferdinand and Isabella after his Second Voyage. This passage is preserved in Columbus's *Libro copiador*.[71]

> I am sending drawings of all the islands discovered so far along with those from last year, all of them on a map I made with no small labor....Your Highnesses will see Spain and Africa on the map and in front of them all the islands discovered on this and the previous voyage. The lines running across indicate the distance from east to west; those going from top to bottom show the distance from north to south. The space between each line represents one degree; I have calculated a degree at 56 2/3 miles, or 14 1/6 nautical leagues; in this way one may count the number of leagues from west to east and from north to south (using the method employed by Ptolemy, who calculated degrees of longitude in terms of degrees on the equator, saying that four equinoctial degrees correspond to five on the parallel of Rhodes) and come up with 36 degrees, since each degree on the map equals 14 1/6 degrees, whether figured from north to south or east to west. From here you may see the length of the route between Spain and the beginning—or end—of the Indies, and you will see the distance between these lands. In this map you will notice a red line running from north to south and passing over the

island of Isabela, at Tin d'España; [72] beyond it are the lands discovered on the earlier voyage, while those found on this voyage are on this side of the line. I hope in Our Lord that every year we shall be able to significantly enlarge the map, because new discoveries will continue to take place.

It is truly unfortunate that this map does not survive. In addition to the light it would have shed on Columbus's conception of the lands he discovered, it would have been of considerable value to the history of cartography. It seems likely that the map was in the style of a nautical chart, so it would have been the first nautical chart to include a grid of latitude and longitude (the earliest surviving nautical chart to include a scale of latitudes is from about 1504).[73] Columbus's idea for continuous updating of the chart anticipates the similar policy at the Casa de Contratación, the Spanish governmental institution that oversaw exploration and colonization from Seville.[74]

We have examined several problems in the vocabulary of discovery, but images provide important evidence as well. The early maps associated with Columbus as well as maps that depict the newly discovered lands in the west[75] shed essential light on the process of understanding the discoveries, particularly the relationship between the new lands and Asia.

Columbus's map of Hispaniola, 1493

The only surviving map generally thought to be from Columbus's hand is a small sketch map of Hispaniola, held to be a fragment from his handwritten journal of his First Voyage. It is preserved in the library of the Duke of Alba in the Palacio de Liria in Madrid (fig. 7).[76] Columbus probably drew the map early in 1493, when he had a good idea of the northern coast of the island. It offers very little in the way of interior detail, which is typical of contemporary nautical charts that were designed for practical use: just the name of the island, *la [e]spañola*, and from west to east, the cape *San nicolas*, the name of the small island *tortuga*, the name of the settlement *natividad[d]*, *monte Christi* and *Civao*, a part of the island the Native inhabitants had told Columbus about. The map is most likely a preliminary sketch, intended as the basis of a more detailed depiction to be completed at a later date, but it is drawn with the assurance we would expect of the Admiral. It is the earliest surviving cartographic depiction of any part of the New World, and shows the first post-Viking European settlement in the New World, the short-lived town of La Navidad.

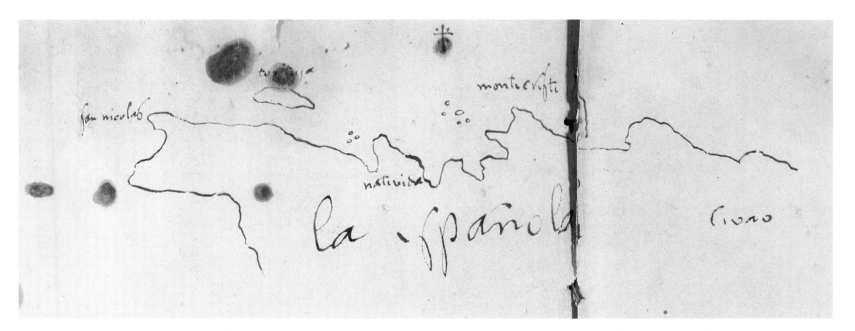

Figure 7. A map of the northern coast of Hispaniola—thought to be the only surviving map drawn by Columbus himself, in early 1493.

The earliest printed images of the newly discovered lands, 1493-1494

Hispaniola also figures prominently in the first printed map-like illustration of the New World, and also in another illustration in the same work, an account of Columbus's First Voyage published in Basel, Switzerland, in 1494. The news of Columbus's discovery spread quickly in Europe:[77] an account in Spanish of his First Voyage was printed twice in Barcelona in April 1493,[78] a Latin translation was printed in Rome the same month, then two Latin editions of Columbus's letter were printed in Basel in 1493-1494, with illustrations.[79] The illustrations were devised by an artist working for the publisher and have no connection with Columbus, but the artist seems to have been quite sympathetic to Columbus and his Spanish sponsors. The map-like image (fig. 8) shows a man who can only be Columbus guiding his ship by a group of close-set islands, and the names of three of the five islands clearly indicate Spanish control of the newly discovered lands: one is called *hyspana* (Hispaniola; literally, "the Spanish [island]"), and two others, *fernanda* and *ysabella*, are named for the Spanish king and queen. The islands are well wooded and have numerous towns, and thus seem welcoming. Another image (fig. 9) shows the settlement of La Navidad being constructed, and all seems prosperous and peaceful. In fact, to modern eyes, the illustration has the feel of a tourist poster, lacking only a slogan like "*Insula hyspana*—where adventure and happiness come together."[80]

Figure 8. A map-like image of the islands of the Caribbean, with Columbus sailing before them—one of the earliest printed images of the newly discovered lands in the West.

Figure 9. The construction of the settlement of La Navidad on Hispaniola from *De insulis nuper in Mari Indico inventis*.

Chart by Juan de la Cosa, 1500

The earliest surviving detailed map of the new discoveries is that of Juan de la Cosa, an experienced navigator and cartographer who had sailed with Columbus on his First and Second Voyages. He was also the chief pilot on a voyage

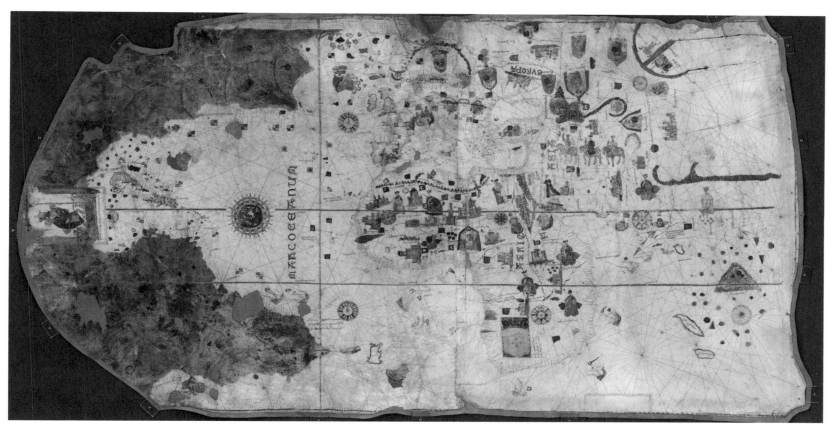

Figure 10. Manuscript nautical chart by Juan de la Cosa made in 1500, the first detailed map to show the new discoveries in the West. The vertical line is meant to demark the division between Spanish and Portuguese possessions in the New World, but here it does so in a way that heavily favors the Spanish.

Figure 11. Detail of the western portion of the nautical chart of Juan de la Cosa.

led by Alonso de Ojeda to South America from 1499 to 1500. The map is hand-drawn and painted on two conjoined sheets of parchment, and is made according to the tradition of a nautical chart—that is, in its framework, it is a practical tool for navigation—but it is so richly decorated that it would never have been taken to sea (fig. 10).[81] It depicts the world from the River Ganges and the island of Taprobana (Sri Lanka) in the east, to the newly discovered lands in the west. The huge landmass of the New World, painted a deep green, is very striking, attracting the viewer's attention much more than Europe, Africa, and Asia, and the map is of fundamental importance in appreciating early understanding of what the lands were that Columbus had first brought to the world's attention.

A vertical line near the eastern tip of South America is to be understood as representing the division between Spanish territory (to the west) and Portuguese (to the east) according to the

Treaty of Tordesillas, agreed to in 1494.[82] The political affiliation of Juan de la Cosa is clear: Portugal is assigned a small peninsula in the east, while the northern coast of the landmass bristles with Spanish flags. (The patches of brown in the New World are holes in the map where the backing shows through.)

On the one hand, the map is important because it was made by someone who was on Columbus's first two voyages, but on the other, it is clear that Juan de la Cosa had his own ideas about the newly discovered lands. Columbus had been certain that Cuba was a peninsula of Asia, but La Cosa depicts it as an island, and to remove any doubt, places the words *Mar oceanum*, "Ocean sea," between Cuba and the mainland (fig. 11). We do not know whether La Cosa had heard any detailed account of Columbus's Third Voyage, but evidently he, like Columbus, was impressed with the volume of rivers flowing from the newly discovered lands. Rather than conclude that the Terrestrial Paradise was the source of those waters, though, he depicted a series of what seem to be drainage basins, each with a lake at its center, and a river flowing from the lake, often to the coast. At the same time, the map seems to contain an homage to Columbus. At the western edge of the map is a large rectangle with a portrait of St. Christopher carrying Christ across a river; nautical charts often have a figure of a saint at their western edge, but given Columbus's conception of himself as *Christoferens*, bearing Christ to the newly discovered lands, it is difficult not to see this image as an allusion to Columbus's mission.[83] This rectangle covers the area between the lands discovered to the north and to the south, and thus allows Juan de la Cosa to avoid indicating whether he thinks there is a sea passage to the east there, or whether land would block such a passage.

The western border of the map, which cuts off the more distant reaches of the land, helps La Cosa avoid committing to either side of another issue, namely whether the huge landmass is part of Asia or something separate. While the cartographer ducks some questions, the map is the work of a well-informed and bold man. It incorporates information about the latest discoveries in both the north and south, made by explorers from England, Spain, and Portugal. To have had access to such a variety of sources, when information about discoveries tended to be secret,[84] bespeaks powerful backers. And the numerous ships on the map, both off the coast of South America and on the route around Africa to India, suggest that more discoveries will be forthcoming.[85]

The Cantino map, 1502

A map made just two years after Juan de la Cosa's, the Cantino map of 1502 (fig. 12) shows a radically different depiction of the New World that demonstrates very clearly how much extrapolation and guesswork were involved in the early cartography of the recently discovered lands.[86] The anonymous maker of the map did not have access to the same reports of the discoveries of John Cabot in North America that Juan de la Cosa did, so huge swaths of green land north of the Caribbean on Juan de la Cosa's map are simply absent on the Cantino map. The shape of what is now called South America is totally different as well (fig. 13).

Alberto Cantino, an Italian diplomat stationed in Lisbon and working for the powerful Este family of Ferrara, purchased the map and smuggled it into Italy. As the map contains the latest Portuguese discoveries, it was a secret state document, making Cantino's procurement of it an act of espionage.[87]

The Portuguese origin of the map is evident in the many Portuguese flags on the coast of Africa and also in eastern South America—on the eastern side of the vertical line marking the boundary between Spanish and Portuguese territory according to the Treaty of Tordesillas. The cartographer's bias can perhaps be seen in the fact that the beautifully painted landscape in South America, with ample forests populated with parrots, which became symbols of South America on maps,[88] is mostly on the Portuguese side of the line. But the cartographer does give full credit to Columbus for his discoveries. The red letters in the northern part of South America read *Toda esta terra he descoberta per manddo del Rey de castella*: "All of this land was discovered by order of the King of Castile." And the text below Hispaniola reads:

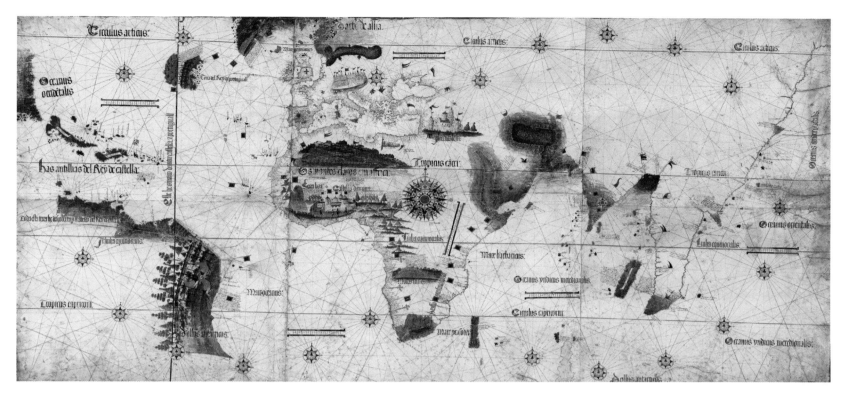

Figure 12. A nautical chart made in 1502 by an anonymous Portuguese cartographer, smuggled out of Portugal by Alberto Cantino and given to Ercole I d'Este, Duke of Ferrara. It is one of the most influential early maps to show the newly discovered lands.

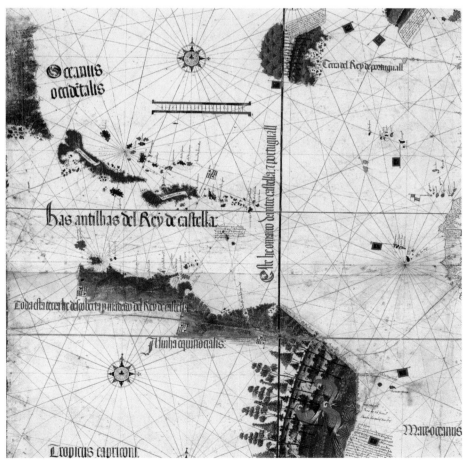

Figure 13. Detail of the western portion of the Cantino chart.

Has antilhas del Rey de Castella descoberta por colonbo almirante que es de las aquales dites ilhas se descubriran por mandado do muyto alto et poderoso principe Rey dom fernando Rey de castella.

These are the Antilles of the King of Castile, discovered by Columbus, the admiral of those islands, which were discovered by order of the very great and powerful prince, King Don Ferdinand, King of Castile.

The cartographer of the Cantino map is more tentative than Juan de la Cosa regarding the newly discovered lands, for in South America he indicates only the eastern coast and does not depict any substantial hinterlands. The most famous problem regarding the depiction of the newly discovered lands on this map is to the north. An island that, from its shape (compare with Juan de la Cosa's map) must be Cuba, is instead labeled *Isabella*, and there is a landmass northwest of this island that looks as though it might be intended for Florida—but Florida was not discovered until 1513, by Ponce de León. It is much more likely that this landmass is intended to represent mainland Asia.[89] The mainland does not bear a name,[90] but it seems that Cuba has been renamed Isabella so that the mainland can represent the mainland Cuba of Columbus's conception: the "Florida" peninsula is the eastern part of Cuba that Columbus had explored, and it is joined to the Asian mainland as Columbus believed. This interpretation is rendered very likely by a look at the eastern tip of Asia on Henricus Martellus's world map of c. 1491 (fig. 5), where a peninsula that is quite similar to that on the Cantino map juts south. The renaming of Cuba as Isabella is an excellent illustration of how difficult it was to interpret the discoveries: in an effort to fit firsthand information with theory, an island was given a whole new identity.

The Cantino map gives further evidence of the confusion suffered by geographers and cartographers in interpreting the discoveries. The landmass at the northwestern edge of the map apparently represents part of Asia, but it does not connect with the Asian land at the eastern edge of the map: there is no land at the same latitude at the eastern edge of the map to join with that at the western edge. This lack of connection reflects unresolved questions about what the newly discovered land is, and that same confusion is reflected in the names of the oceans. The ocean in front of the northwestern landmass is labeled *oceanus occidentalis*, the Western Ocean, and the ocean east of India is labeled *oceanus orientalis*, the Eastern Ocean. The waters to the north of the Eastern Ocean are labeled *oceanus occiderorientalis*, the West-East Ocean.[91] This "West-East Ocean" is clearly a hypothetical construct, a guess separating two landmasses whose relationship was still not understood.[92]

Alessandro Zorzi sketch map, c. 1506-1525

An important illustration of Columbus's conception of his discoveries following his Fourth Voyage is provided in a map drawn by Alessandro Zorzi, a Venetian traveler and scholar who collected accounts of voyages of exploration. The map is a marginal illustration to an Italian translation of a letter Columbus wrote to Ferdinand and Isabella from Jamaica on July 7, 1503,[93] and Zorzi claims by way of the title of the manuscript that his information comes from Columbus's brother Bartholomew. It had been argued in the past that this map, and two others that accompany it in Zorzi's manuscript, were drawn by Bartholomew,[94] but the map seems rather to be Zorzi's attempted interpretation of the Columbus brothers' geographical ideas.[95]

The map (fig. 14) shows Africa on the right, and the *Mondo novo* (South America) along the lower margin in the center of the image, with the principal Caribbean islands above. The *Mondo novo* is joined by land to eastern Asia, and the outline of eastern Asia, it should be pointed out, is very similar indeed to that in the Yale Martellus map of c. 1491 (fig. 5), tending to confirm that Martellus's maps had influenced Columbus's ideas of the world's geography. On Zorzi's map, however, the eastern coast of Asia has placenames from Columbus's Fourth Voyage.[96] According to this idea, when Columbus was sailing up the eastern coast of what was actually Central America in 1502-1503, he had reached his long-sought

Figure 14. A sketch map made by Alessandro Zorzi in the first quarter of the sixteenth century, showing his interpretation of Columbus's ideas about his discoveries.

Asia. The map is also of value for demonstrating graphically that in the early sixteenth century, it was possible to consider a landmass a "new world" that was connected to one of the traditional three parts of the world (Europe, Asia, Africa).

World map by Martin Waldseemüller, 1507

The earliest detailed printed map to show the newly discovered lands in the west was that of Giovanni Matteo Contarini, published in 1506.[97] The next year two more were published, one by Martin Waldseemüller and another by Johannes Ruysch. Waldseemüller's map,[98] which was printed on twelve sheets designed to be assembled into a large wall map (fig. 15), boldly depicts all 360° of the earth's circumference. The map is closely based on the world map by Henricus Martellus (fig. 5), with the addition of the newly discovered lands in the west from a map very similar to the Cantino chart (fig. 12), namely the Caverio chart of c. 1504.[99] But at the same time that Waldseemüller largely copied

Figure 15. World map of 1507 by Martin Waldseemüller. This is the first map to show the newly discovered lands as landmasses separate from Asia, and also the first to apply the name America to any part of the New World.

his depictions of the newly discovered lands from a map like the Cantino, he had a very different conception of them. Waldseemüller and his colleague Matthias Ringmann published a pamphlet titled *Cosmographiae introductio* (*Introduction to Cosmography*) to accompany the map, and in chapter 9 of that work, after briefly describing Europe, Africa, and Asia, they explain why they are baptizing the southern part of the newly discovered lands "America." More important than the new name is their bold statement that those lands are both separate from and on an equal footing with Europe, Africa, and Asia:[100]

> Now, these parts of the earth [i.e., Europe, Africa, and Asia] have been more extensively explored, and a
> fourth part has been discovered by Amerigo Vespucci (as will be set forth in what follows). Inasmuch as both

Europe and Asia received their names from women, I see no reason why anyone should justly object to calling this part Amerige, i.e., the land of Amerigo, or America, after Amerigo, its discoverer, a man of great ability.... Thus the earth is now known to be divided into four parts.

It is tempting to see the moment these words were conceived as the moment the New World was truly discovered, in the sense of being first understood to be a separate continental landmass. And Waldseemüller depicts them as such on his map, with an ocean to their west. At the same time, to designate as a discovery what was really a lucky guess is to go too far. Information about the newly discovered lands was still very scanty: the Pacific had yet to be seen by a European explorer, and Waldseemüller still labels Cuba as Isabella on his map. Indeed, the very choice to name the newly discovered lands "America" seems to have been based on an exaggerated understanding of Vespucci's importance in the process of discovery. Ideas about the lands to the west would continue to change as more information was brought by explorers, and even Waldseemüller's ideas, as we shall see shortly, changed—but the name America somehow stuck.[101]

World map by Johannes Ruysch, 1507

A handsome world map by Johannes Ruysch appears in some copies of the 1507 Rome edition of Ptolemy's *Geography*, and more consistently in the 1508 Rome edition. These editions of the book contain chapters by Marcus Beneventanus describing the new discoveries, and Ruysch's map illustrates them.[102] Ruysch, like Contarini and Waldseemüller, boldly shows all 360° of the earth's circumference at a time when large parts of the world, including the Pacific Ocean, were unknown (fig. 16). South America, labeled *Terra Sancte Crucis sive Mundus Novus*, "Land of the Holy Cross or New World," is entirely separate from Asia. Ruysch is quite clear about this, for he writes that this land *a plerisque alter terrarum orbis existimatur*, "is considered by many to be another orb of lands." The phrase *terrarum orbis*, "orb of lands," was usually used to describe the known world consisting of Europe, Asia, and Africa. Classical authors had applied the phrase *alter orbis* to Britain and Taprobana (Sri Lanka),[103] so the phrase does not necessarily imply (as it seems to) continental dimensions, but it does certainly indicate separateness from Europe, Asia, and Africa. Thus the claim that the lands are an *alter terrarum orbis*, like Waldseemüller's designation of it as a fourth part of the world, is a watershed in the understanding of the nature of the newly discovered lands. We do not know whether Ruysch was influenced by Waldseemüller on this point; he does say that others hold this opinion, so influence from Waldseemüller is possible.

Ruysch in effect acknowledges that this conclusion is a bold one, given that he carefully indicates in a vertical banner that the western extent of the land is not known:[104]

Spanish sailors came as far as this and called this land a new world because of its size, since indeed they did not see it all, nor up to this time have they surveyed further than this limit. Therefore here it is left unfinished, especially since it is not known in which direction it tends.

While Ruysch was correct that the southern portion of the newly discovered lands was entirely separate from Europe, Asia, and Africa, the map still speaks volumes about the difficulty of the continuing struggle to understand the new discoveries. Ruysch makes both Greenland and Newfoundland (labeled *Terra Nova*) peninsulas of northern Asia, and he does not depict the island of Japan (which he knew as Sipango), because he thought it was to be identified with Hispaniola:[105]

Marco Polo says that 1500 miles east of the harbor of Zaiton is a vast island generally called Sipango, whose inhabitants are idolaters, who have a king of their own, and who are tributary to no one. The greatest abundance of gold and of all kinds of gems is there to be found. But because the islands discovered by the Spanish sailors occupy this locality, we do not dare to locate this island there, thinking that what the Spaniards

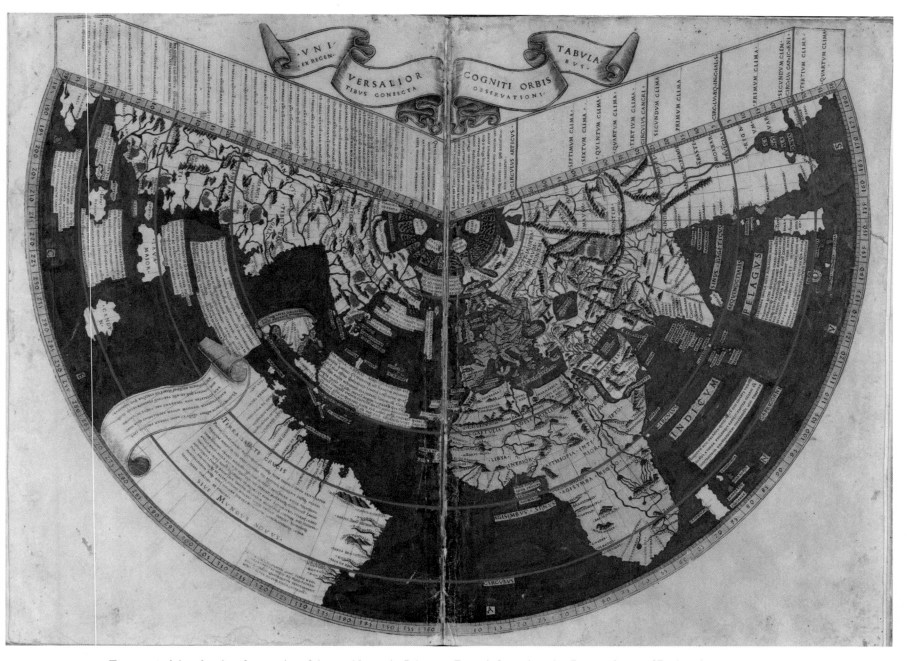

Figure 16. A hand-colored exemplar of the world map by Johannes Ruysch from the 1508 Rome edition of Ptolemy's *Geography*. Ruysch, like Waldseemüller, declared the southern part of the newly discovered lands to be separate from previously known parts of the world.

call Spagnola they call Sipango, inasmuch as the particular things described as existing in Sipango are found existing in Spagnola, except the idolatry.

The question of Cuba on Ruysch's map is particularly revealing. On the one hand, Ruysch follows the Portuguese tradition of placing a large landmass west of Hispaniola, and this landmass is certainly to be identified with Cuba, in accordance with Columbus's conviction that Cuba was part of the mainland.[106] The cartographer omits the island of Isabella, the doublet of Cuba that appears on the Cantino map, but shows open ocean between Cuba and the Asian mainland, so he is not entirely convinced by Columbus's theory that Cuba was Asia. At the same time, we can see him hedging his bets, for there is a peninsula on the eastern coast of Asia at the same latitude and with a configuration similar to that of Cuba. Ruysch seems to be offering two different scenarios—Cuba as a large island separate from Asia, and Cuba as a peninsula joined to Asia—on the same map.

World map by Francesco Rosselli, c. 1508

Francesco Rosselli (1445-c. 1513) was a painter of manuscripts and engraver of maps and prints, and ran a shop that was the earliest known map store. In about 1508 Rosselli engraved a world map on a new oval projection; it is a printed map, but the example illustrated here (fig. 17) was painted over by hand.[107] On this map Rosselli not only shows all 360° of the earth's circumference, but also depicts it from pole to pole, and thus is the first to indicate a southern coast for South America—though that coast is pure speculation. The uncertainty still prevailing about the lands in this region is indicated by the three large hypothetical islands that have materialized off the southeastern coast. In the north, the newly discovered lands are still shown being connected to Asia. Rosselli has somehow understood what happened to Cuba, and he restores that name to the island shaped like Cuba that was called Isabella on the Cantino chart. As a result, the large landmass that represents Cuba on the Cantino and Ruysch maps is gone, and on Rosselli's map directly west of Cuba we have (at the right-hand edge of the map) Japan. This is a potent indication of the inadequacy of early sixteenth-century knowledge of the size of the world, and in particular of the problems resulting from their ignorance of the existence of the Pacific Ocean, even while cartographers like Rosselli dauntlessly portrayed the full circumference of the earth.

Along the eastern coast of mainland Asia is a dense concentration of placenames, and these come from Columbus's Fourth Voyage.[108] That is, places that Columbus visited that were actually on the eastern coast of Central America are here located on the eastern coast of Asia.[109] In this respect Rosselli's map is very similar to Alessandro Zorzi's sketch

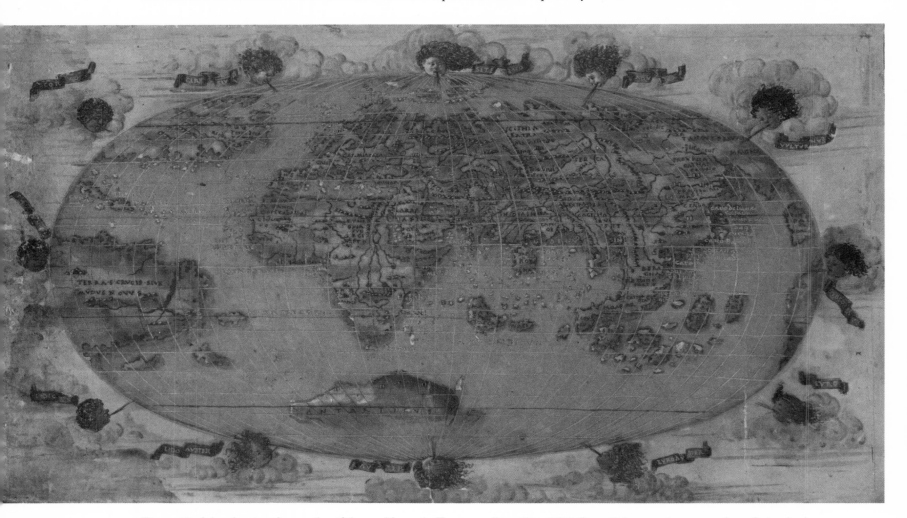

Figure 17. A hand-painted exemplar of the world map by Francesco Rosselli, c. 1508. Rosselli locates placenames from Columbus's Fourth Voyage on the eastern coast of Asia, following Columbus's belief that that's where he had been exploring, when in fact he was in Central America.

map (fig. 14), though Zorzi showed South America as connected to Asia, which Rosselli does not. Moreover, in Rosselli's attempt to understand the relationships between the lands reported by different sources, he created an image of the world that entails that Columbus had sailed right by Japan.

Martin Waldseemüller's Carta marina of 1516

Nine years after publishing his 1507 world map, Waldseemüller made a new one, also printed on twelve sheets designed to be assembled into a large wall map (fig. 18).[110] Aside from their close similarity of size and format, the two maps are entirely different. Waldseemüller cast aside almost all of the information from his 1507 map; he based the new map on more modern sources and even on a different cartographic system, that of nautical charts rather than Ptolemy's *Geography*. The many differences between the two maps have been discussed elsewhere;[111] we will focus here on just one. The depictions of the newly discovered lands in the 1507 and 1516 maps are based on the same source, namely the Caverio chart of c. 1504 mentioned earlier (similar to the Cantino chart illustrated in fig. 12). But Waldseemüller's

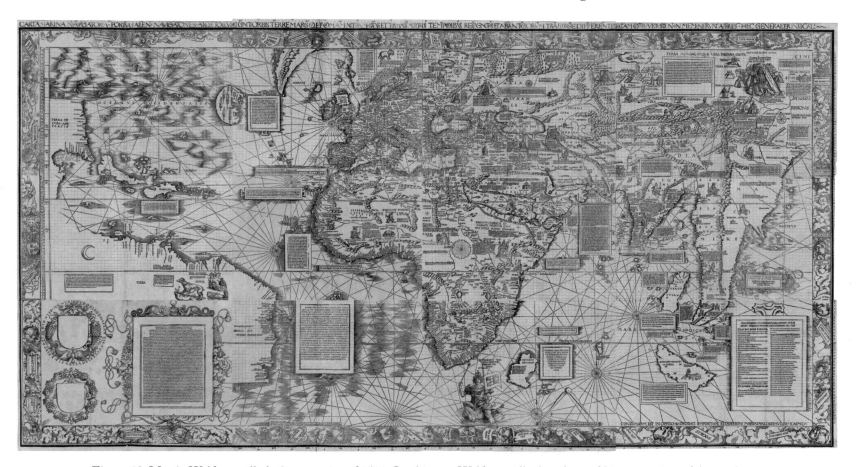

Figure 18. Martin Waldseemüller's *Carta marina* of 1516. On this map Waldseemüller has changed his conception of the newly discovered lands with respect to his 1507 map, and now indicates that they are part of Asia.

conception of them on the two maps is very different. On his 1507 map he clearly indicates an ocean separating the newly discovered landmasses from Asia. But on his *Carta marina*, the northern landmass is labeled *Terra de Cuba · Asie partis*, "The land of Cuba, part of Asia," and he declines to indicate the western shore of South America, leaving open the possibility that it too is connected with Asia. Waldseemüller has now adopted Columbus's conception of the newly discovered lands, abandoning the idea that they are a separate continent, and also the name "America."

In an age of GPS and digital cartography, it is not easy to appreciate just how complex and difficult it was in Columbus's time to interpret discoveries of new lands—to understand the relationship between these newly discovered lands and those known earlier, to revise ideas about the world's geography to accommodate the new discoveries, and to portray that new understanding on a map. The process involved guesswork, extrapolation, and errors. It was messy.

In the years following Columbus's First Voyage, the image of the newly discovered lands underwent multiple dramatic changes, and at this early period, those changes were not always in the direction of greater accuracy. Columbus had the gifts of great vision, great determination, and great ability as a navigator, and it was he who succeeded in bringing the new lands to the attention of Europe. The task of understanding the discoveries was far too large for one man, and it is no mark against Columbus's talents that he thought he was in Asia. The process of building upon and interpreting his discoveries was in fact the work of thousands, and took decades,[112] and maps continued to depict America as joined to Asia well into the second half of the sixteenth century.[113] Exploration and discovery are slow and arduous tasks, both physically and intellectually.

A view of the port of Seville, depicting boats en route to and from America. Attributed to Alonso Sánchez Coello, painted between 1575 and 1600.

Mystery

John W. Hessler

A Peculiar Form of Logic:
The Structure of Medieval and Renaissance Law

*Rummaging through this pile of documents was a little like opening a chest
filled with bundles of papers that had lain untouched for eight centuries....*

—Georges Duby, History Continues

olumbus's *Book of Privileges* is a collection of legal documents, royal charters, and grants, brought together by the explorer into a cartulary during the course of his four voyages of discovery, and whose contents laid the foundations for the exploration, conquest, colonization, and exploitation of what were, at least to Europeans, newly discovered lands. The word cartulary is a term that scholars use for such a collection, which was generally copied by a notary or scribe, and then bound into a book for safekeeping.

The charters and grants found in Columbus's *Book of Privileges* are generally in the form of letters from Ferdinand, King of Aragon (ruled 1479-1516), and Isabella, Queen of Castile (ruled 1474-1504), to Columbus directly, or papal bulls from Pope Alexander VI, also in the form of letters, granting certain rights to the King and Queen. The first documents in the collection were actually written almost a century before the first of Columbus's four voyages, by former kings of Spain, and relate to royal titles given to his family. Some of the most important are legal writs that outline a business agreement between the monarchs and the explorer, in which Columbus was granted the ability to sail and to take some of the profits that would certainly come from his voyages, to what they all assumed would be Asia, or some of the many islands known to be off the continent's coast.

After Columbus's First Voyage, the documents found in the collection expand on the privileges initially granted, and authorize Columbus to claim the lands he has found by all means available. Dating from 1493 to 1502, this expansion of rights allowed him to make treaties on behalf of Spain, to negotiate trade deals with any indigenous rulers, to dominate by using occupation and setting up temporary colonies and encampments, and finally, if need be, to wage war. This was further enforced by letters from the papacy granting similar rights to the Spanish Crown.

To understand the documents found in the *Book of Privileges* from a legal and historical perspective, we must delve into the form in which they have come down to us and in which they are preserved in the cartulary known as the Washington Codex, which is the copy of the documents shown in this facsimile and that the Library of Congress owns ("Washington" referring to Washington, D.C., where the codex, or book, is housed). Documents of the type found in the codex are always written according to the particular conventions of the chancery, or court, in which they were drafted, and according to the scribal traditions from which they descend. In the case of the Washington Codex copy of the *Book of Privileges* (fig. 19), we will find several variations from these normal conventions that add to the mystery of how they were constructed, and that will lead us to question the purpose for which this particular copy of Columbus's cartulary was intended.

Of all the issues associated with the study of medieval and Renaissance legal manuscripts, charters, and cartularies like those found in Columbus's *Book of Privileges,* perhaps the most challenging for modern readers is their language and ancient traditional form, passed down from generation to generation of scribes with little change. Like the legal documents of today, the grammar and jargon in which they are written are highly specialized. Those drawn up for Columbus by the notaries in late fifteenth- and early sixteenth-century Spain have a particular structure that had developed from legal practices that evolved over very long spans of time, dating back to the traditions of the Roman Empire.[1]

This long history of legal practice and interpretation, descended from the great jurists and lawyers who argued in the courts and in the forums of Imperial Rome, makes its first modern appearance in Italy in the late eleventh century with the rediscovery of a group of texts called the *Corpus of Justinian* (*Corpus Iuris Civilis*). The locus of this reintroduction of Roman law to the European culture of the Middle Ages has a complicated history that scholars are just beginning to unravel.[2] The *Corpus of Justinian*, which is the largest collection of Roman law to survive from antiquity, is made up of the opinions of Roman jurists and the decisions of emperors that span the entire breadth of what might be dealt with in a courthouse today, from commentaries and decisions about marriage, property rights, business contracts, and criminal behavior, all the way to considerations of lawsuits about water allocations, animal grazing lands, taxes to be paid to the imperial and local governments, and the rights of colonized and enslaved peoples.[3]

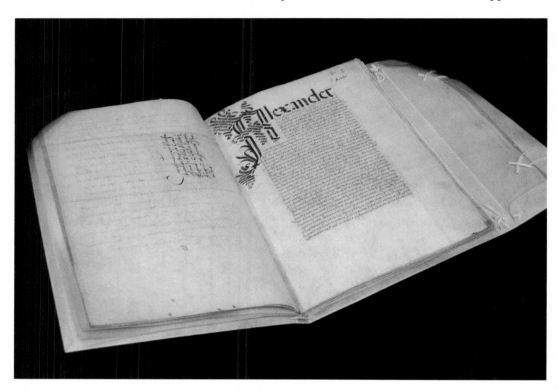

Figure 19. The Washington Codex, as it is preserved in the Library of Congress.

The *Corpus* was first recorded in the form in which it was later introduced into medieval Italy by a team of compilers brought together by the Emperor Justinian in the beginning of the sixth century A.D. The texts themselves were lost for centuries, and their subject matter certainly would not appeal to most modern readers, but they occupy a critical place in the history of European law and governance.[4] The manuscripts that make up the *Corpus* were first studied and brought into the legal curriculum in Bologna, Italy, one of the earliest of medieval universities to take up the study of law as we might recognize it today.

According to one of the great twentieth-century scholars of Roman and Canon law, Stephen Kuttner, the importance of this reintroduction of ancient law into medieval Europe cannot be overestimated. "Medieval philosophy would have blossomed," he wrote, "even if Aristotle's *Posterior Analytics* had never been found. But it is unthinkable that a science of law could have taken shape in the medieval West without the rediscovery of Justinian's *Digest* about 1070 A.D. The central monument of ancient Roman jurisprudence presented a model and challenge to the medieval mind for which the eleventh century was rather ill-prepared."[5]

Before this period there does not appear to have been any evidence of the study of law as a coherent and intellectually rigorous discipline in the West, nor could there have been such a discipline until the reappearance of the *Corpus of Justinian*, which was, as Kuttner says, "the beginning of everything," and the start of a new revolutionary period in the history of Europe. At first, this was a tenuous revolution at best, and "everything hung by a slender thread, since only a single complete manuscript of Justinian's book survived,"[6] but gradually, as a century or so went by, more manuscripts came to light, and the foundations of law took hold, leading to the establishment of jurisprudence and the professionalization of the study of law in the large medieval universities, cities, and royal courts throughout Europe.

Those who took up the legal profession tended to center themselves, for the most part, in royal courts and the Papacy in Rome, leading to the development of particular forms of legal documents and a bureaucracy staffed by trained scribes and notaries to produce and interpret them. These documents granted certain forms of status, property rights, and other legal privileges, all of which became central to the governing institutions of the time and necessary for conducting trade and commerce, both locally and internationally, which blossomed in the fifteenth century.

None of this is to say, however, that legal practices did not exist before the rediscovery of the *Corpus*, for even before its opinions made their way into the various legal codes, the writing of charters and the scribes that produced them were well established, and followed local traditions and monastic conventions. The Papal Chancery in Rome, which may have been the first medieval institution to issue written legal documents, modeled itself on the ancient Roman Imperial Chancery and was copied throughout Europe by both local Episcopal and royal chanceries.[7] The role of the papal chancery and its interactions with secular royal courts in granting rights of colonization during the age of discovery, plus its role in defining the Spanish operations in the New World, is one of a delicate balancing act between the ideological and dogmatic concerns of a Vatican bent on converting the populations to Catholicism, and that of keeping the peace between the imperial powers of Portugal and Spain.[8]

The first real legal code to appear in medieval Spain was brought together by King Alfonso X, known as the Wise (ruled 1252-1284), in 1265, and was written in the Castilian vernacular of Spanish. The code, called *Las Siete Partidas* (The Seven-Part Code), did not go into effect in Spain until 1348. Alonso Díaz de Montalvo subsequently edited and published it in Seville in 1491, followed by Gregorio López in the mid-sixteenth century. Lopez produced the most important commentary on the text.[9] His edition was the text most often cited in Spanish America and influenced the legal codes developed throughout Latin America. They were even in effect in places in the United States such as Louisiana,[10] well into the nineteenth century.[11] The laws themselves came from a variety of sources, including Roman, canon, and local feudal laws, along with important Islamic influences.[12]

Roman law was transmitted to Spain through many routes, entering Spanish humanist circles through commentaries and the publication of primary classical texts. One important book that influenced Christian humanists associated with the Spanish Crown, after it was printed in Rome in 1471, was Cicero's *De Legibus* (*On Laws*), which Luis de Vives (1492-1540) commented on.[13] In the preface to his book on *De Legibus*, published in 1519, Vives praises the legal details of the Romans and the power that law gives to those who understood it. No other work of pagan authors, he wrote, was more worth being read, re-read and learned by heart.[14]

Legal documents that granted or transferred various kinds of privileges or property rights, called charters, were drawn up by notaries, lawyers, and scribes in huge numbers from the early Middle Ages through the seventeenth century, and represent by far the largest category of documents that survive.[15] They are among the most rewarding of ancient documents for historians to work with, but at the same time, although plentiful, they are some of the most difficult written evidence to understand because of their locally varying language. Marriages, the sale of land, permission to dig a well—these are the kinds of common events they relay to posterity. For the historian, these bits of everyday life give profound insight into the goings-on in long-vanished villages, monastic communities, and the networks of trade and exchange that grew up between them.

The historian Georges Duby provides perhaps the best description of what it is like to encounter these kinds of documents:[16]

> I was alone. I had managed to have a carton [of charters] brought to my table. I opened it. What was this box going to turn up? I withdrew the first packet of documents. I untied it and slipped my hand between the sheets of parchment. Taking one of them, I unfolded it, and already I felt a peculiar pleasure: these old skins are often exquisite to touch. Along with the palpable delight goes the sense of entering a secret preserve. When the sheets are opened up and flattened out, they seem to fill the silence of the archives with the fragrance of long-vanished lives. One can almost feel the presence of the man who, eight hundred years earlier, took up his goose quill, dipped it in ink and began to form his letters at an unhurried pace, as if engraving an inscription for eternity—and the text is there, before one's eyes, as fresh as the day it was written. In all the intervening years, who else has set eyes on these words?
>
> Another pleasure, and an exciting one, is that of deciphering the text, which is in fact nothing more than a game of patience. At the end of the afternoon you come away with a small handful of facts, a small haul. But they are yours alone, for no one else knows how to ferret them out, and the hunt matters more than the quarry.

Many of the surviving documents of this kind are in the form of letters from popes, kings, queens, and local officials that have a particular grammar. They contain certain turns of phrase that granted them legal status and allowed them to be accepted as a form of proof and justification granted to the holder. The surviving collections of these documents, which typically are made up of copies of the originals, were a means of collecting and organizing the most important documents owned by an institution or individual. In this way the originals could be put aside for safekeeping, to be consulted only if there were some question regarding the authority of those found in the cartulary. It is these kinds of letters and papal bulls (letters from popes) that we find in the *Book of Privileges*, copied by notaries from the originals or certified copies, and brought together by Columbus for his use and for his family's records.

Cartularies from the late medieval and early modern period are at times difficult to work with and to construct an historical narrative out of. They are selections of charters and privileges that the owner thought important at the time and chose to preserve. This editing and filtering of documents sometimes produces a group of texts that may not have a great deal to do with one another, or that may have gaps and whose context is difficult for historians to fill in. Besides this evidential problem there is also the question of ordering. Why are the documents collected in the particular order in which they appear in the cartulary? Is it a random ordering based on something as simple as when the scribe finished copying them, or does it have some reasoning behind it that might tell us something about the owner?

Problems and questions like these are among those that we face when confronting the Washington Codex in which, as we will see, many of the documents are missing important legal formulas and language, and in which the order of the documents seems to make little historical, categorical, or chronological sense. Further, because of their local nature, and because the various granting institutions developed specific practices, the documents that have survived are of some complexity; it has taken scholars time to work out the detailed iconography and linguistic conventions used by notaries of the day.[17]

The study of charters is called "diplomatics" and comes from the word *diploma*, which in Latin simply means a document that has been folded twice.[18] The modern study of these texts and their collection into cartularies has a long history and one that began with the explorations of the Benedictine monk Jean Mabillon (1632-1707), who in the seventeenth century tried to determine the authenticity of the ancient charters he found in the abbey of Saint-Denis in Paris.[19] Because charters often confer property rights and important economic favors, in the Middle Ages and early Renaissance they were often forged.[20] Mabillon, using techniques that he mostly invented, found that many of the oldest Merovingian charters associated with the abbey were indeed fakes.[21]

In order to determine the authenticity of the documents he found in the archive, Mabillon used a variety of techniques that are still in use today, examining the handwriting, or paleography, the parchment and vellum on which they were written, and the particular forms of address that the charters used to describe the relationship between the parties mentioned.[22] Mabillon detailed his techniques in a book called *De re diplomatica* (*On Diplomatics*), published in 1681 (figs. 20, 21, 22).[23] Since that time scholars have refined his methods, and with increasing knowledge of how medieval and Renaissance scribes worked, they have been able to date and authenticate charters with more confidence.[24]

As mentioned earlier, the charters found in the *Book of Privileges* are of a particular form, and most were drafted by the Castilian chancery with the formulas and procedures developed in the mid-fifteenth century by the notaries who worked for Juan II of Castile, Isabella's father. The documents found in the *Book of Privileges* are most often in the form of a letter and, as with most charters of the period, they are divided into three parts:[25] the protocol in which the parties who are the principals in the agreement or in the granting of the privileges are named and greeted; the corpus, or text, which conveys the purpose of the charter and includes any details about prohibitions and whether the grant is limited in time or perpetual; and the eschatocol, or closing protocol, which includes the names of those present at the issuing of the grant or privilege, the date, and a formulaic ending.

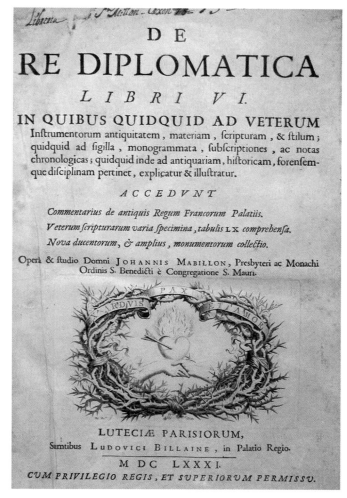

Figure 20. Title page of *De re diplomatica*.

Finally—and this is perhaps the most important part of the charter itself, and what grants the document authenticity and the power of law—there would be marks of authentication, designed to convey the authority of the individual to grant the charter and to guarantee its genuineness. Copies such as those found in cartularies like Columbus's collection should also contain information from the notary declaring that he saw the original and made a faithful copy of it to the best of his ability.

In the Washington Codex, the first royal charter of importance to scholars interested in both legal history and in how the first of Columbus's voyages came about is called the Santa Fe Capitulations (folios 11r-11v). It stands out from the rest of the charters for several reasons. First and perhaps most important, it granted to Columbus a large number of rights and privileges associated with his First Voyage and provided the basis for a business contract between the explorer and the Spanish Crown. Like all charters and privileges, it begins simply enough:[26]

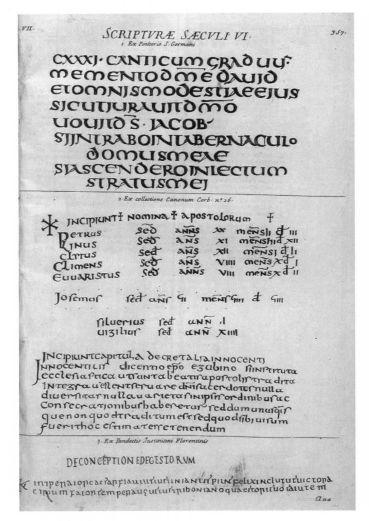

Figure 21. An example of the paleography found in cartularies, this from *De re diplomatica*.

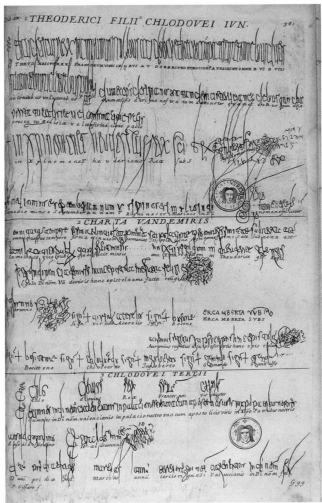

Figure 22. An example of notary conventions, from *De re diplomatica*.

> The things requested and that Your Highness give and grant to Sir Christopher Columbus in partial reward for what he has discovered in the Ocean Seas and will discover on the voyage that now, with the help of God, he is to make on the same seas in the service of Your Highness, are the following…

This was written on April 17, 1492, in response to Columbus's proposal to sail west to Asia on a commercial and exploratory voyage, and it granted to him five privileges that aroused controversy in the Spanish royal court.[27] To understand how the process of drawing up such documents worked at the time, we need to look at how they were drafted and at the conventional formulas employed by the chancery. The final form of the privileges granted to Columbus as set down in the Santa Fe Capitulations is the result of a combination of what was possible to grant according to Spanish law and a series of negotiations between a representative of Columbus and the king's secretary, Juan de Coloma. Columbus appointed his friend, the Friar Juan Pérez, who was at the time prior of the Franciscan monastery at La Rabida, Spain, to negotiate his demands for his first voyage.

The capitulations ended up commissioning Columbus as admiral, viceroy and governor general. It further granted him the right to one-tenth of all gold, spices, and merchandise that might be acquired on the expedition that everyone thought would take him to Asia. It also allowed him to invest up to one-tenth of his own money in the vessels that would engage in trade relating to the voyage, and to keep one-tenth of the profits that might come from them. And lastly, it gave him ultimate jurisdiction over any lawsuits that might arise from any of this commerce. The text of the document goes step by step granting him these rights and privileges—for example, in the case of the gold and precious stones:

You wish him to have and to take all and any merchandise, whether pearls, precious stones, gold, silver, spices and any other things and merchandise of whatever kind, name, or sort it may be, that is bought, exchanged, found, acquired, and obtained within the limits of the admiralty that Your Highness from now on grant to Sir Christopher Columbus, deducting all the relevant expenses incurred, so that, of what remains clear and free, he may keep one-tenth for himself and do with it as he pleases, reserving the other nine-tenths for Your Highnesses.

It pleases Their Highnesses. Juan de Coloma.

After each privilege, the line "It pleases Their Highnesses" appears, followed by the witnessing signature of the king's secretary. These are the verbal approvals of the monarchs of each of the privileges. Lastly, the charter contains the witnessing signature that was then used by the registrar of the chancery, Juan Ruiz de Calcena, who drew up an official copy that was then signed by the monarchs in the form "I, the King" and "I, the Queen." It is typical of charters since the Middle Ages in not mentioning their names explicitly.

Because the rights conferred on Columbus by the Santa Fe Capitulations seemed so extraordinary to members of the royal court, Columbus, on receiving his copy, immediately asked to have some clarifications made to the document. This resulted in the creation of a second document, known as the Granada Capitulations (folios 13v–15r), which clarified the titles granted to Columbus. In conferring the titles of Admiral, Viceroy, and Governor General, the text of the Santa Fe Capitulations is economical and does not spell out explicitly who should recognize this privilege, something that placed Columbus in a difficult position with the court. Because of this the Granada Capitulations take a much different tone:

With this our writ or its transcript certified by a public notary, we order Prince Sir Juan, our most dear and beloved son, and the princes, dukes, prelates, marquises, counts, masters, priors and commanders of the orders; royal councilors, judges of our appellate court, and judges and any other justices of our household, court and chancery; subcommanders and commanders of our castles, forts and buildings; all municipal councils, royal judges, corregidores, municipal judges, sheriffs, appeals judges, councilmen, parish delegates, commissioned and noncommissioned officers, municipal officials, and voting citizens of all towns and villages of these our kingdoms and domains and of those you may conquer and acquire; captains, masters, mates, warrant officers, sailors and ships' crews; and each and every one of our citizens now and in the future, that, having discovered and acquired any islands and mainland in the Ocean Sea, once you or your designated representative have performed the oath and formalities required in such cases, from then on you shall be accepted and regarded for the rest of your life, and your sons and successors after you forevermore, as our admiral of the Ocean Sea and viceroy of the islands and mainland that you, Sir Christopher Columbus, discover and acquire.

The invoking of the various royal categories is common in royal grants that are given in perpetuity. Here the list is expanded to include all Spaniards and any residents in Spanish territory, all of whom are listed in order of rank, including Prince Juan, son of Ferdinand and Isabella (he died in 1497 after Columbus's Second Voyage).

The Granada Capitulations were updated several times throughout Columbus's voyages, and further stipulations were made in them regarding Columbus's titles. The chancery takes the extraordinary step of granting him complete access to the original capitulations, normally held in the chancery, if any other questions regarding his position and/or challenges to his authority should arise.

If it should be necessary for you, and you should request it of them, we command our chancellor, notaries and other officials who preside over the desk with our seals to give, issue, forward and seal our letter of privilege with the circle of signatures, in the strongest, firmest and most sufficient manner that you may request and find necessary.

Columbus must have had a great deal of difficulty in getting his status accepted by members of the royal court and other officials related to the chancery, for the practice described here called the "circle of signatures" was a medieval one, and had fallen out of use by the end of the fifteenth century.[28] The circle of signatures (*privilegio rotundo*) requires the witnesses to the charter to sign the document with their names around the seal of the monarchs. The Granada Capitulations are also signed "Rodericus, doctor," which is the notarial abbreviation for Rodrigo Maldonado de Talavera, the chief legal counsel to the king and queen. His signature suggests that because of the controversy that arose around the rights granted to Columbus in the Santa Fe Capitulations, additional checks on the legal language were needed.

In the Washington Codex we find that Columbus brought together charters, writs, mandates, and other letters, all of which give deep insight into how his voyages were planned, funded, and executed. In the cartulary we find a wide variety of subjects addressed, from memos allowing the use of prisoners and those facing banishment to colonize the New World, to the seizing of vessels and ships to transport the prisoners, and the distribution of wheat from the royal granaries to feed them.

One of the most critical documents for the later history of the Americas and the indigenous peoples who lived there was drafted on April 23, 1497, and gave Columbus instructions for the colonization of the Indies (folios 18v-20v). This one document provides a case study of the operations of Columbus in the New World and a concise statement of the problems he and the indigenous population faced. The instructions to Columbus begin:[29]

> When, God willing, you are in the Indies you shall endeavor with all diligence to encourage and lead the natives of the Indies to serve us and remain benignly under our sovereignty and subjection in peace and order, and especially to convert them to the Catholic faith. They and those who are going to live in the Indies shall be administered the holy sacraments by the monks and priests who are already there and those going now, so that God our lord may be served and their consciences may be satisfied.

With this short statement begins the subjugation and attempted conversion of the Native peoples of Columbus's New World.

In addition to bringing the Native population under the reign of the Spanish monarchs and converting them to Catholicism, Columbus was told to found a settlement and, in order to provide food for the Spanish colonists, to find land for the herding of animals and the planting of European crops (folios 18v-20v):

> Near this new settlement or the one that is already established or in some other location that seems well suited to you, establish and introduce plowing and animal husbandry, so that persons who are or will be residing on the island can sustain themselves better and more economically.

> In order to accomplish this, give to the farmers now going to the Indies up to fifty cahices of the wheat and barley being sent there, on loan for sowing, and up to twenty yokes of oxen, mares, or other plow stock. Farmers who receive the grain shall plow, sow, and obligate themselves to return grain to you at harvest time in addition to paying tithe on what is harvested.

The farmers may sell the remaining grain to the Christians for as much as they can, provided that the prices do not cause undue hardship for those purchasing it. If the latter should occur, you, our admiral, or your representative must set and enforce a maximum price.

Columbus established several colonies, the first being La Navidad, which was located in present-day Haiti. The Taíno destroyed the colony, so in 1493, on his Second Voyage, he established the town of Isabella.[30] The indigenous Taíno occupied five independent kingdoms in 1492 and were the first New World peoples that Columbus and his crews encountered. For many years they resisted both the conversion to Christianity and the planting of European crops, but gradually succumbed to both the smallpox brought by the Spanish settlers and the violence associated with resistance to European rule.[31]

Scholars believe that the Taíno originally migrated from Venezuela to the Caribbean and across the Antilles as early as 400 B.C., establishing themselves in fishing and agricultural communities, where they raised yucca, maize, and sweet potatoes. The population reached its peak, nearly three million, just before the arrival of Europeans.[32] Columbus found the Taíno to be generous and peaceful, writing that "they do not carry arms nor do they seem to know them…they will certainly make good servants."[33] When he saw that the Taíno chieftains possessed gold, he assumed that there was a great deal of the long sought-after metal to be found on the island, and so he established a small colony using the crew of one of his wrecked ships. The notion that gold was abundant is reflected in the letter from Ferdinand and Isabella (folio 19r):

> …you shall establish another settlement or fortress on the island of La Espanola, on the other side of the island from the one already in existence, near the gold mine in the place and form that seems best to you.

Neither the Taíno nor the island itself had gold mines at the time, and the gold that the Taíno did possess had been collected in nugget form, a rare find that would be washed out of outcrops around the island.[34] Later, in 1496, when evidence of gold was found in the Ozama River on the southern coast of the island, the colonists forced the Taíno to mine for several months a year.

It was not only the indigenous Taíno who began to die in great numbers, but also the Spanish. The monarchs write that, "…concerning the settlement of estates for those who die in the Indies, it seems to us the procedure should be observed that you describe in a section of your report to us." Ferdinand and Isabella quote Columbus directly in the charter (folio 20r):

> Many foreigners and citizens have died in the Indies, and I ordered, by virtue of the powers that I have from Your Highnesses, that they should draw up wills and that these should be executed. I gave responsibility to Escobar, citizen of Seville, and Juan de León, citizen of La Isabella, faithfully to discharge all this by paying what the deceased owed, if their executors had not paid it, as well as recovering all their property and wages. All this must be recorded by magistrates and public clerks. Everything accumulated should be placed in a chest with three locks: the executors will have one, a monk another, and I the third. The money of the deceased shall be placed in this chest and remain there for up to three years, so that their heirs will have time to come for it or send to claim it. If they do not claim it in this time, it should be distributed in good works for souls.

Lastly, we hear about the taxes to be levied on the indigenous peoples and how their payment was to be tracked. This letter, from Ferdinand and Isabella, provides the modern-day reader with an amazing insight into a legal bureaucracy fully engaged in responding to its own needs in these earliest of New World colonies, and looking to quickly establish Spanish rule, with little care or concern for the indigenous populations (folio 20r):

It seems to us that the Indians who have agreed to pay the ordered tax should wear a token of brass or lead that they can hang from their neck. The design or mark on this token should be changed each time one pays, so that it will be known if someone has not paid. Every time persons are found on the island without this token hanging from their neck, have them arrested and given some light penalty.

The fact that the Taíno did not have a writing system made it difficult to keep track of the taxes the indigenous people paid; hence the system of the medallion was invoked. The token envisioned here would be made by the mint Columbus was to establish on the island (folio 20v):

In order to coin money we order that you take the persons, dies, and tools necessary, for which purpose you will have complete power, with the condition that the money coined in the Indies conforms to the ordinances that we now order to be made about the coining of money.

It is important to understand the legal implications of taxation for the Taíno and Spanish alike. According to Spanish law of the period, anyone taxed by the Crown became a royal subject and therefore not subject to the former constraints of their tribal rules, laws and customs. This taxation effectively voided the power of the Taíno chieftains, or *caciques*, and undermined their authority. Later on in the sixteenth century, many indigenous peoples would use the idea that they were royal subjects in an attempt to protect themselves from persecution by the Spanish by claiming the rights of Spanish subjects.[35]

The subject of taxes was a difficult one for Columbus, as the Taíno methods of tribute to be paid to their tribal *caciques* did not fit with the Spanish economic system and way of collecting taxes. The indigenous peoples paid their taxes in goods and services, the Spanish in coin or gold. Traditional Native payments were made in things like chilies and feathers, not something the Spanish thought useful or valuable. In fact, the only good that the colonists thought worthwhile monetarily was the cotton thread the Taíno produced.[36]

Other documents in the cartulary relate directly to Columbus himself—for example, his request for permission to establish a hereditary trust (folios 36r-38r) dating from 1497. Columbus requested this in order to preserve the wealth and status he had attained through his voyages, and to allow his family to maintain them should he not return. The king and queen are quite specific in what Columbus may pass down:

You may include in this trust any subjects, jurisdictions, buildings, properties, heritable offices, mills, and pasture lands that you hold from us by right and inheritance and of all the above everything you possess now and that you are entitled to have, and may acquire from now on, whether by gift, or by grant, or by renunciation, purchases, trades, exchanges, permutations resulting from any other honorific or lucrative titles, or by any other manner, whatever the cause or reason may be.

Because this trust was so sweeping in its grants to Columbus and his heirs, the monarch included an important statement that bypassed some Spanish law of the period:

We desire and it is our wish that this be obeyed, notwithstanding the laws stipulating that hereditary trusts cannot have effect even if they are made by virtue of any writs and rescripts that have been given about it; and likewise not withstanding any laws, constitutions, codes, edicts, uses, customs, proceedings, and actions, be they common or municipal, given by the kings our ancestors that contradict it.

This in effect protected Columbus's trust from any laws that had been previously enacted, and guaranteed that it could not be lost or forfeited except in the case of the crimes of "lese majesty, sedition or heresy."

Privileges, charters, and instructions from Ferdinand and Isabella are not the only documents to be found in the *Book of Privileges*. In fact, the first two documents that are bound into the Washington Codex, as it has come down to us today, are letters from Pope Alexander VI.

Papal bulls are letters, much like those we have been speaking about so far, and are named for the small lead seals, or *bullae* in Latin, that hang from silk threads or hemp string (fig. 23) from the fold at the bottom of the letter called the *plica*.[37] The form of papal bulls, like those of the charters, has a particular form developed over centuries of scribal and notarial practice. The papal chancery that issued such letters has a long history stretching back deep into the Middle Ages. The earliest surviving papal charter is a grant made to the church of Ravenna by Pope Paschal I on 11 July 819. The document is written on papyrus, which was used by the papacy for official documents long after vellum and parchment appeared in the rest of Europe.[38] Transitions in the writing material used for charters occurred several times in the long history of chanceries in Europe, and happened in the Spanish royal chanceries in the generation before Columbus's *Book of Privileges*. Because of costs, these chanceries gave up vellum and parchment and began using paper for all official documents.

Historians divide the history of the papal chancery into four periods, the first beginning with the earliest popes through Hadrian I. The second period starts in 781, the third with Pope Leo IX in 1049. It is distinguished by many reforms and changes in the form that papal letters took, and the addition of specific types of seals and authentication signs that would distinguish between great bulls that granted perpetual

Figure 23. Papal Bull and Land Grant Charter from 1493, showing the hemp string or silk hanging from the bottom fold.

privileges and simple letters. The fourth period starts with Innocent III in 1198 and ends with the election of Martin V in 1417, after which time little change occurred in the form of the papal privileges.[39]

The papal chancery, from an early period, issued several different forms of letters.[40] The most important, called a Great Bull or Solemn Privilege, was a very large document requiring many forms of authentication. A second type, closely related to charters issued by royal and Episcopal chanceries, was simpler but had some defining characteristics that made it very different from a great bull. One of the phrases that appears in a simple bull and never in the solemn privilege is written in the initial protocol as *Salutem et apostolocam benedictionem* (Greetings and apostolic benediction). Solemn privileges have no greeting like this, and the initial protocol ends with the words *In perpetuum* (In perpetuity).

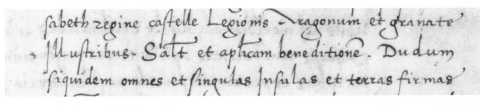

Figure 24. *Salutem et apostolocam benedictionem* greeting in the Papal Bull *Dudum siquidem*.

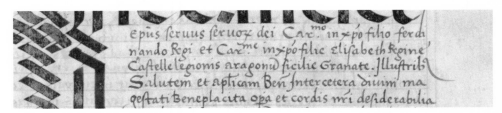

Figure 25. *Salutem et apostolocam benedictionem* greeting in the Papal Bull *Inter cetera*.

If we examine the papal bulls found in the Washington Codex *Book of Privileges*, we can see quite clearly that they are simple privileges, as both have the greeting in their protocols (figs. 24 and 25).

After Ferdinand and Isabella had been informed of the results of Columbus's first voyage, they asked their ambassadors at the Vatican to attempt to gain a papal endorsement for further voyages, and for Spanish sovereignty over the lands that Columbus had encountered and claimed for Spain. In response, the Spanish Pope Alexander VI issued a series of letters, the first three of which came in May 1493, with a follow-up coming in September of the same year.

Papal bulls are typically named by the words that come immediately after the *Salutem et apostolocam benedictionem* greeting; the two bulls that we find bound into the Washington Codex are called *Inter cetera* (May 1493) and *Dudum siquidem* (September 1493). The September letter is written on paper, unlike all the other documents in the Washington Codex, which are on vellum. The presence of the September Bull in the Washington Codex makes it unique among the four more or less complete manuscripts of the *Book of Privileges* that survived from Columbus's time.

Of the four principal copies of the *Book of Privileges* (the other copies are called the Veragua Codex, Genoa Codex, and Paris Codex), the history of the Washington Codex is by far the most unknown and puzzling. Purchased by the collector Edward Everett in Florence in 1818, it was sold to the Library of Congress by his son William in 1901.[41] Although the Washington Codex has many commonalities with the other copies, it lacks most of the notarial certifications and justifications that give the documents their legal status and import. For example, the Papal Bull from May 1493 begins in the Washington Codex with:

> Alexander, bishop, servant of the servants of God, to the illustrious sovereigns, our very dear son in Christ, Fernando, and to our very dear daughter in Christ, Isabel, the king and queen of Castile, Leon, Aragon, Sicily, and Granada, greetings and apostolic benediction.

Because this is a copy of a papal bull, however, it should begin instead with some remarks from the notary claiming its authenticity, as in the Genoa Codex, where this same document begins:

> In the name of God, amen. This is a transcript well and faithfully copied from a document written on parchment in the Latin language, embossed with a red wax seal, placed in a wooden box, tied with green silk ribbon, and apparently certified and signed by a certain papal notary, the content of which, word for word, is as follows.

> Pedro Garcias, by the Grace of God and the apostolic see, bishop of Barcelona, royal judge and councilor. To each and everyone who sees, reads and hears this public document, eternal health in the Lord and prosperous success.

> By these letters we inform you and whoever of you there may be that we had in our hands, held, felt, viewed, and diligently inspected the apostolic letters of the most holy father in Christ and of our Lord, Alexander VI, by divine providence pope, with his genuine leaden bull hanging from it with red and saffron colored silk

ribbons in the custom of the Roman court. We inform you that they are indeed whole and entire, not corrupted, crossed out, or in any part suspect, but free of every kind of suspicion, as they appeared, whose contents and tenor follow word for word.

The importance of holding the documents and seeing before one's eyes cannot be overestimated in early modern law, and these kinds of manuscript omissions in the Washington Codex suggest a certain haste in copying. The idea that they would have been left out of the manuscript indicates that for whatever purpose it was intended, it could in all probability not have been a working legal copy meant as proof of privilege. Although in the beginning of the Washington Codex (folios 2v-3r) we find a kind of blanket notarial declaration by Martin Rodriguez, a public notary, this declaration was written much later in 1502, and it is questionable to assume that he saw all the originals.

That particular declaration was written on January 5, 1502, just before Columbus's fourth voyage, when he was beginning to think about his legacy and his family's future. It is the latest dated document in the cartulary, even though many of the other copies contain documents relating to the Fourth Voyage. This fact seems to suggest that the Washington Codex is an incomplete copy, possibly made from the four originals that Columbus is thought to have made between his third and fourth voyages.

The contents of the two bulls in the Washington Codex have led to a great deal of speculation on the part of historians about whether or not Columbus, and hence the Spanish Crown, knew that he had, in fact, discovered a New World. Both of the papal letters in the Washington Codex lay the groundwork for what would become the papal policy toward the Spanish claim in the Americas, but they go further in that they give the Spanish rights to not only "all the mainlands and islands" that Columbus had claimed for Spain during his first voyage, but also to any other lands that he might find to the west in the Ocean Sea. The "Ocean Sea" refers to the widely held belief that a sea stretched directly from Europe to the coasts of China and India, leaving no place for the large landmasses of North and South America that stood in the way.

After Columbus had already left for his second voyage, the additional bull from September was issued. It appears that this letter was in response to the possibility that Columbus's second voyage might extend the territories claimed by Spain beyond the geographical regions formerly granted. The bull, after first confirming what the previous papal letter granted, states (folios Ar-Bv):

> But since it may happen that your representatives, captains, or vassals, while voyaging toward the west or south, might bring their ships to regions in the east and there discover islands and lands that belonged or belong to India, with the desire to further bestow gracious favors upon you, through our similar accord, our knowledge, and fullness of our power, and by apostolic authority and by the tenor of these letters, in all and through all, like what was written in our previous letters and that was mentioned previously, we do in the same way amplify and extend our previous gift, privilege, assignment, and letters, with all and singular the clauses contained in the said letters, to all islands and lands whatsoever, found and to be found, discovered and to be discovered, that are or may be or may seem to be in the route of navigation or travel toward the west or south, whether they be in western parts, or in the regions of the south and east and of India.

There are several important things to note about what the papal notaries are granting to Spain here. First, they are giving permission to claim for the monarchy all lands that have been discovered and that might be discovered in the future. Second, based on the text, which says that these lands that may be discovered by sailing west or south can also be in "the east," we can conclude that the Vatican in 1493 assumed the earth to be a sphere.[42]

Scholars have made strong interpretations of this later bull, including the idea that it might be the first surviving document to mention the New World in its geographical claims. The historian Seymour de Ricci (1881-1942), in a

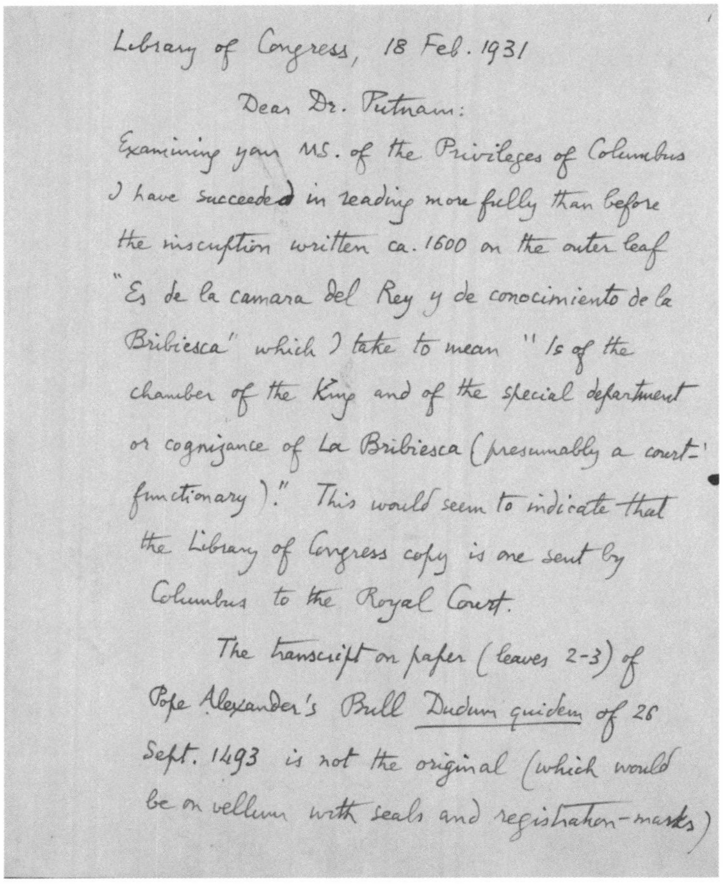

Library of Congress, 18 Feb. 1931

Dear Dr. Putnam:

Examining your MS. of the Privileges of Columbus I have succeeded in reading more fully than before the inscription written ca. 1600 on the outer leaf "Es de la camara del Rey y de conocimiento de la Bribiesca" which I take to mean "Is of the chamber of the King and of the special department or cognizance of La Bribiesca (presumably a court-functionary)." This would seem to indicate that the Library of Congress copy is one sent by Columbus to the Royal Court.

The transcript on paper (leaves 2-3) of Pope Alexander's Bull Dudum quidem of 26 Sept. 1493 is not the original (which would be on vellum with seals and registration-marks)

Figure 26a

2

nor is it a copy made in Spain (for the ~~writing~~ writing is clearly Italian). It has been folded as a letter and forwarded as a letter. On the reverse of the second leaf of the Bull is the address to Ferdinand and Isabella.

I take these two leaves to be an unofficial transcript sent direct in 1493 from Rome to the Spanish king, either by his agent or by the Vatican authorities.

These leaves were already in the book ca. 1600 when the Spanish archivist wrote the title Las Bullas.

The Bull Dudum quidem is known by two other early copies, but which do

Figure 26b

Library of Congress, 18 Feb. 1931

Dear Dr. Putnam:

Examining your MS. of the Privileges of Columbus I have succeeded in reading more fully than before the inscription written ca. 1600 on the outer leaf "Es de la camara del Rey y de conocimiento de la Bribiesca" which I take to mean "Is of the chamber of the King and of the special department or cognizance of La Bribiesca (presumably a court-functionary)." This would seem to indicate that the Library of Congress copy is one sent by Columbus to the Royal Court.

The transcript on paper (leaves 2-3) of Pope Alexander's Bull Dudum quidem of 26 Sept. 1493 is not the original (which would be on vellum with seals and registration-marks) nor is it a copy made in Spain (for the writing is clearly Italian). It has been folded as a letter and forwarded as a letter. On the reverse of the second leaf of the Bull is the address to Ferdinand and Isabella.

I take these two leaves to be an unofficial transcript sent direct in 1493 from Rome to the Spanish king, either by his agent or by the Vatican authorities.

These leaves were already in the book ca. 1600 when the Spanish archivist wrote the title Las Bullas.

The Bull Dudum quidem is known by two other early copies, but which do not seem to have the same importance as this one.

I fancy this is—if really written in 1493, as I believe it to have been—the earliest MS. extant record of the discovery of America.

Yours very truly
Seymour de Ricci

3

not seem to have the same importance as this one.

I fancy this is — if really written in 1493, as I believe it to have been — the earliest MS. extant record of the discovery of America.

Yours very truly

Seymour de Ricci

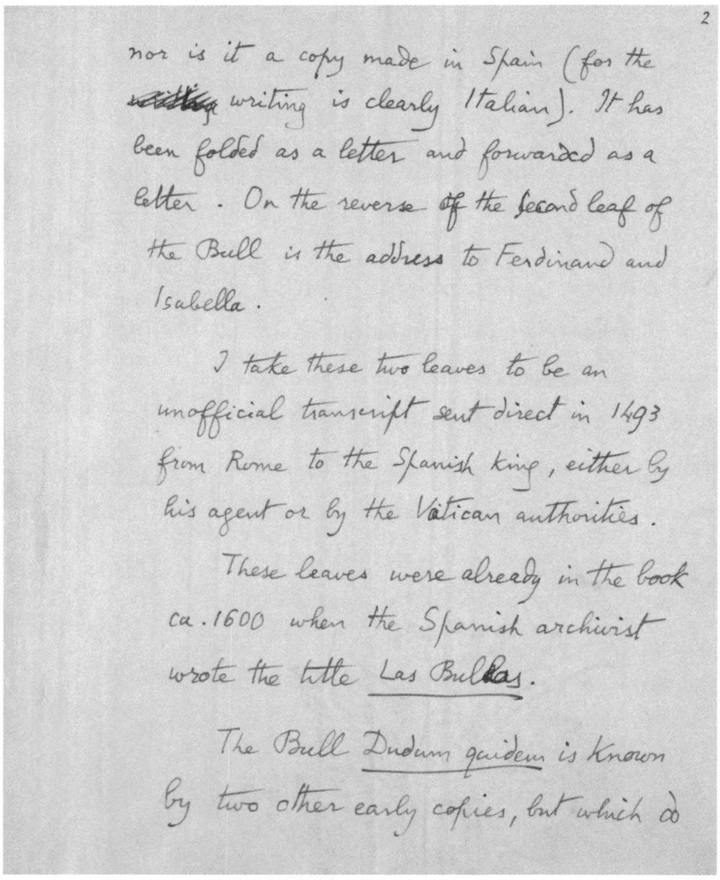

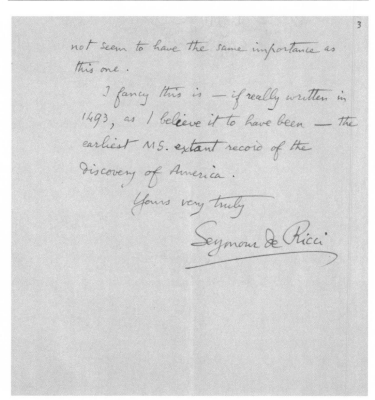

Figure 26c

Figures 26a, b, c. Seymour de Ricci's letter on the significance of the Papal Bull *Dudum siquidem* contained in the Washington Codex.

letter dated February 18, 1931, to the Librarian of Congress Herbert Putnam (figs. 26a, b, c), wrote of this papal letter, "I fancy this is—if really written in 1493, as I believe it to have been—the earliest MS. extant record of the discovery of America." The claim de Ricci is making has to do with the increased expanse of the lands mentioned in the bull. De Ricci does not appear to be claiming that either Columbus or the papacy knew explicitly that they had discovered the land that would be called America, but simply that the geographical breadth of what the papacy was granting to Spain encompassed the New World. This claim, while difficult to accurately verify, seems to hold true in the limited way de Ricci held it, making the Washington Codex the oldest surviving document to mention the New World.

Many questions about the Washington Codex remain unanswered, including the purpose for which it was created, whom it was created for, and its history before Edward Everett purchased it in Florence in 1818. Beyond that there is the question brought to the attention of Herbert Putnam by Seymour de Ricci as to whether or not the Papal Bull *Dudum siquidem*, from September 1493, is the oldest surviving manuscript to mention the discovery of what would be America.

The Washington Codex remains a mystery, but if one had to speculate on its purpose, it appears to have been a copy of one of the original cartularies that Columbus had prepared, perhaps a working copy for informational and archival purposes. The four principal surviving codices—the Veragua, the Paris, the Genoa, and the Washington—can be divided into two categories based on the dates of the documents they contain.[43] The first includes only the Veragua Codex, which is a shorter and older redaction of the documents from around 1498. The second category includes the remaining three, which were begun on January 5, 1502, and completed after March of that same year. Unlike the Veragua Codex, this group contains documents that date from after 1498 and includes texts relating to Columbus's Fourth Voyage. It is important to note that the Washington Codex contains only one such dated document, a notarial statement from 1502 that is intended to lend authenticity and legal status to the newer documents added to the cartulary. Because of this, it appears that the Washington Codex is either incomplete, or that whoever needed and commissioned the copy was uninterested in the later documents.

Regardless, the Washington Codex is a truly remarkable document relating to the history, discovery, and exploration of the New World. It shows a side of the age of discovery that injects large doses of everyday realism into the otherwise heroic adventures.

It is quite probable that we may never know the answers to the questions surrounding this codex, although scholars will continue to search for them. But whatever their solutions to these puzzles may be, this *Book of Privileges* has its rightful place in the Library of Congress next to that other great mystery of early American history, the Waldseemüller World Map of 1507, which displays Columbus's newly discovered lands as a separate continent, is the first to show a Pacific Ocean, and is the first map to name America.

Facsimile

How the Washington Codex Was Written

The copying of the documents in the Washington Codex was accomplished by scribes and notaries attached to the royal Spanish court. These scribes were part of a chancery, or court, that traveled with the king and queen throughout the regions they ruled over. The movement of the court is reflected in the titles of many of the documents, such as the Granada and Santa Fe capitulations, whose names tell us where they were written.

The scribes who wrote the *Book of Privileges* started their careers as adolescent apprentices in the domestic households of the royal secretaries. Many would remain at this level for their entire careers, but those who showed talent, and were selected to travel, took an oath of vassalage to the queen or king and became what are known as *continos,* members of the royal staff. They began in the chancery simply enough, with tasks such as taking dictations and making unimportant entries in the royal account books. Notaries who showed an outstanding ability for accuracy would be given more difficult assignments, making fair, or clean, copies of drafted materials and receiving training in more detailed legal matters. The truly exceptional would become deputy registrars, rotating through various positions in the chanceries with the outside chance of someday becoming one of the many secretaries to the king and queen. This may not sound like an exciting career, but it was respectable and well paid, and it was these men who wrote many of the most important surviving documents that historians today use to reconstruct much of the everyday world of the Renaissance and Middle Ages.

The scribes who worked on the documents in the Washington Codex wrote on vellum, which is an animal skin. Look closely at the facsimile and you can see a slight difference in color, reflecting the difference in the hair or fur side of the skin and that closest to the flesh. During Columbus's time the Spanish chanceries had adopted paper as their official medium, reserving vellum, because of its expense, for only the most important presentation and ceremonial items. It is strange, therefore, that the simple legal documents found in this *Book of Privileges* should appear on vellum—yet another mystery in a book seeming to be full of them.

The pages in the Washington Codex are numbered as folios (abbreviated as fo. or ffo.) rather than pages. A folio is the number given to a single sheet bound into a book; it has both a front side (*recto,* or right, abbreviated as r) and a back side (*verso,* or left, abbreviated as v). Numbers are written on the front sides only. (One should note that on the original codex there exist penciled page numbers added by a recent scholar; these have been removed digitally from this facsimile in order to present the codex in as close to original form as possible.)

The paleography, or handwriting, in the Washington Codex reflects the work of a few different scribes or notaries who wrote in iron gall ink. It is typical of that found in Spanish manuscripts of the early sixteenth century. Iron gall ink is generally either brown or black and is prepared by adding iron to an acid solution that is normally extracted from oak galls, which are outgrowths found on oak trees caused by the parasitic larvae of wasps, midges, and flies. In many medieval and Renaissance manuscripts, this ink causes preservation problems and headaches for conservators, as over time the acid slowly eats its way into the vellum or paper, leaving holes in the shape of the handwriting.

Many of the documents in the Washington Codex do not contain titles in the cartulary itself, and are written continuously by the scribe who copied them without any line breaks or separations, making it difficult for the modern reader to see where one document begins and another ends. Readers seeking a translation of the full codex—which is replete with legal terminology—will find an authoritative one in Helen Nader and Lucian Formisano, *The Book of Privileges Issued to Christopher Columbus by King Fernando and Queen Isabel*, published in 1996. For this volume, we present instead a short description of each document, the date of its composition, if known, and the voyage of Columbus's it is associated with. We also include the numbers in the Nader and Formisano 1996 translation that identify and cross-reference the documents in the Washington Codex with those in the other surviving copies of the *Book of Privileges*. (The documents in the other codices are not bound in the same order as the Washington Codex.)

As with the other codices, the Washington Codex was written in Spanish. The Papal Bulls, being issued from the Vatican, are in Latin. But the Washington Codex is unlike all of the other surviving copies of Columbus's *Book of Privileges* in one important way. It contains an additional Papal Bull found in none of the others: the *Dudum siquidem* of September 1493. This document is believed by many scholars to contain the earliest known mention in manuscript form of the lands of the New World. It is translated in its entirety following this listing of contents, and will provide the reader with a sense of the language and form of these documents, as well as the range of the powers granted to Columbus and to the Spanish Crown.

Contents of the Washington Codex

Nader No.	Folio	Voyage	Date	Document
N/A	A$_{add}$r-B$_{add}$v	2	26 Sept 1493	Papal Bull, *Dudum siquidem*
14	1r-2v	2	June 1493	Papal Bull, *Inter cetera*, dated June 1493, written May 1493
N/A	2v	N/A		Title Statement, *Cartas, Previligios…Don Christoval Colon…*
65	2v-3r	4	5 Jan 1502	Notarial declaration of the transcription made for Columbus, Seville
40	3r	3	23 April 1497	Warrant to Francisco de Soria to deliver to Columbus a copy of the privileges
41	3r	3	23 April 1497	Notarial description, Burgos
42	3r-3v	3	5 July 1435	Notarial declaration, Valladolid
43	3v-4r	N/A	no date	Juan II acknowledgment of charter appointing Alfonso Enriquez admiral
45	4r-5r	N/A	4 April 1405	Charter from Enrique III appointing Alfonso Enriquez admiral
46	5r-6v	N/A	17 August 1416	Juan II confirmation of Alfonso Enriquez
47	7r-8r	N/A	6 June 1419	Amplification of charter appointing Alfonso Enriquez
48	8r-9v	N/A	12 Nov 1489	Certificate of collation of authenticated copy of appointment of Alfonso
4	9v-11r	1	23 May 1493	Preface to 1493 confirmation of Granada Capitulations
1	11r-11v	1	28 March 1493	Santa Fe Capitulations
50	11v-12v	3	23 April 1497	New preface to Granada Capitulations
4 (repeated)	12v-13v	3	23 May 1493	Preface to confirmation of Granada Capitulations
2	13v-15r	1	30 April 1493	Granada Capitulations
5	15r-16v	1	28 April 1493	Appendix to the confirmation of the capitulations, Barcelona
51	16v-17v	3	23 April 1497	New confirmation of Columbus's appointment as admiral and viceroy

35	17v–18r	3	12 June 1497	Settlement of Columbus's share of expenses, Medina del Campo
33	18r–18v	3	30 April 1497	Order for representatives to ascertain Columbus's share of profits
18	18v–20v	3	23 April 1497	Instructions to Columbus for colonization of the Indies
20	20v–22v	3	15 June 1497	Instructions to Columbus about colonists; supplies and provisions
12	23r–24v	2	10 April 1495	Permission for other persons to take Spanish settlers to La Española
34	24v–25r	3	2 June 1497	Revocation of document 12's permission
26	25r–25v	3	23 April 1497	Remission of taxes and tolls on exports and imports from the Indies
27	26r–27r	3	6 May 1497	Further tax remissions
28	27r–27v	3	6 May 1497	Treasury office memo to Crown officers that tax remission will take effect
22	27v–28v	3	22 June 1497	Writ allowing criminals to settle on La Española
23	28v–29v	3	22 June 1497	Order that persons liable to banishment be sent to La Española
24	29v–30r	3	22 June 1497	Order to receive prisoners and deliver them on board ship
29	30r	3	22 June 1497	Warrant for seizure of ships required for the Indies
31	30v	3	22 June 1497	Delivery order for wheat for the Indies from royal barns
38	30v–31r	3	23 April 1497	Warrant to Francisco de Soria to give Columbus transcripts of documents
16	31r	3	23 April 1497	Authority for Columbus to take 330 colonists on the royal payroll
17	31r–31v	3	23 April 1497	Writ for payment of wages on the admiral's warrant
30	31v–32r	3	9 May 1497	Mandate for reimbursement of cash advances made by Columbus
19	32r	3	23 April 1497	Permission for Columbus to increase number to 500 on royal payroll
21	32r–32v	3	22 July 1497	Permission for Columbus to apportion land among the colonists
36	33r–33v	3	22 July 1497	Appointment of Bartoleme Colon as interim governor of the Indies
37	33v–34r	3	23 Dec 1497	Authority for Columbus to draw on royal profits to pay wages
32	34r	3	23 Dec 1497	Authority to the Bishop of Badajoz to contract for provisions
11	34r–34v	2	16 August 1494	Mandate ordering people in the Indies to obey Columbus
7	34v–35v	2	28 May 1493	Writ ordering captains and mariners to obey Columbus
8	35v	2	28 May 1493	Authority for Columbus to appoint someone to act in his absence
9	35v–36r	2	28 May 1493	Writ giving Columbus sole right of appointing his officers
39	36r–38r	3	23 April 1497	Permission for Columbus to establish a hereditary trust
3	38r–38v	1	30 March 1493	Letter from the monarchs inviting Columbus to court at Barcelona
13	38v–39r	2	3 June 1493	Letter from Isabella inquiring about a sailing chart she asked Columbus to make
10	39r–39v	2	16 August 1494	Letter from monarchs in reply to Columbus's letters
15	39v–40v	2	23 April 1494	Letter from monarchs promising Columbus great rewards
6	40v–42v	2	24 May 1493	Warrant to Columbus to outfit the Second Voyage

Dudum siquidem

26 September 1493

Translation of the Papal Bull

(see the facsimile pages preceding the first folio)

Alexander, bishop, servant of the servants of God, to the illustrious sovereigns, his dear son in Christ, Ferdinand, king, and his very dear daughter in Christ, Isabella, queen of Castile, Leon, Aragon, and Granada, greetings and apostolic benediction.

A short while ago of our own free will, out of our certain knowledge, and the fullness of our apostolic power, we gave, transferred, and assigned forever to you and your heirs and successors, the kings of Castile and Leon, all islands and lands, discovered and to be discovered, toward the west and south, that were not under the actual temporal rule of any Christian powers. Further we placed with you and your heirs and successors, and appointed and deputized you as lords of them with full and free power, authority, and jurisdiction of every kind, as more fully appears stated in our previous letters, the terms of which we wish to be understood as if they were inserted word for word in the present document. But since it may happen that your representatives, captains, or vassals, while voyaging toward the west or south, might bring their ships to regions in the east and there discover islands and lands that belonged or belong to India, with the desire to further bestow gracious favors upon you, through our similar accord, our knowledge, and fullness of our power, and by apostolic authority and by the tenor of these letters, in all and through all, like what was written in our previous letters and that was mentioned previously, we do in the same way amplify and extend our previous gift, privilege, assignment, and letters, with all and singular the clauses contained in the said letters, to all islands and lands whatsoever, found and to be found, discovered and to be discovered, that are or may be or may seem to be in the route of navigation or travel toward the west or south, whether they be in western parts, or in the regions of the south and east and of India.[a]

We grant to you and your forenamed heirs and successors full and free power through your own authority, exercised through yourselves or through another or others, freely to take material possession of these islands and countries and to hold them forever, and to defend them against whoever may oppose you. We grant this with the strict prohibition and warning to all persons, no matter of what rank, estate, degree, order or condition, that under penalty of excommunication latae sententiae, and that would occur ipso facto,[b] that no one without your express and special permission or that of your forenamed heirs and successors shall, for no matter what reason or pretense, presume in any way to go or to send to these regions for the purpose of navigating or of fishing, or of searching for islands or lands. This is granted in spite of any apostolic constitutions and ordinances, and any gifts, grants, powers, and assignments of the aforesaid regions, seas, islands, and countries, or any portion of them, made by us or our predecessors to any kings, princes, or any other persons, orders, or knighthoods, for no matter what reasons, even for motives of charity or the faith, or the ransom of captives, or for other reasons, even the most urgent. This is notwithstanding also any repealing clauses, even though they are of the most positive, mandatory, and unusual character; and no matter what sentences, censures, and penalties of any kind they may contain. We grant this providing however, that these grants have not gone into effect through actual and real possession, even though it may have happened that the persons to whom such gifts and grants were made, or their representatives sailed there at some time through chance. Therefore should any such gifts or grants have been made, considering their terms to have been sufficiently expressed and inserted in our present decree, we through similar accord, knowledge, and fullness of our power do wholly revoke them and as regards the countries and islands not actually taken into possession, we wish the grants to be considered as of no effect, notwithstanding what may appear in the aforesaid letters, or anything else to the contrary.[c]

Decreed in Rome, at St. Peter's, on the 26th day of September, in the year of the birth of our Lord one thousand four hundred and ninety-three, the second year of our pontificate.

Graciously, by order of our most holy lord, the Pope.

Johannes Nilis. P. Gormaz.

September.

---

[a] This passage effectively expands the territory that can be claimed by Spain to all geographic regions that might be encountered by Columbus. It is this section of the Bull that mentions the geographic region containing the New World, and that some scholars believe is the oldest surviving manuscript to do so.

[b] This technical section of the Bull is based on religious and Canon Law. The phrase *latae sententiae* means "as a direct consequence of the act," which is further magnified by the phrase *ipso facto*, or "after the fact." In effect, the passage threatens to excommunicate anyone who violates the provision stated immediately after the act is performed. This punishment occurs without a hearing, or without any action having to be taken on the part of the authorities; it is the act of violating the provision that immediately engages this result.

[c] In this section the Vatican effectively repeals any grants it may have made to any power, person, or group of the regions that the Spanish and Columbus may have discovered or may discover in the future.

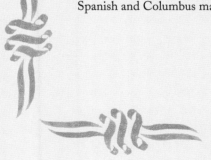

Treslado de

Las Bullas del Papa Alexandre 6º de laconcession de
las Jndias y los titulos, Priuilegios ycedulas Reales que dieron
a Xpoual Colon /

Es dela camara del Rey ydeams
a mº dela sobresca /

✝

Alexander epus seruus seruox dei. Carissimo
Jn xpo filio ferdinando regi. et Carissime Jn xpo filie Eli
sabeth regine castelle Legionis Aragonum et granate
Jllustribus. Salt et aplicam benedicione. Dudum
siquidem omnes et singulas Jnsulas et terras firmas
Jn uetas et Jnueniendas uersus occidentem et Meridiem
que sub actuali dominio temporali aliquox dominorum
xpianox constitute non essent uobis heredibusq3 et
Subccessoribus vris Castelle et Legionis Regibus imperpe
tuum motu proprio et ex certa sciencia ac de aplice potestat
plenitudine donauimus concessimus et asignauimus uosq3
ac heredes et Successores prefatos de illis inuestiuimus
illazq3 dominos cum plena libera et omnimoda potestate
auctoritate et Jurisdictione constituimus et deputauim
prout in nris inde confettis litteris quax tenores ac si
de uerbo aduerbum presentibus insererentur haberi volum
pro sufficienter expressis plenius cotinetur Cum autem
contingere posset quod nuntij et capitanei aut vassalli vri
uerssus occidentem aut meridiem nauigantes ad partes
orientales aplicarent/ ac Jnsulas et terras firmas quesndie
fuissent uel essent zepperirent Nos uolentes etiam vos
fauoribus prosequ gratiosis motu et sciencia ac potestat
plenitudine similibus donationem concessionem assi
gnationem et litteras predictas cum ommibus et singulis
Jn eisdem litteris cotentis clausulis ad omnes et singu
las Jnsulas et terras firmas inuetas et Jnuenjendas

ac detectas et detegendas que nauigando aut itinerando
uersus occidentem aut meridiem huiusmodi sint uel
fuerint aut apparuerint siue in partibus occidenta
libus uel meridionalibus et orientalibus et Indie
existant auctoritate aptica tenore presencium In
omnibus et per omnia perinde ac si in litteris pre
dictis de eis plena et expressa mentio facta fuisset
extendimus pariter et ampliamus vobis ac heredibus
et successoribus vris predictis per nos uel alium seu
alios corporalem Insularum ac terrarum predictarum po
ssessionem propria auctoritate libere apprehendendi
ac perpetuo retinendi illasque aduerssus quoscumque impe
dientes etiam defendendi plenam et liberam facultatem
concedentes ac quibuscumque personis etiam cuiuscumque
dignitatis status gradus ordinis uel condicionis sub exco
municacionis late sentencie pena quam contrafacientes
eo ipso incurrant districtius inhibentes ne ad partes pre
dictas ad nauigandum piscandum uel inquirendum In
sulas uel terras firmas aut quouis alio respectu seu
colore ire uel mittere quoquo modo presumant absque ex
pressa et speciali vra ac heredum et successorum predictor
licencia. Non obstantibus constitucionibus et ordina
tionibus apticis ac quibusuis donacionibus concessionibg
facultatibus et asignacionibus per vos uel predecessores
vros quibuscumque Regibus principibus Infantibus aut
quibusuis alijs personis aut ordinibus et Milicijs de
predictis partibus maribus Insulis atque terris uel aliqua

eorum parte etiam ex quibusuis caussis etiam pietatis
uel fidei aut redemptionis captiuorum et alijs quarum
cumque urgentissimis et cum quibusuis clausulis etiam
derogatoriarum derogatorijs fortioribus efficacioribus
et insolitis etiam quascumque sentencias censuras et penas
inse cotinentibus que suum per actualem et realem
possessionem non essent sortite effectu licet forsam
aliquando illi quibus donationes et concessiones huiusmodi
facte fuissent aut eorum Nuntij ibidem nauigassent
quas tenores illarum etiam presentibus pro sufficienter
expressis et inseztis habentes motu sciennia et po
testatis plenitudine similibus ommino renouamus
ac quo ad terras et insulas per eos actualiter non
possessas pro infectis haberi volumus / nec non ommibus
illis que in litteris predittis volumus. non obstare ceteriisque
cotrarijs quibuscumque. Dat Rome apud Sanctum
petrum Anno in carnacionis dominice Millesimo qua
dringentessimo nonagessimo tercio. Sexto Kal Octobris
Pontificatus mei Anno Secundo. gratis de mandato S. d. n.
ppe Jo. nolis. P. Gormaz

Alexander

epus seruus seruoꝝ dei Carmo in ✝po filio ferdi
nando Regi et Carme in ✝po filie Elisabeth Regine
Castelle legionis aragonu sicilie Granate Illustrib
Salutem et aplicam Ben Inter cetera diuine ma
gestati Beneplacita opa et cordis nri desiderabilia
illud effeto potissimu existit ut fides chatho
lica ✝piana Religio nris prefertim temporibus
exaltetur et ubeꝗ amplietur et dilatetur amma
rumꝗ salus procuretur ac barbare nationis deprimātur et ad fidem
ipam reducantur Undecum ad hanc sacram petri seḋ diuina fauen
te clemencia meritis licꝫ imparibus euocati fuimus Conoscentes vos tam
ꝗ veros chatholicos Reges et principes quales semper fuisse nouimus et a no
bis preclare gesta toti pene iam orbi notissima demostrant ne duỉ id ex optare
ꝗ oi cognatu studio et diligencia nullis laboribus nullis impensis nullisꝗ par
cendo piculis etiam proprium Sanguinem effundendo efficere ac onem animu
vriȝ omesꝗ cognatus ac hoc iam dudum dedicasse. Quem admoḋ recupatio
Regni granate A tiramde Sarraceno et odiernis tporibus per vos cum tanta
diuini nominis gloria facta testatur digne ducimur nõ merito et debemus illa
uobis etiam sponte et fauorabiliter concedere perque hmoi sanctum et launda
bile ac in mortali deo aceptum propositum in dies feruenciori animo ad ipius
Dei honorem et ipij ✝piam propagationem proseꝗm Valeatis. Sane accepi
mus quoḋ uos qui dudum animo proposueratȝ aliquas insulas et trias fir
mas remotas et incognitas ac per alios hatteṅ non reptas querere et in
venire ut illaȝ incolas et habitatores ad colemdum redemptorem nrem et
fidem catholicam proffitenḋ reduceretis hattenus in expugnatione et re
cuperatione ipius regni granate ptimu ocupati hmoi sanctum et laudabile
ppositum vrm ad optatum finem perducere nequiuistis. ȝ tanḋ sicut domi
no placuit Regno predicto recuperato. Volentes desiderium ad implendum vrm
Dilectum filium Christoforum colon virum iṫa ꝗ et plurimu comendan
dum ac tanto negotio aptum cum nauigiys et homim bȝ ad similia in
tentis non sine maximis laboribȝ et periculis ac expensis destinatis
ut trias firmas et insulas remotas et incognitas hmoi per mare ubi
hattenus nauigatum nõ fuit diligenter inquireret. Qui tanḋ diuino
auxilio facta extrema diligencia in mari oceano nauigantes certas in
sulas remotissimas et etȝ terras firmas que per alios hatteṅ repte non
fuerant invenerẽ inquibus ꝗ plime gentes pacifice biuentes et ut asitiṫ
nudi incedentes nec carnibus uescentes inhabitant et ut p facti nuntiy

ri possunt opinari gentes ipe insulis et terris predictis abitantes
credunt unum deum creatorem in celis esse. Ac ad fidem Catholicam amplexand et moris bonibus imbuend satis apti videntur
spesqz habetur quod si erudirentur nomen Saluatoris dni nri ihu xpi
in terris et insulis predictis facile induceretur ad profactus Christofor
in una ex principalibz insulis predictis iam unam turrim satis
munitam inqua certos xpianos qsecu iuerant in custodiam et ut
alias insulas et terras firmas remotas et incognitas inquizerent
posuit costrui et edificare fecit. Inquibus quidem insulis et terris iam
Reptis aurum aromata et alie quamplurime Res preciose diuer-
si generis et diuerse qualitatis reperiuntur. Onde omnibz diligenter
et presertum fide exaltacione catholice et dilatacione pro ut de
cet Catholicos Reges et principes consideratis more progenitorz
nrorz clare memorie regum terras firmas et insulas preditas
illarumqz incolas et habitatores uobis diuina fauente clemencia
subicere et ad fidem Catholicam reducere pposuistis. Nos igitur
huiusmoi urum sanctum et laudabile ppositum plurimum in domino Co-
mendantes ac Cupientes ut illud ad debitum finem perducatur
et ipm nomen Saluatoris nri inpartibus ill inducatur hortamur
uos plurimum in dno et per sacri lauacri Susceptionem qua mandatis
aplicis obligati estis et uiscera mie domini nri ihu xpi hardent re
quirim ut cum expiditionem huiusmoi oino persequi et assume pna
mente orthodoxe fidei zelo intendatis populos in huiusmoi insulis et
terris degentes ad xpianam religionem suscipienda inducere
uelitis et debeatis. nec picta nec Labores ullos unqz tpe uos de
terreamfirma spe fiducidqz concepts qd deus omnipotens copnat
uros feliciter psequitur et ut tanti negotij quintiam aplice pre lar
gitate donati liberius et audatius assumatis Motu proprio nonad
uram ut alterius pro uobis sup hoc nobis oblate peticionis instanciam
sz de nra mera libertate et certa sciencia ac de aplice potestatis ple
nitudine omnis insulas et terras firmas inuentas et inueniendas de
tectas et detegendas uersus ocidentem et meridiem fabricando et
Constituendo unam lineam apolo artico s. septemtrion ad polum am
tarcticum. s. meridiem siue terre firme et insule inuente et inuenien
de sint uersus indiam aut uersus aliam quacumqz partemqz linea distet
aqualz insularz que uulgariter nuncupantur delos acores et cabo uirde
Centum leucz uersus occidentem et meridiem. Ita quod omnis in
sule et terre firme reperte et reperiende detecte et detegende dpre
facta linea uersus occidentem et meridiem palium regem adprincipem
xpianum no fuerint actualiter possesse useqz ad diem natiuitatis

domini nostri ihu xpi proxime preteritum a quo incipit annus presens
Millesimo Quadragentesimo nonagesimo tercius quando fuerunt per
nuntios et capitaneos vros in uente aliquos predictaru insularum ante
omnipotentis dei nobis in Bto petro concessa ac vicariatu ihu xpi
qua fungimur in terris cum omnibus illaru dominiis Ciuitatibus Castris
Locis et uillis iuribusque et iurisdicionibus ac pertinentiis. Vniuersis
nobis heredibusque et successoribus nostris Castelle et legionibus Regibus in
perpetuum tenore presentium donamus concedimus et asignamus
nosque et heredes ac successores prefatos illaru dominos cum plena libera
et omnimoda potestate ante et iurisditione facimus constituimus et de
putamus decernentes nichilominus et per huiusmodi donationem con
cessionem et assignationem nostram nulli xpiano principe. Qui actua
liter prefatas insulas aut terras firmas possederit usque ad predictum
diem natiuitatis domini nostri ihu xpi ius quesitum sub latum intelligi
aut aufferri debere et insuper mandamus nobis in virtute Sancte obe
dientie ut sic et pollicemini et non dubitamus pro nostra maxima de
uotione et regia magnanimitate nos esse facturos ad terras firmas
et insulas predictas viros probos et deum timentes doctos prefatos
in fide catholica et in bonis moribus imbuendi destinare debeatis.
omnem debitam deligentiam in premissis adhibentes ac quibuscumque
personis Cuiuscumque dignitatis etiam Imperialis et Regalis statu pra
dus hor dinis ut conditionis sub excomunicationis late sense pena quam
Eo ipso si contra fecerunt incurrant discriptus inhibemus ne ad insu
las et terras firmas inuentas et inueniendas detectas et detegen
das uersus occidentem et meridiem fabricando et constituendo Li
neam a pollo articum ad pollum antarticum siue terre firme et insu
le inuente et inueniende sunt uersus indiam aut uersus aliam quacumque
partemque lineam distet a qualibet insularum harumque uulgariter nuncupantur de los
Acores et Cabo uerde centum leng uersus occidentem et meri diem
ut prefertur imertib tenendis uel quamuis alia de causa accedere presu
mant absque nostram a chere du et successoru nostroru predictoru licentiam
speciali non obstantibus institutionibus et ordinationibus apostolicis Ce
terisque contrariis Quibuscumque in illo aqua impia et dominationes ac
bona cuncta procedum confidentes quod diligente domino actus uros
si huiusmodi sanctum et laudabilem propositum prosequemini breui tempore
Cum felicitate et gloria tocius populi xpiani nostri labores et cogita
tus exitu fellicissimum consequemtur. Verum quia dificille fo
ret presens litteras ac singula queque loca in quibus expediens fuerit deferri uo
lumus ac motu et sciencia similibus decernimus quod illaru transumptis
manu publici Notarii inde rogati suscriptis et sigillo alicuius persone

In ecclesiastica dignitate constitute seu Curie ecclesiastice munitis et
prorsus fides in Juditio et extra ac alios ubith adhibeat q prentibus
adhiberetur si eet exibite ul ostense Nulli ergo oio hominum liceat
hanc paginam nre comendationis hortacionis Requisitionis dona
tionis concessionis asignationis constitucionis deputationis decre
ti mandati inhibicionis et uoluntatis infeimpere uel ei ausu te
merario contraire Siquis autem hoc attentare presumpserit
indignationem omnipotentis dei ac Btorum Petri et pauli a
postolorum eius senouerit incursurum · Date Rome apud
Sanctum Petrum anno incarnationis domine Millesimo qua
dringentesimo nonagesimo Tercio quarto nonas Maii Pontificatus
nri Anno Primo · Gratis demandato sanctissimi dominiin
pape · P · Rmo · A · denuncialis · P · Jo · bufo · A · con senino · L
podo · Cratai · D · galleti · registrata in camera aplica de
merimus ·

Este es traslado de dos escripturas escriptas en
pargamino de cuero la una abtorizada de ciertas ce
dulas e cartas e titulos del almirante delas yndias ante
ciertos allos e firmadas e oxinadas de martin Rodriguez
es criuano publico de Seuilla En thenor delas quales una
en pos de otra es este e tesigue ·

El abto quel al
mirante don Xpo
ual colo fizo pa
abtorizar sus
preuilleios

En la muy leal ciudad de seuilla martes cinco dias del
mes de Enero año del nascimiento de nro saluador Jhu
xpo de mill e quios e dos años · En este dho dia e ora de bis
peras estando en la posada del señor almirante que es en esta dha
cibdad en la Collacion de Sancta maria ante esteuan dela Ror
e pero Luys motero allos ordinarios en esta dha cibdad de Seuilla
por el Rey e por la Reyna nros señores e en presencia de my martin
Rodriguez escriuano publico dla dha cabdad de Seuilla e delos
testigos deyuso escriptos que a ello fueron presentes parescio en de
presente el muy magnifico señor don xpoual colon almirante ma
yor del mar oçeano visorrey e gouernador delas yslas e tierra
firme e presento Ante los dhos allos ciertas cartas e preuillejios

al çedulas delos dhos Rey e Reyna nros señores escriptas enpapel e
pergamjno e firmadas de sus Reales nōbres E selladas con sus sellos
deplomo pendiente enfilos de seda e colores e decera colorada enlas espal
das e referendadas de çiertos ofiçiales de su Real casa segud por
ellas epor cada vna dellas pareçia su thenor delas quales vna enpos
de otra es este que se sigue.

el Rey e la Reyna

ffrancisco de Soria lugar tenjente denro almjrante
mayor de castilla nos vos mandamos que dedes e fagades dar al
don xpoual colon nro almjrant del mar oçeano vn traslado ab
torizado en manera que faga fe de qualesquier cartas e merçedes e p
villejos e confirmaçiones quel dho almjrant mayor de castilla tiene
del dho cargo e ofiçio del almjrante por donde el e otros por el llevan
e cobran los derechos e otras cosas a ello perteneçientes con el dho cargo
por que avemos fho merçed al dho don xpoual colon que aya e goze delas
merçedes e honrras eperrogatiuas elibertad e derechos e sala
rios enel almjrantadgo delas yndias que ha e tiene e goza el dho
nro almjrante mayor enel almjrantadgo de castilla. lo qual ha se
e cumplid luego como fueredes requerido con esta nra carta syn que
enello pongades escusa nj dilaçion alguna. E sy asi nolo hizier des
e cumplier des mandamos al nro asistente e otras justiçias dela
çiudad de seuilla que vos apremen e premen al lo que sy fazer e cum
plir e no fagades ende al. fecha enla çibdad de burgos
a veynte e tres dias del mes de abril de noventa e siete años
yo el Rey yo la Reyna por mandado del Rey e dela Reyna. fer
nand aluares.

Este estraslado de vna escriptura escripta enpapel
e signada e firmada de escriuano e notario publico
segud por ella pareçia su thenor dela qual dise enesta
guysa En la villa de vallid estando ay la corte e chançilleria

Del Rey nro Señor martes cinco dias del mes de Jullio del año del nas
cimyento de nro Saluador ihu xpo de mill e quatrocientos e treynta
e çinco años ante los Señores oydores del dho Señor Rey estaua
hasiendo Relaciones en los palacios e casas del señor don gutierre
de toledo obpo de palencia oydor dela dha abdiencia en el palacio
e lugar acostunbrado e donde continua mente se suelen haser
e fasen abdiencia publica e Relaçio los dhos Señores oydores
en presençia de nos Jua mjñz de leon e pero garcia de madrigal
escriuanos del dho Señor Rey e dela su abdiencia e que nota
rios publicos en la su corte y en todos los sus Reynos e seño
rios e delos testigos de yuso escriptos parescio gonçalo frrs
de medina procurador aqui en la corte del dho Señor Rey e en nonbz
y en boz del señor Almjrante don fadriq cuyo procurador se
dixo e presento ante los dhos Señores oydores e hizo leer por
nos e ante nos los dhos escriuanos vna carta de preuilleio del dho
Señor Rey Rodado escripto en pargamjno de cuero e firmado
de su nonbre e sellado con su sello de plomo pendiente en fi
los de seda el thenor del qual es este que se sigue Don Juan
por la gra de dios Rey de castilla de leon de toledo de galisia
de seuilla de cordoua de murcia de Jahen del algarue de alge
sira e señor de vizcaya e de molyna A todos los por la dha
maestres delas ordenes duqes condesticos omes e alos del mj
Conseio oydores dela mj abdiencia e alldes e notarios e justi
cias e ottos oficiales dela mj corte e chancillia e dela mj
casa e rastro e Adelantados e merinos mayores caualleros
escuderos e A todos los conçeios Regidores e alldes e alguasi
les merinos e prestameros prebostes e ottas justicias e ofi
ciales quales quier dela muy noble çibdad de Seuilla e de
todas las ottas çibdades villas e lugares delos mjs Reynos
e señorios e alos capitanes dela mar e al mj armador dela
flota e pattones e comytres dela sus galeas e alos maestres
e marineros e mareantes e ottas personas quales quier
que navegaren por la mar e tierra e todas las ottas quales quier
personas de qualquier estado e condiçio preemjnencia o digni
dad que sean Aquien Attañe e Attañer puede lo de yuso es
cripto Aquien esta mj carta de preuilleio o el traslado della
abtorizado signado de escriuano publico fuere mostra
da e a cada vno devos Salud e gra Sepades que vi de vna
carta de preuilleio e sellada e to dada con mj sello de
plomo pendiente que por mj mandado fue dado A don alonso

enRiquez mj tio nj almjrante mayor de lamar escripta en
pargamjno de cuero su thenor del qual es este q se sigue
En el nonbre de dios padre fijo spu sancto que son tres per
sonas e vn solo dios verdadero q reyna por siempre jamas e dela
bien aventurada virgen gloriosa sancta maria su madre A quien yo
tengo por Senora e por abogada en todos mjs fechos e a onrra e ser
vicio del bien aventurado Apostol Santiago luz e espejo de todas las
españas patron e gujador de los Reyes de castilla mjs Antecessores e mjo
e de todos los sanctos e sanctas dela corte Celestial y por q es na
tural cosa todos los q bien biuen alos Reyes con linpia voluntad
en lo qual han grad trabajo e afan que Reciban por ende grad gua
lardon dello por q sea grad Refrigerio e consolacion de sus Afanes
E otrosi por que esta bien Alos Reyes de dar gualardon Alos q bien biz
ven. lo vno por hazer lo q deuen. lo otro por q sea enxeplo a los q lo
Supieren e oyeren por q mejor mjs te lo sirua. E el Rey Golo faze
ha de catar en ello tres cosas. la primera q mde es agjlla q hase. la se
gunda qen es aquel aquen la ha se e como gela merece. e la tercera q es
el proo el daño q le puede venjr si la hiziere. Por ende yo Acatando e
considerando to do esto e otrosi los muchos e buenos seruicios q vos don
Alonso enrriquez mj tio e mj Adelantado mayor de lamar hesistes al Rey
don Juan de esclarecida memoria mj Abuelo q dios de Sancto paraj so
e al Rey don enrriq mj padre e Señor q dios perdone e avedes fecho e fa
se des Amj de cada dia. E el linaje don de vos venj des e el debdo que con
bus cofe e quen vos Gors e por vos dar gualar don dellos quiero q Sepan
por este mj preujllejo todos los oms q agora son e Sera da quj Allant
Como yo don Juan por la gra de dios Rey de castilla de leon de toledo de ga
lisia de Seujlla de cordoua de murcia de jahen del algarbe de algesira e
Señor de Vizcaya e de molina. Vi vna carta del dho Señor Rey don En
rriq mj padre e mj Señor q dios perdone escripta en papel e firmada de
su nonbre e sellada con su sello en las espal das fecha e nesta guj sa
Don enrriq por la gra de dios Rey de castilla de leon de toledo de ga
lisia de Seujlla de cordoua de murcia de jahen del algarbe de alge sira e
Señor de Vizcaya e de molina por hazer bien e mrd a vos don alfonso en
rriquez mj tio por los muchos e buenos e leales e señalados seruis que
hesistes al Rey don Juan mj padre e mj Señor q dios perdone e avedes
fecho e fase des Amj de cada dia e por vos dar gualar don dellos fa
go vos mj almjrate mayor de lamar e quiero y es mj mrd q Seades de aquj
a delante mj almjrante mayor de lamar Segud lo solia ser el almjdan
te don diego hurtado de mendoça q es finado e q aya des el dho mj a
delantado Con todas las Rentas e derechos e juris diciones q le perteneçen

e perteneſcer deven en qual quier manera Segud mejor e mas aupli
mente lo avia el dho don diego hurtado e los otros almyrantes e fasta
aqui han seydo e por esta my carta mãdo A los perlados y mae
estres condes ricos oms cavalleros escuderos e A todos los conçe
jos e alguasiles e merinos e prestameros e prebostes e otras
justiçias quales quier dela muy noble çibdad de Sevilla e de todas
las otras çiudades e villas e lugares de los mis Reynos e senorios e
A los capitanes de lamar e al my Armador e A la flota e patrones e co
mytres delas mis galeas e a los maestres marineros e marçantes e
otras personas quales quier q Andouieren e navegaren por lamar e a qual
quier e quales quier dellos q vos Ayan e obedezcan A vos el dho don
Alfonso enrriquez por mi almyrante mayor dela mar e en todas las
cosas e cada vna dellas q al dho officio de almyrantadgo perteneçen
e que vos Acudan e fagan Re e dizconto das las Rentas e derechos que
por rason del dho officio vos pertenecen e perteneçer vos deven bien e
aupli da mente en guisa q vos no mengue ende cosa alguna Segud que
mejor e mas aupli da mente avia e obedeçian e Re cudia al dho almyra
te don diego hurtado e A los otros almyrantes e fasta aqui hã seydo
e por esta my carta vos doy todo mi poder aupli da ment pa q podades
vsar del dho dela jurisdiçion ceuil e criminal q al dho dofficio de
almyrantadgo perteneçe e perteneçer deve en qual quier ma
nera en todos los drechos de lamar o si para dar cas de Repre
sarias e juzgar todos los pleytos q en ella conteçieren como los
puertos y en los lugares dellos fasta do entra el agua Salada e na
vegan los navios e que vos el dho almyrante aya de poder de poner
e ponga vos vros alcaldes e alguasiles e escrivanos e officiales en
todas las villas e lugares de los mis Reynos que son puertos de mar
e para q conozcan e libren todos los pleytos criminales e ceviles que
Acaesçieren en lamar y en el tiempo de llegaren las cecientes e
menguantes Segud e en la manera q mejor e mas aupli da mente
los otros mis almyrantes passados lo pusieron e pusieron en la
dha çibdad de Sevilla e por esta my carta mando A los del my conseo
e a los oydores de la mi abdieçia e alcaldes de la mi corte e A todas las
otras justiçias delas dhas villas e lugares de los puertos de lamar
e de los mis Reynos que se no entre metan de conoçer ny librar
los dhos pleytos ny perturbar a vos ny a los dhos vros officiales en la
dha vra jurisdiçion q pusieron por vos para conoçer dllos dhos
pleytos en la manera q dha es e Sobresto mãdo al my chanciller
mayor e notarios e escrivanos e otros officiales quales quier que
estan dla tabla de los mis Sellos q vos den e libren e Sellen mis

cartas e preuillegios las mas fuertes e firmes e bastantes e co
mayores firmesas que fueren menester e Seguid fuero dadas alos
ottos almjrantes vros Antecessores o aqual quier dellos q mas cun
plidamete lo ouieron e los vnos ni los ottos non ffagades ende al por
alguna manera Sopena dela mj mrçd e desto man de dar esta mj ca
firmada de mj nonbre e sellada con mj sello dela poridad. Dada
enla çibdad de toro a quatro dias del mes de Abril año del nasçimj̃ de
nro Senor ihu xpo de mjll e quatroçentos e çinco Anos. yo Jua ma
tinez chançeller del rey la ffiz escreuir por su mãdado. yo el
Rey. Registrada. E agora el dho don Alonso enrriquez mj
tio e mj almjrante mayor dela mar pidiome por mrçd que le a
firmase e lla dha carta del dho Rey mj Senor e mj padre q dios per
done e las merçedes en ella contenjdas que gelas mãdase guardar faz
cuplir en todo e por todo Segud q en la dha carta se cottiene man
dandole dar mj carta de preuillegio escripta en pargamjno de cuero
e sellada con mj sello de plomo pendiente para q mejor e mas cupli
damente el pudiese gozar e gozase del dho offiçio del almjrantadgo
e delas dhas mrçds enla dha carta del dho Senor rey mj padre con
tenjdas e ottosi q le fuesen guardadas e ouiese todas las jurisdiçiones e fran
quezas e preuillejos e libertades q le perteneçia e perteneç
çer deuen en qual quier maña por razon del dho almjratadaz
go Segud q mejor e mas cuplidamente lo ouieron los ottos mjs
almjrantes sus Antecessores o qual quier dellos y en la dha carta
del dho Senor rey mj padre e mj Senor q dios perdone se cotiene. Et
yo el sobre dho rey don Jua por haber bien e mrçd al dho don alõso
enrriquez mj tio e mj almjrante mayor dela mar touelo por bien e con
firmole la dha mrçd del dho rey mj padre e las mrçds en ella con
tenjdas e mando q valan e sean guardadas en todo e por todo bie
e cuplidamente Segud q en la dha carta se cotiene. E por este
mj preuillejo e por el treslado del signado de escriuano publi
co sacado con autoridad de Juez o alcalde mãdo a todos los perla
dos maestres priores delas ordenes e condes e ricos omes e
comendadores e subcomendadores Caualleros e escuderos e a los
del mj conseio e oydores dela mj abdiençia e a allos Alcaldes alguaz̃
les dela mj corte e a todos los conçeios e alldes e alguasiles jueces
e merinos e prestameros e prebostes e alcaydes delos castillos
e casas fuertes e llanas e dotras justiçias e ofiçiales e al
portellados quales quier dela muy noble çibdad de Seuilla
e de todas las otras çibdades e villas e logares delos nros reynos

al señorios e alos capitanes dela mar e patrons e comitres e na
vecheles e maestres delas naos e galeas e al my armada or dela
flota e alos marineros e mareantes e a todos los omes dela mar
etio e a todos los otros que andan en la my flota e fuera della en qual
quier manera o en quales quier navios que ando vieren daqui adelante
de qual quier estado o condiçion que sean que ayades e aya e he
cabades e te caban al dho alonso enrriquez my tio por my almyra
te mayor dela mar e todas las partes delos dhos mys reynos
e señorios e que vsedes conel e el dho oficio de almyrantadgo e su
jurisdiçion çevil e criminal e vengays a sus llamamientos e enpla
samientos o delos quel pusiere segund que mejor e mas cumplida men
te vsaro e vsaste con los dhos almyrantes e fuero en tiempo delos reyes
donde yo vengo o con qual quier dellos. otrosi enla dha carta
del dho rey my padre e my señor que dios perdone se contiene e que
le acudades e fagades le acudir con todas las otras rentas e derechos
que al dho oficio de almyrantazgo pertenesçen e pertenesçer deven e
qual quier manera o por qual quier razon que sea. e otrosy colo
dho de los casos e fagades su mandado ansi como de my almyrante
mayor dela mar e como fariades por my cuerpo mysmo e por my persona
real. e otrosi tengo por bien e mando que si alguno o algunos dela
dha mar o delos dhos tios hisieren en la mar o enel tio o fuera por
que menester se aga a ser derecho del o justiçia enel o enellos o si le
fueren desobidientes al dho don alonso enrriquez my tio o a sus ofi
çiales quel por si pusiere enla mar o enel tio o en tierra al dho al my
rante pueda ha ser o man dar ha ser e faga la justiçia enel o enellos
e deles dar o man dar dar ala pena o penas que de derecho meresçie
ren aver. e tengo por bien que todas las ganançias al dho o my almy
rante ovier o viere o hisiere enla my flota o por la mar que aya yo
las dos partes e el dho my almyrante la terçia parte yendo el por
su cuerpo mesmo enla dha flota avn que la dha flota o parte della
se aparte por su mandado o sin su mandado. e otrosi que todas
las galeas que yo mandare armar sin flota para ganar que la ganan
çia que dieren que aya yo las dos partes y el dho almyrante la ter
çia parte. otrosi tengo por bien e mando que todas las galeas e
naos e galeotes e leños e otras fustas quales quier que armare a
otras partes de que yo aya de aver el quinto que yo aya las dos partes
del dho quinto y el dho my almyrante la terçia parte del. e otro
tengo por bien que cada que el dho my almyrante hisiere armar por
my mandado e pueda sacar e saque quatro omes dañados de
qual quier malefiçio porque devan ser açenados de muerte que este

presos qualesquier q̃ fueren o biuiere enla dh̄a cabdad de seuilla
o en ottos puertos qualesquier de los n̄ros reynos e señorios flotã dos
e por flotar o pueda el dh̄o mj almjzante cargar la tercia parte q̃l
q̃ en ellos para si segud el precio o precios q̃ vinjere flotã dos o flotã
ren. Otrosi tengo por bien q̃l dh̄o mj almjzante que aya el dh̄o
mj almjrantazgo e abelase e jurisdicon cebil e crimjnal bien e
amplida mente en todos los puertos e lugares de todos los mis rey
nos e señorios q̃ sean puertos de mar asy como la dh̄a cabdad de
Seuilla con todas las fuerças e derechos q̃ al dh̄o oficio de almj
rantadgo pertenescen e pertenescer deven en qualquier manera
e otro si q̃ aya e pueda vsar e vse el o los q̃ por si pusiere dela
dh̄a jurisdicon cebil e crimjnal en qualquier manera en todos los
dh̄os puertos dela mar o las villas e logares dellos asi para dar
cartas de represarias e juzgar todos los pleytos q̃ enla dh̄a mar
etio̅ a me scierē como en los dh̄os puertos e villas e lugares dellos
fasta donde entra agua salada o navegan los navios e q̃l dh̄o
almjzante ponga sus alldes e alguasiles e scriuanos e oficiales
e y todas las villas e lugares de los mjs reynos e señorios q̃ son puer
tos dla mar para q̃ conozca e libre todos los pleytos crimjnales e
ceuiles q̃ acaes scieren enla mar o en el rio por donde llegare la
cre scente o menguare segud y enla manera q̃ mejor e mas ampl
damente los ottos almjzantes o qualquier dellos los pusieren dla
dh̄a cabdad de seuilla. e mãdo a los sobre dh̄os almj conseso coy
dores dela mj abdiencia e alldes dela dh̄a mj corte e a todas las ottas
justicias delas dh̄as villas e lugares delos dh̄os puertos dla mar
de los dh̄os mjs reynos q̃ se no ss̃e metan de conocer n̄ librar
delos dh̄os pleytos nj de perturbar nj perturben al dh̄o mj almjzãte
nj a los dh̄os sus oficiales q̃l por si pusiere para conocer delos
dh̄os pleytos enla manera q̃ dh̄a es la dh̄a jurisdicon ceuil nj cri
mjnal nj parte della e de fixen do firme mente e njnguno nj alguis
no sean osados de yr nj pasar contra la dh̄a carta del dh̄o señor
rey mj padre e mj señor q̃ dios perdone nj contra las mercedes nj fra
q̃sas nj libertades en ella nj en este dh̄o mj preuilleso contenjdas
nj en otra parte dellas agora nj daquj adelant para gelos q̃bra
tar o menguar njnguna nj alguna dellas. e qualquier o quales
quier q̃ lo contrario fisieren o contra ello o contra parte dello
fuesen o pa sasen avria la mj ira e pecharmeyan en pena
por cada vegada q̃ contra ello fuesen o pa sasen dos mjll dobllas
castellanas de fino oro o de justo peso e al dh̄o mj almjrãte
e mjo o al que su boz tubiese todos los daños e menoscabos

que por ende rescibiesen doblados e demas delos cuerpos e alo que
tomasen me tornaria por ello. e mando alas dichas justicias e arenda
uno de vos en vros lugares e jurisdiciones que prendades en bienes de aq
llos que contra ello o contra parte dello fueren o passaren o sieren yz
o pagar por la dicha pena delas dichas dos mill doblas de oro cada uno por
cada vegada e las guarden para hazer dellas lo que la mj mercet fuere
e toda que ey mi mercet es e fago mercet en mendar al dicho mj almirante e mayor
o aquien la dicha su boz toviere de todos los dichos dampnos e menos u bos
e por la dicha razon se cabieren dello des como dicho es. E demas por
qual quier o quales quier por quien fincare delo asi fazer e cumplir man
do al ome que este mj preuilleso mostrare o el traslado como dicho es
uos en plaza que parezcades ante mj do quier que yo sea uos los dichos
concesos por uros procuradores suficientes e uno o dos delos of
ciales del cada cabdad o villa do esto acaesciere personal mente con
pro curacion delos otros oficiales uros conpañeros del dia que uos en pla
zare en quinze dias primeros siguientes sola dicha pena a de diez
por qual razon non cumplir des mj mandado e demas sola dicha pena aqual
quier escriuano publico que para esto fuere llamado que de ende al que uos
la mostrare testimonio signado con su signo por que yo sepa en como
se cumple mj mandado e desto le mande dar al dicho don alonso enrriq
mj tio e mj almirante mayor este mj preuilleso escripto en parga
mino de cuero todado e sellado con mj sello de plomo colga
do con filos de seda. Dada en la villa de valliz diez e siete dias de
agosto año del nascimjento de nro saluador ihu xpo de mill e quatro
cientos e diez e seys años. E yo el sobre dicho rey don juan reynate
en uno con la reyna doña catalina mj madre e mj señora e mj tuto
ra e regidora delos mjs reynos con la ynfanta doña catalina mj her
mana en castilla y en leon y en toledo y en galizia y en seuilla y en
cordoua y en murcia y en jahen y en baeça y en badajoz y en el algar
be y en algesira y en biscaya y en molina otorgo este preuillejo y
confirmolo. El ynfante don juan primo del dicho señor rey
e su mayor domo mayor confirma. Don enrriq su hermano primo
al dicho señor rey maestre de santiago confirma. Don luys de
guzman maestre de la orden de la cavalleria de calatraua confirma
Don pedro señor de monte alegre vassallo del rey confirma. Don
luys dela cerda conde de medina celi vassallo del rey confirma.
Don pablo obispo de burgos chançeller mayor del rey confirma. Don lope
de mendoça arçobispo de santiago capellan mayor del rey con
firma. Don fray alonso obispo de   confirma. Don
juan obispo de segouia confirma. Don diego obispo de cuenca

confirma. Don gonçalo de çuñiga obispo de palencia confirma. Don
diego gomez de Sandoual adelantado mayor de murçia confirma.
don Juan Ramirez de Arellano Senor delos cameros vasallo del rey
confirma. Don garci fernandez marrique Senor de Aguilar vasallo
del Rey confirma. Yñigo lopez de mendoça Senor dela vega vasallo
dellRey confirme. yo Juan fernandez de palençia escriuano del
dicho Senor Rey fize escreuir por su mandado enel Año de seno el
dicho Señor Rey E Reyno. ferdinan bachalleri legibus. Alfonsi legista.
E agora el dicho don alonso enrriquez almjrante mayor dela mar
pidiome por merçed qle confirmase el dicho preuillejo de merçed aqui con
tenjdo eqele mandase guardar entodo bien e cunplidamente Se
gund qenel se contiene E yo el sobre dicho Rey don Juan por fazer bien
e merçed al dicho don alonso enrriquez mj tio e mj almjrante mayor
de la mar e acatando el debdo q comjgo ha e los muchos e buenos e
Señalados seruiçios qhizo al Rey don Juan mj Abuelo e al Rey don
enrrique mj padre e mj Señor q dios perdone e fase almj dela va
da e touelo por bien E porende de mj propio motuo e çierta çiençia
e mj Voluntad e merçed de confirmar e confirmole el dicho preuillegio
etodas las merçedes enel contenjdas E dogelo Agora de nuevo (s)ytodo
Seguid y enla manera q enel dicho preuillejo se contiene E qpueda
vsar e vse al dicho ofiçio de almjrantadgo contoda la Justiçia e
jurisdiçion alta e baxa çeuil e criminal e el mero mjsto jmperio
e todas las otras cosas e cada vna dellas enla dicha carta depre
uillejo Suso encorporada cotenjdas Evse dello. e de cada co
sa dello e los q por ey pusiere Asy enla mj corte e chançelleria
e casa e Rastro como fuera della. E pueda fazer E faga el
los q por ey pusiere todas las otras cosas e cada vna dellas
Contenjdas ela dicha carta depreuillejo Suso encorporada las
quales yo Agora do e otorgo E libre e plenaria Jurisdiçion
e poderio e cunplida Auctoridad Segud q volahe. E defie
do firme mente poresta mj carta depreuillejo y porel traslado
Signado de escriuano publico Sacado con auctoridad dejuez o
de alcalld qel algud Adelant njnguno nj algunos no sea osado
deleyr nj pasar cotra el dicho preuillejo nj cotra parte del para
gelo Cbrantar o dmjnguar en alguna cosa delo qel se cotie
ne que aqualqujer o qualesquier qlo hisieren o cotra el o cotra
parte del fuesen o pasasen avrian la mj yra e demas pecharme
yan las penas ela dicha carta depreuillejo Suso encorporada cotenjdas
E al dicho don alonso enrriquez mj tio e mj almjrante mayor o al
quel que Suboz touiese todos los daños e menoscabos que por

çey ⁊ ꝑ escatuesse y eso mjsmo pagar le han diez mjll mrs de pena para
su camara al dho don alon so enrriquez mj tio en mj almjzant
en los quales dhos dies mjll mrs de pena qujero y es mj md ⁊ voluntad
q cayan por ese mjsmo fecho qual qujer q vinjere o tentare venjr con
tra lo conten̄j d enes te mj preuj o contra cosa o part dello ꝯ yo le
fago md al dho al fonso enrriquez mj tio ⁊ mj almjzant mayor
o a qujen el quj siere ⁊ por bien tobiere. ⁊ sobresto mand a los ꝯ
bre dhos perlados maestres dlas ordenes comendadores ⁊ subcomen da
dores duqs ⁊ condes ⁊ ricos oms ⁊ a los dl mj conse jo ⁊ oydores dela
mj abdiencia ⁊ all dos ⁊ notarios ⁊ alguasiles ⁊ justi cias ⁊ otros ofi
çiales dla mj ꝯrt ⁊ chancilleria ⁊ de la mj casa ⁊ castro ⁊ a los
mjs adelantados ⁊ merinos ⁊ prestameros ⁊ prebostes ⁊ otras jus
ti cias ⁊ ofiçiales quales qer dla muy noble çabdad de seujlla
⁊ de to das las çabdades ⁊ villas ⁊ lugares dlos mjs reynos ⁊ señorios
⁊ a los capitanes de la mar ⁊ al mj armador dla flota ⁊ patrones
⁊ comjtres dlas mjs galeas ⁊ a los maestres ⁊ marineros y mareant
tes ⁊ otras personas quales qer q an do vjere ⁊ navegare por la
mar ⁊ a to das las otras personas de qual qujer estado o condiçion
o preemjnencia o dignidad q sean q esta mj carta de preujllejo o vie
ren o el traslado della signado de amo dho es q guarden ⁊ cumplan
⁊ fagan guardar ⁊ cumplir al dho don alonso enrriquez mj tio
⁊ mj almjrante mayor d la mar o al q lo oviere d aver por el este
dho preujllejo. ⁊ to das las mds en el conten̄j das en to do bien ⁊ cum
plida ment segud y ena manera q en el se contiene ⁊ q le no vaya
nj pasen nj consientan yr nj pasar contra el nj contra part dell so
la dha pena ⁊ por alguna fa son q sea so pena dla mj md ⁊ de la
pena conten̄j da en la dha carta d preujllejo suso en corporada a cada
uno por qujen fin care dello. ⁊ de mas faser ⁊ cumplir ⁊ mand al mj cha
çiller ⁊ mayor del mj sello de la poridad ⁊ a los dl mj conse jo ⁊
oydores dela mj abdiencia ⁊ all dos ⁊ notarios delos mjs conta dores
mayores ⁊ a los dmjs ofiçiales y escrivanos q estan dla tabla dlos
mjs sellos q en sobre to das las cosas suso dhas o sobre qual
qujer o quales qujer dellas el dho mj almjrante o los q por su pu
viere les pidieren quales qer mjs cartas ⁊ preuj todados o otros
quales qer q gelos den ⁊ libren ⁊ pasen ⁊ sellen los mas firmes
⁊ bastantes q a cumplidos ⁊ q pidieren ⁊ menester oviere por a
to d lo lo suso dho para cada cosa e part dello ⁊ ꝯla e pena
con ello ⁊ non faga des nj faga ꝯ nj al so la dha pena
⁊ dmas por qual qujer o quales qujer dllos por qen
fin care dlo de asi faser ⁊ cumplir mand al ome que vos esta

mj carta de preujlleio mostrare oel qual el trasllado sjgnado
como dho es q vos enplaze q parezcades Antemj enla mj
corte los vcesos por vros dros buradores elos oficiaales e las
otras personas syngulares personalmente al dia q vos enplaza
rede fasta qinze dias primeros sygujentes Ca da vno A del siz
por qual Rason no conplido mj manda e Sola dha pena e al
qual coer es guano pun e paza esto fuere llamado Eq el ende
al q vos la mostrare testimonjo Sygnad co su sygno porque
yo sepa en vmo Se cunple mj mandado E esto leman e daz al
dho mj alnjrate mj tio esta mj ca de preuj escripta en parg
mjnto e cuero firmada de mj nobre e Sella do con
mj sello de plomo pe dient enfilos de seda. Dada Ela cib
dad de segouja a seys dias de junjo Ano del nascimj de nro Sal
vador ihu xpo de mjll e quatrocetos e diez e nueve Anos yo
el Rey yo el Gobre delo Rey don Jua Reynante enno co la Rey
na doña maria mj esposa y conla ynfanta doña catalyna mj her
mana encastilla y enleon y engalisia y cey toledo y en Seujlla
y encordoua y enmurcia y en Jahe y enbacca y en badajoz y el
Algarbe y en algesira y enbizcaya en molyna cotorgo este pre
ujlleio y confirmolo. El ynfante don jua primo del dho señor
Rey ynfante de Arago maestre de Santiago confirma. El yn
fante don pedro primo del dho Señor Rey co firma. Don Alonso ey
tquñez tio el Rey Almjzante mayor de la maz confirma. Don
Ruy lopez daualos condestable e castilla Adelantado mojr de
murcia confirma. Don luys de gusman maestre dela orde dela
canalleria de calatraua confirma. Don luys dela cerda ce el
de medina celj vassallo del Rey co firma. Don jua alonso pimetel
Conde debenaventa vasallo del Rey co firma. Don pedro señor
de monte Alegre vasallo el Rey co firma. Don lope e men do m
riz obpo de Santiago capellan mayor co firma. Don Fo driz
go de velas obpo de palencia cofirma. Don alonso obpo de
Siguenca confirma. Don jua obpo e Segoja co firmal. Don juan
obpo e Auila co firma. Don aluaro obpo de cuenca co firma. Don fer
nando obpo de cordoua co firma. Don Fre gomez Administrador dela
iglia de palencia chanciller mayor de la Reyna de castilla co fir ma
Don Rodrigo obpo de Jahen confirma. Et yo jua feran de guada
lajara la fiz escrevjr por Su mandado del Rey nro señor. Fernad
bartalla Integro Registrada Laqual dha Carta depreuj
del dho señor Rey presentada e leyda en la manera q dha es
el dho go calo fuñz en nonbre del dho señor Almjzante dixo Alos

dhos Senores oydores que por quanto el dho Senor Almyrante en
tendia yle hera nece sario enbiar la dha carta de preuy ala presentar
eyalgunos lugares donde cumplia aservicio del dho Senor Rey edel bien
comun delos susReynos e senorios e delos subditos enaturales ellos
eguarda y observacion del dho Almyra tadgo edel dho almyrant e que se
temia ula con la dha carta depreuy se podria perder e danyficar ossi por
Robo como por furto e por agua e por otra causa e caso fortituy to o
peligro alguno que podria acaescer edello se podria seguir deservicio
al dho senor Rey e al dho Senor almyrant Reçebir enello daño por
ende dixo que pedia e pidio alos dhos Senores oydores ela mejor manera
eforma e podia edevia de derecho que del su officio el qual ynploravan man
dasen e diesen licencia ad nos los dhos Jua martinez e pero garçia como s
para que ambos a dos juntamente como personas publicas sacasemos e
hisiesemos sacar dela dha carta depuy del dho Senor Rey original un tras
la do o dos o mas quantos cumpliesen e fuesen menester al dho Senor Al
myrant e ge los diesemos sygnados d cadauno de nos
juntamente Rey manera que hisiese fe concertandos con la dha tal depreuy
original e que al tal traslado o traslados que ansy diesemos e cada dos el mes
mo sygno dela dha carta depreuy del dho Senor Rey al dho Senor
Almyrant o al que lo oviese de aver porel e porque fuese demas firmes
dote dios pidio alos dhos Senores oydores que diesen e ynterpusiesen a
ello su decreto e autoridad para que los tales tras lados depues la dos
a nos los dhos escrivanos Rey diesemos dello sygnados como dho es
valiesen e fisiesen fe dquier que paresçiesen en juy sio e fueza del
Rey como valdria o haria se la dha carta depreuy original enso
contenyda paresciendo. E luego los dhos Senores oydores visto el
dho pedimyento tomaro la dha carta depreuy original ensus manos e
vieron la e cataro la y examynaro la e por quanto alpresente nola
hallaro rota ny cassa ny chancellada ny sospechada ny en al
guna parte della dha dosa ny sospechosa mas antes paresçiente
de todo abisio por enel acatan d lo sobre dho todo dixeron que
mandavan e mandaro e dieron licençia ad nos los dhos Jua como no
dleon e pero garçia d madrigal escrivanos sobre dhos para que
ambos a dos juntamente como personas publicas ha casemos e fisie
semos sacar dela dha carta depreuy del dho Senor Rey original un
tras la do o dos o mas quantos cumpliesen e fuesen menester al dho
Senor Almyrate e ge los diesemos sygnados d nros sygnos con
cartandos con la dha carta de preuyllejo original e en manera que
hisiesen fe y el tras la do o traslados que nos los dhos anos diesemos dello
al dho Senor almyrante como dho es e los dhos Senores oydores dixero

e ynterponjan e ynterpusiero en d'autoridad e decreto si y en
quanto y enla mejor manera e forma q podia e devia de dere cho
para q los tales tras lado o tra slados q ansi diesemos dello sig
na dos valiesen e fisiesen fe doquier q paresçiesen en juy zio e
fuera del q. e a q cata' cumplida mente valiria e faria
fe la dha carta de preuyllejo original del dho señor Rey pares
ca en ll. testigos q fuero presentes a todo lo que dho es el lira dicho
juan lopez de myra'da e los bachilleres diego muñoz alldes delos fijos
dalgo e luys Rodrigues e fernand mateos e alonso lopez de seuylla e
luys go'çalez de cor doua escriuanos del dho señor Rey e desto en como
paso el dho gonçalo fernã'dez en nombre del dho señor almjrante pidio
a nos los dhos escriuanos q le diesemos este tras lado de la dha carta
de preu original del dho señor Rey con la dha Autoridad e decreto
para guarda e conserbaçion del dho almjrate e delas dhas sobre dhas
q fue fecho y pa so dia e mes e año antelos testigos sobre dhos q d
e/uso es criptos. e nos los dhos Jua' m'ñz de leon e pero garçia de
madrigal escriuanos sobre dhos por virtud dla dha liçençia e ma'da
m'to a nos fecho e da do por los dhos señores oydores dela dha Autori
dad e decreto por ellos a y ynterpuesta fesimos escreujr e sacar
e sacamos este dho tras la do de la dha carta de preu original del dho
señor Rey amos a dos juntamente e le co'certamos con la dha carta e su
original de verbo a verbo q alynso seran escriptos e fuero presentes
al dho con cartanos vieron e oyero leer e co'çertar este dho tras
la do con la dha carta d preu original los quales dhos testigos que
fuero presentes llamados al dho concertar con estos q se sigue
ff'n m'ñz de villalpa'do escriuano dla dha Abdiençia e andres de
vallid e fernand de medina giado del dho Jua' m'ñz de leo'. va escripto
sobre Rayd e en vn lugar donde dise po ren de grad qual az do o diz
e. e escripto este renglon q o diz m'j e escripto entre renglones o diz
qual ber nabiso o diz en la dha maz e entre renglones o diz dha q
sobre Rayd o diz publico que para. entre renglones. de. e o
diz de origaz. e escripto sobre Rayd o diz tenorio notario y e
tre renglones escripto o diz m'j o diz Jua' lopez no le e pez cay. e yo
el dho Jua' m'ñz de leon escriuano e notario publico sobre dho
q esto q dho es presente fuy con el dho po' garçia de madrigal
escriuano ante los dhos señores oydores en vno los dhos dho's t.s.
e dello presente fueron e por el dho ma'dam'to e liçençia delos dhos
señores oydores en vno con el dho pero garçia escriuano fize escre
uir e sacar este tras la do de la dha carta de preu del dho señor
Rey con la dha Autoridad en estas tres folias e media de pergamjno

de acero con esta en nueva (mj) signo de abaxo de cada plana va
puesto mj nonbre e çertado d'este traslado con la dha carta de preuilleso
original del dho señor rey en vno anel dho pero garcia escriuano en vn
presençia delos testigos q esta escriptura hase mençio q fuero presen
tes al dho q certa mj e pore el fise aqnj este mjo Signo q es atal
eytestimonjo de verdad. Juan mjne. E yo el dho pero garcia d
madrigal escriuano en bta publico Griso dho que d'esto q sobre
dho es presente fuy con el dho juan mjns de leon escriuano Ante los dhos
señores oydores en vno con los dhos testigos q d'ello fuero psenta
e por el dho ma dami el dçia delos dhos señores oydores en vno del
dho juan mjno escriuano fise escriuir e sacar este traslado dela
dha carta de preu del dho señor rey con la dha auctoridad en
estas tres fojas e media de pargamjno de acero con mas este pedaço
en va este mj signo e debaxo de cada plana va puesto mj nonbre
e con certado d'este traslado con la dha carta de preu original del dho
señor rey en vno anel dho jua mjns (vaj). en presençia delos
testigos q enesta escriptura hase mjnçio q fueron presento al
dho vn certa mj e por el fise aq este mjo Signo en testio d
verdad pero garcia. Este traslado fue d certado d la dha
escriptura original donde fue sacado Antelos testigos q d'ello fue
ron presentes en vierno trese dias del mes de noviembre Año del
nasçimiento de nro Salua de ihu xpo de mjll e quatro acentos e
ochenta e nueve Años testigos q fuero presents al leer e d
certar d'este dho traslado sacado dela dha escriptura Alonso
de valle e diego de mesa allos St nuño de mendoça e fernão
de esquivel e jua de montaños escriuano del rey nro Señor
co estos. E yo gonçalo garcia de villa mayor escriuano del rey
mo señor e su notario publico en la su corte y en todos los
sus reynos e señorios present fuy en vno col los dhos testigos
Al certar este dho traslado cola dha escriptura donde fue
Sacado el qual fise escriuir e por e fise Aqnj este
mjo Signo a tal eytestimonjo. gõ gã con al rey.

En el nonbre de la sancta trinidad y
eterna vnidas padre e fijo y espu Sancto tres
personas Real mete distintas en vna essençia diuina que
biue e reyna por siempre son fin At ala bien aventura de

virgen gloriosa nra señora Santa maria su madre d̄ quien
nos tenemos por señora e por abogada en todos los nros fechos e en
honrra y reuerencia suya e del bien aventurado Apostol señor
Santiago luz y espejo delas españas patron e guiador delos reyes
de castilla e de leon. E Ansi mismo a honor y reuerencia de to
dos los otros Santos y Santas dela corte celestial. por que
aunq̄ Segund natura nopuede el ome cumplida mente conoscer q̄
cosa es dios por el mayor conocimje̅to q̄ al mu̅do puede aver
puede lo conoscer biendo y co̅te̅mplando Sus marauillosas o
bras y fechos q̄ hizo e hase de cada dia pues q̄ todas las obras
por Su poder son fechas e por su saber gouernadas e por su bo̅
dad mantenjdas e Ansi el ome puede entender q̄ dios es comjenço
e medio e fin de todas las cosas q̄ el se ley acerca y el ma̅tiene ca̅
da vna en aquel estado e las ordeno. et todas le han menester y el
noha menester dellas y el las puede mudar cada q̄ quisiere se
gund su voluntad e no puede caber en el q̄ Se mude nj Se canbie ca en
alguna maña y el es dho rey Sobre todos los Reyes porq̄ del ha
ellos nonbre y por el Reynan. y el los gouierna y ma̅tiene los
quales Son virrios cada vno en su reyno puestos por el Sobre
las getes pa los mantener en justicia y en birtud temporal me̅te
la qual se muestra cumplida me̅te en dos maneras. la vna dellas
espiritual Segu̅d lo mostraro los proffetas y los Santos a gen
do nro señor gra̅ de saber todas las cosas cierta me̅te e las
haser entender. La otra manera es Segu̅d natura Asy como lo
mostraro los omes Sabios q̄ fuero̅ conoçedores d̄las cosas natu
ral mente. e a los Santos dixero̅ el rey es puesto en la tierra e e̅
lugar d̄ dios para cu̅plir la justicia e dar a cada vno Su drecho
y por ende lo llamaron Coraço̅ y Anjma del pueblo e Asy como
el Anjma esta en el Coraço̅ del ome e por el biue el cuerpo e Se
ma̅tiene Asy en el rey esta la justicia q̄ es bien y ma̅tenj mje̅to
del pueblo de su Señorio et Asy como el Coraço̅ es vno y por el
Reçiben todos los otros mjenbros vnjdad pa ser vn cuerpo. bie̅
Asy todos los d̄l Reyno maguer Sean mūchos porq̄ el rey de ue es
y es vno. y por esto de uen ser todos vno con el pa lo Segujr
e ayudar e ylas cosas q̄ ha de fasr en natural me̅te dixero̅ los
Sabios q̄ los reyes Son cabeça del Reyno porq̄ Asy como d̄la cabeça
naçen los Sentidos porq̄ se ma̅dan todos los mjenbros del cuerpo
bien Asy por el ma̅damj̅enar del rey q̄ es Señor y cabeça de todos
los d̄l Reyno Se deuen ma̅dar e gujar e lo obedescer. et tan
grande es el drecho y poder d̄los reyes q̄ todas las leyes e d̄rechos

tienen. ¶o su poderio porque del no le ha a los omes mas de dios
cuyo lugar tiene e las cosas temporales. al qual e las otras
cosas principal mente pteneçe de Amar y honrrar y guardar
sus pueblos. y e los otros señalada ment de ve tomar y
honrrar a los q lo mereçen por seruiçios q les ayan fecho. y por
ende el Rey o el principe entre los otros poderes q han nota sola
mente pue du mas de ven haser graçias a los que las mereçen
por seruiçios q les ayan fecho y por bondad q hallen e llos
y porq entre las otras virtudes anexas a los Reyes segud di
xeron los sabios es la justiçia la qual es virtud e verdad de las
cosas. por la qual mejor e mas enderesada ment se matiene
el mundo. y es asi como fuente don de mana todos los derechos
e dura siempre e la voluntad de los omes justos e nuca des fa
lleçe. e da a cada parte a cada vno ygual mente su derecho. e com
prende en si todas las virtudes prinçipales y nay de lla gran
vtilidad porq hase biuir verdad mente y en paz a cada
vno segud su estado syn culpa e syn yerro. e los buenos se
hasen por ella mejores. ¶e cabed galardon por los benefi
çios q hisieron e los otros por ella se enderesa e se me dan. e la
qual justiçia tiene en si dos partes prinçipales la vna es Comu
tiba q es entre vn ome e otro. e la otra es distributiua en la
qual con sisten los galardones y renumeraçiones de los bene
fiçios e virtuosos trabajos e seruiçios q los omes hasen a los Reyes
e prinçipes e a la cosa publica de sus Reynos. porq segud dise
las leyes dar galardon a los q bien e lealmente syruen es cosa
q conuiene mucho a todos los omes mayor ment a todos los Reyes
e prinçipes e grandes señores q tienen poder de lo haser. e de llos
es cosa propia honrrar e subliimar a aquellos q bien e lealmente
los syruen o cuyos virtudes e serviçios lo mereçen. y en galar
donar los benefiçios fechos los Reyes q lo hasen muestran ser
cono o dres de la virtud e otro si justiçieros. e la justiçia no es
tan solament en escarmentar los malos. mas en galardonar
a los buenos. e de mas desto nay de llo otra muy grand vtilidad por
q da voluntad a los buenos para ser mas virtuosos e a los malos
para en mendarse e guardar q no se hase podria al contra
rio. e porq entre los otros q galardones e Remuneraçiones
q los Reyes pue den haser a los q bien e lealmente los syruen es
honrrarlos e subliimarlos entre los otros de su linaje e los
ennobleçer e de corar e honrrar q les hase otros muchos bienes
e grandes mercedes. ¶por ende de tratando e considerando esto e lo suso

Dn̄ queremos que sepan por esta n̄ra carta d preuᵉ alt por su
tras la d signll d de escriuano publico todos los q̄ agora son
o seran daqui adelant como nos don fernãdo alt doña ysabel po
la grã d dios Rey e Reyna d castilla de leon d aragõ de sicilia
de granada d toledo de valencia de galisia d mallorcas d sevilla d
cerdeña de cordoua de corcega d murcia de jahen de los algarbes
de algesira alt de gibraltar e de las yslas de canaria conde y condᵉ
sa de barcelona señores de viscaya e de molina duqs de athenas
e d neopatria condes d Ruysellon e d cerdama marqses de ori
tan e d de gociano · Vimos unos capitos firmados d n̄ro nōbre
alt sellados cõ n̄ro sello fechos estᵉ guysa ·

Las cosas suplicadas e que vras altesas dan e otorgan d dõ
xpoual colon en alguna satisfaçõ d lo q̄ ha descubierto e de las
mares oceanas e del viaje q̄ agora cõl ayuda de dios ha de faz
n̄rellas en seruiᵉ d vras altezas son las q̄ se syguē

Primera mēte q̄ vrãs altesas como señores son de las dhãs
mares oceanas fasē dende agora al dho dõ xpoual colõ su al
mirante en todas aqllas yslas y tras firmes q̄ por su mano o jn
dustria se descubriran o ganaran en las dhas mares oceanas ya
durant su vida e despues del muerto a sus herederos e subceso
res de uno en otro perpetua mēte cõ todas aqllas premjnēcias
e prerrogatiuas perteneçientes al tal ofiçio e segud q̄ don
alonso enrriquez v̄ro almirant mayor de castilla e los otros pre
deçessores d dho ofiçio lo tenjã en sus districtos / pla ze a s̄s
sus altesas · juan de coloma

Otrosy que vras altesas hasen al dho dõ xpoual su visorey
e gouernador general en todas las dhas yslas e trras firm
mes e yslas q̄ como dho es el descubriere e ganare en las dhas
mares e q̄ p̄ᵃ el rexjmj̄ d cada una e qual qer dellas fa
ga electiõ de tres personas para cada ofiçio e que vrãs al
tesas tomē e escojan uno el q̄ mas fuere su seruᵐᵒ alt ansy se
rã mejor regidas las trras q̄ n̄ro señor le dexara hallar e
ganar a seruiçio d vras altesas · pla ze a sus altesas ·
jua̅ d coloma

Yten q̄ todas e quales qer mercaderias siqujer sean perlas
piedras preçiosas oro plata e espeçieria alt otras q̄ es qer

cosas e mercaderias de qualquier especie nombre e manera
q̃ sean q̃ se conpren trocaren hallaren ganaren e ovieren
dentro delos limytes del dho almyrantadgo q̃ desde agora sus
altezas hasen m̃d al dho don xpoual q̃ quiere que aya
elleve para si la desena parte de todello quitadas las costas
todas q̃ se hizieren enello · por manera q̃ delo q̃ quedare linpio
e libre · aya e tome la desma parte para si nismo e haga della
asu voluntad q̃ dando las otras nueve partes pa vras altezas
plase a sus altezas · Juan de coloma ·

Otrosi que si acaubsa delas mercaderias q̃l traera delas dhas
yslas e tiras q̃ asy como dho es se ganaren o descubrieren
o delas q̃ entruego de aquellas se tomaren aca de otros mer_
caderes nacieren pleyto alguno enel lugar donde el dho comercio
e trato seterna e hara q̃ si por la premynecia de su ofiçio de al
myrant le pertenecera o no oyr del tal pleyto · plega a vras al
tesas q̃l o su teniente e no otro juez conozca del tal pleyto et
asy lo provea dende agora · plase a sus altesas sy perte
nece al dho ofiçio de almyrante segun q̃ lo tenia el almyrãte
don alonso enrriquez e los otros sus antecessores en sus distri
tos e sy en de justo · Juan de coloma ·

Yten que en todos los navios q̃ se armaren para el dho trato e
negociacion cada e quando e quantas veses se armaren que
pueda el dho don xpoual colon sy quisiere contribuyr et
pagar la ochaua parte deto de loq̃ se gastare enl armason
e que tanbien aya e lleve del provecho la ochava parte delo que
resultare dela tal armada · plaze a sus altesas · Juan de
coloma

Son otorgados y despachados con las respuestas de vras al
tesas en fin de cada un capitulo en la villa de santa fe dela
vega de granada a diez e siete dias de abril del año del nasci
mi de nro saluador ihū xpo de mill e qtrocientos e noventa e dos
años · yo el rey · yo la reyna · por mandado del rey e dela reyna
Juan de coloma · Registrada calcena ·

E agora por quanto vos el dho don xpoual colon nro al
myrante del mar oceano e nro visorey e gouernador dela
tierra firme e yslas nos suplicastes e pedistes por merçed

que porque mejor et mas cumplida mente vos fuese guardada la
dha carta de md a vos e a vros fijos e descendientes que vos la
confirmasemos e aprouasemos e vos mandasemos dar nra carta
el preui della o como la nra md fuese et nos Acata do lo suso dho
e los muchos e buenos e leales e grades e continuos seruis que vos el
dho don xpoual colon nro almirante e visorey e gouernador
delas yslas e tra firme descubiertas e por descubrir en la mar o
ceano e en la parte delas yndias nos aves de fecho y esperamos e nos
hareys espeçial mente en descubrir e tener Anro poder et nro
Señorio a las dhas yslas e tra firme mayor mente porque es
peramos que con ayuda de dios nro Señor se fundara en mucho
Seruiçio suyo e honrra nra et pro e vtilidad de nros Reynos et Se
ñorios porque esperamos ayuda de dios e los pobladores yn
dios delas yslas e yndias se convertira A nra sancta fe ca
tholica tobimos lo por bien et por esta dha nra carta de preuille
jo o por el dho su trasladado Signado como dho es de nro pro
prio motuo e çierta çiençia e poderio Real absoluto de que
en esta parte queremos vsar e vsamos confirmamos et aproua
mos para agora et para siempre jamas a vos el dho don gonçal
colon e a los dhos vros fijos e nietos e descendientes de vos e
dellos et a vros herederos la sobre dha nra carta suso encor
porada e la md en ella contenida e queremos e mandamos y es nra
md e voluntad que vos bala e sea guardada a vos e a vros fijos
e descendientes agora e de aqui adelant ynviolable men te segun
agora et para siempre jamas en todo e por todo bien e cumplida
mente segund e por la forma e manera que en ella se contiene
et sy neçesario es agora de nuevo vos façemos la dha md e de
fendemos firme mente que ninguna ni algunas personas no sea
osados de vos yr ni venir contra ella ni contra parte della por
vos la quebrantar et menguar en tpo alguno ni por alguna maña
Sobre lo qual mandamos al prinçipe don Ju nro muy caro
e muy Amado fijo e a los ynffantes duques perlados marqueses
condes ricos omes maestres delas ordenes priores comenda dores
et subcomenda dores e a los del nro consejo e oydores de la nra abdi
ençia alcaldes Alguasiles e otras justiçias quales quier dela nra casa
e corte e chançilleria e a los alcaydes delos castillos e casas fuertes
e llanas e a todos los conçejos asistentes corregidores alldes
alguasiles merinos prebostes e otras justiçias de todas las
çibdades e villas e lugares delos nros reynos et señorios e a
cada vno dellos que vos guarde e fagan guardar esta dha nra

Carta de preuillejo e confirmacion e la ca de merced enella conte
nj da e contra el thenor e forma della no vos vayan ni passen ni co
sientan yr ni pasar entodo alguno ni por alguna manera so las pe
nas enella contenjdas delo qual vos mandamos dar esta dha nra
carta de preuj e confirmacion escripta en pargamjno de cuezo e fir
mada de nros nombre e sellada e nro sello de plomo pendiente en
filos de seda de colores laql mandamos al nro chanciller mayor e noto
rios e alos otros oficiales que estan ala tabla delos nros sellos que sellen
e libren e pasen loqual todo que dho es enlos dhos capitulos suso
encorporados y enesta nra confirmaço contenjdos queremos y es
nra md e voluntad que se guarde e cumpla dis segud que enellos se
contiene e los vnos ni los otros no fagades ni fagan ende al por al
guna manera sopena dela nra md de diez mjll mrs parala nra
camara a cada vno que lo contrario fisiere e demas mandamos al
ome que vos esta nra carta mostrare que vos enplase que parezcades ante
nos enla nra corte doquier que nos seamos del dia que vos enplasare
fasta qnse dias primeros siguientes sola dha pena sola qual man
damos a qualquier escriuano publico que para esto fuere llamado
que ende al que gela mostrare testimonio signado consu signo por
que nos sepamos encomo se cumple nro mandado dada enla çibdat
de burgos a veynte e tres dias del mes de abril año del nasci mj
e nro saluador ihu xpo de mjll e quatrocientos e noventa e
syete años yo el rey y ola reyna yo ferna daluarez de
toledo secretario del rey e dela reyna nros señores la fise es cre
vir por su mandado antonj doctor ferna daluarez iua vela
quez y enlas espaldas del dho preuj estaua escripto lo siguiente
syn chancilleria e syn derechos por mandado de sus altesas

En el nonbre de la santta trinjdat eterna vnj
dat padre y fijo y espu sancto tres personas real
mente distintas e vna essencia dinjna que bive e rey na
por siempre sin fin e dela bien aventurada virgen gloriosa sa
cta maria nra señora su madre aquien nos tenemos por señora
e por abogada en todos los nros fechos e ahonra e reuerencia
suya e del bien aventurado apostol señor santiago luz y
espejo delas españas patro e guiador delos reyes de castilla e de
leon e asi mjsmo a honrra e reuerencia de todos los otros san
tos e santtas dela corte celestial porque avnque segud natura
no puede el ome cumplida mente conoscer que cosa es dios por el

Otro preuj real
al mj don Xual
encorporada en
el lamj de al
mj visorrey e
gouernador de tha
en el dho año de
jUcccc xc vij.

mayor conosçimyento q̃ del mundo pueda aver pues delo vno cer
viendo e adtenplando sus maravillas cobras e fechos q̃ hi
zo e haze de cada dia pues q̃ todas las obras por su poder son fechas
e por su saber governadas e por su bondad matenjdas las vel
ome puede entender q̃ dios es comyenço e medio e fin de todas las
cosas e q̃ el se en acierran y el mantiene a cada vna dellas estado e
las ordena e todas le han menester y el non ha menester dellas y el
las puede mandar cada vez q̃ huysiere segud su voluntad y no pue
de aver el q̃ se mude nj se canbie en alguna maña y el es dicho rey
sobre todos los reyes porq̃ del han ellos nobre e por el reynan
e el los govierna e mantiene los quales son vicarios suyos ca
da vno en su reyno puestos sobre las gentes para los matener en
justiçia y en verdad temporal mente lo qual se muestra cunplida
mente en dos maneras la vna dellas espiritual segud lo mostraro
los profetas y los santos a quien dio nro señor gra de saber
las cosas çiertamente e las ha syentender la otra manera es
segud natura asi como lo mostraro los omes sabios q̃ fuero cono
çedores dellas cosas natural mente ca los santos dixero q̃el
rey es puesto enla tierra en lugar de dios para cunplir la justiçia e
dar a cada vno su drecho e por ende le llamaro coraçon e alma
ca asi como el anjma esta el coraço del ome y por el bive el cuerpo
y se matiene asy por el rey esta la justiçia q̃ es vida e matenj
de su señorio ca asy como el coraço es vno y por el te caben todos
los otros mjenbros vnj dad para ser vn cuerpo bie asy todos los del
reyno maguer sean muchos con vno por q̃ el rey deve ser y es vno
y por esto deven ser todos vnos con el para le servir e ayudar en
las cosas q̃ ha de hazer y natural ment dixeron los sabios
q̃ los reyes son cabeça del reyno porq̃ asy como dela cabeça naçe los
sentidos por q̃ se mandan todos los mjenbros del cuerpo bien
asy por el mandamjento q̃ naçe del rey q̃ es señor y cabeça de todos
los del reyno se deven mandar e gujar y lo obedeçer y tan
grande es el ordo poder delos reyes q̃ todas las leys y los derechos
tienen so su poderio por q̃ a el no lo han delos omes mas de dios
cuyo lugar tienen en las cosas temporales al qual q̃ e las otras
cosas principal mente perteneçe de amar y honrrar e guardar
sus pueblos y entre los otros señala damente deve amar y
honrrar a los q̃ lo mereçe por servjçio q̃ le ayan fecho y por de
el rey y el prinçipe entre los otros poderes q̃ ha no tan sola
mente pue de mas deve hazer gras a los q̃ las mereçe por ser mas
q̃ le ayan fecho e por bondad q̃ halle en ellos y porq̃ en te las otr

virtudes anexas a los Reyes segund dixeron los sabios es la justicia
la qual es virtud e verdad delas cosas por la qual mejor e mas en dre-
resçada mente se mantiene el mundo y es asi como fuente e don de manan
todos los derechos e dura por siempre enlas voluntades delos omes justos
e nunca desfallece e da a cada parte a cada vno ygual mente su derecho
e es en presençia en si e todas las virtudes prinçipales y nasçe della muy
grand vtilidad por que se biuir cuerda mente y en paz cada vno e que
esta do sin culpa e sin yerro. E los buenos se la sen por ella mejor
resçiben de galardon por los bienes que fizieron y los otros por ella se
reçelan y en miedo estan. la qual justiçia tiene en si dos partes prinçipales
la vna es comutatiua que es entre vn ome e otro. la otra es distributiua la qual considera los galardones e remuneraçiones a los buenos e
virtuosos trabajos e seruiçios que los buenos fazen a los Reyes e prinçipes e
a la cosa publica de sus reynos e por que segund dize la ley. dar
galardon a los que bien e leal mente siruen es cosa que conviene mucho a
todos los omes mayor mente a los Reyes e prinçipes e grandes señores
que tienen poder de lo fazer e en ellos es propia cosa honrrar e sublimar
aquellos que bien e leal mente los siruen e sus virtudes e seruiçios
lo meresçe. y en galardonar los buenos fechos los Reyes en lo fazen
muestran ser conosçedores dela virtud. otrosi justiçieros. E la
virtud dela justiçia no esta sola mente en escarmentar los malos.
mas avn en galardonar a los buenos. E demas desto nasçe della
otra grand vtilidad por que da voluntad a los buenos para ser mas buenos e a los malos para emendarse. e que de al Rey no se le podria
de acaesçer por contrario. y por que entre los otros galardones y remuneraçiones que los Reyes pueden fazer a los que bien e leal mente
les siruen es honrrar los e sublimar los entre los otros de su
linaje e los ennoblesçer e decorar e honrrar e les fazer otros
muchos bienes e graçias e merçedes. por ende considerando e acatando
lo en so dicho queremos que sepan por esta nuestra carta de preuilegio por su
treslado signado de escriuano publico todos los que agora son e seran daqui adelante. Como nos don fernando e doña ysabel por la
graçia de dios Rey e Reyna de castilla de leon de aragon de siçilia de
granada de tole do de valençia de galisia de mallorcas de seuilla
de çerdeña de cordoua de corçega de murçia de jahen de los algarbes de algesira de gibraltar e delas yslas de canaria conde e condesa de barçelona e señores de vizcaya e de molina duques de athenas
e de neopatria condes de ruysellon e de çerdania marqueses de oristan
e de goçiano. Vimos vna carta merçed firmada de nuestros nombres e
sellada con nuestro sello fecha en esta guisa. Don fernando

Doña ysabel por la graçia de dios Rey e Reyna de castilla e leon
de aragon de çiçilia de granada de toledo de valençia de ga
lisia de seuilla de çerdeña de cordoua de corçega de murçia
de jahen selos algarbes dalge zira degibraltar e delas yslas
de canaria Conde e condesa debarçelona Señores deviz caya e
de molyna Duques de Athenas e deneopatria Condes de Ruyse
llon e de çerdanya marqueses de oristan e degoçiano porque
quanto vos xpoual colon por nuestro mandado Avedes deyr adescobrir
e ganar con çiertas fustas nuestras y con nuestras gentes çiertas yslas
e tierra firme enla mar oçeana e se espera que con la ayuda de
dios se descubriran e ganaran algunas delas dhas yslas
e tierra firme enla dha mar oçeana por vuestra mano e yn dustria
e aquesto es cosa justa e Rasonable e pues vos poneys al dho pe
ligro por nuestro serviçio sea de ello remunerado Acreçentar e
vos honrrar e fazer como por lo en so dho es nuestra merçed e voluntad
que vos el dho xpoual colon despues que ayades descubierto
e ganado las dhas yslas e tierra firme enla dha mar oçeana
o qualesquier dellas que seades nuestro almyrante delas dhas yslas
e tierra firme que asi descubrieredes e ganaredes Al sea de nuestro almy
rante e visorrey e governador enellas e vos podades den de
en adelante llamar e yntitular don xpoual colon e asi
vuestros fijos e subçessores en el dho ofiçio e cargo se puedan
yntitular e llamar don el almyrante e visorrey e gover
nador dellas e para que podades vsar e exerçer el dho ofiçio
de almyrantadgo con el dho ofiçio de visorrey e governador
delas dhas yslas e tierra firme que asi descubrieredes e ga
naredes por vos o por vuestros lugares tenientes e oyr e librar
todos los pleytos e cabsas çeviles e criminales tocantes al
dho ofiçio de almyrantadgo e de visorrey e governador segund
hallaredes por derecho e segund lo Acostumbran vsar y exer
çer los almyrantes de nuestros Reynos e podades punir e castigar
los delinquentes e vsedes delos dhos ofiçios de almyrantadgo
e visorrey e governador vos e los dhos vuestros lugares tenientes
e llevedes los derechos e salarios a los dhos ofiçios e a cada vno dellos es Anexo
e conçernientes e tayades e llevedes los derechos e sa
larios a los dhos ofiçios e a cada vno dellos Anexos e
conçernientes e perteneçientes segund e como los lleva
e Acostumbra llevar el nuestro almyrante mayor e el almyrantadgo
de nuestros Reynos e por esta nuestra carta o por su traslado signado
de escriuano publico mandamos al prinçipe don Juan nuestro

muy claro et muy amado hijo e a los ynfantes duques perlados
marqueses condes maestres de las ordenes priores comendadores e a
los del nro conseso e oydores de nra abdiencia alldes e otras justicias
quales quier dela nra casa e corte e chancilleria e a los subco
mendadores alcaydes delos castillos e casas fuertes e llanas e a
todos los cavalleros e asystentes corregidores e alldes e alguasi
les merinos veynte e quatros cavalleros escuderos oficiales e
omes buenos de todas las cabsas e villas e lugares delos nros rey
nos e senorios e alos que vos conqystardes e ganardes e alos ca
pitanes maestres de otra maestres e oficiales marineros e getes
dela mar nros subditos e naturales que agora son e seran de
aqui adelante e a cada vno e qual ser della que syendo por
vos descubiertas e ganadas las dhas yslas e tierra firme dela
dicha mar oceana e fecho por vos o por qyen vro poder oviere
el juramento e solepnidad que en tal caso se te qyere vos aya
e tengan dende en adelante para en toda vra vida e despues
de vos a vro hijo et subcesor e de subcesor en subcesor para
siempre jamas por nro almirante dela dicha mar oceana e por vi
so rey e governador delas dichas yslas e tierra firme e vos
el dho don xpoual colon descubrierdes e ganardes e vsen de vos
e en los dhos vros lugar tenientes que en los dhos oficios de almira
tadgo e visorrey e governador pusierdes e en todo lo a ellos
concerniente e vos recudan e fagan recudir con la qytacion e
derechos e otras cosas alos dhos oficios anexas e pertenes
cientes e vos guarden e fagan guardar todas las honrras
e gras e mrds e libertades e premynecias e perrogatinas e esen
ciones e munidades e todas las otras cosas e cada vna dellas
que por razon delos dhos oficios de almirante e visorrey e governador
devedes aver e gozar e vos deven ser guardadas e todo bien e
cumplida mente e en gyusa que vos non mengue ende cosa alguna e
en ello ny en parte dello enbargo ny contrario alguno vos non
pongan ny consientan poner ca nos por esta nra carta desde a
gora para entonces vos fasemos mrd delos dhos oficios de al
mirantadgo e visorrey e governador por juro de heredad para
siempre jamas e vos damos la posesion e casy posision dellos e
de cada vno dellos e poder e abtoridad para los vsar e exercer
e llevar los derechos e salarios a ellos e a cada vno dellos ane
xos e pertenescientes segund e como dho es e sobre lo qual todo
lo que dho es sy necesario vos fuere e gelo vos pidierdes man do
al nro chanciller et notarios e a los otros oficiales que estan

la tabla delos nros sellos q̃ vos den en libro o pasen e sellen
nra carta de prem̃ j todas las mas fuerte e firme e bastante q̃
les pidierdes e o pudierdes menester / et los vnos nj los otros no fa
gades nj fagan ende al por alguna manera Sopena dela nra m̃d
e de diez mjll mrs para la nra camara a cada vno q̃lo contrario
hiziere et demas mandamos al ome q̃les esta nra carta mostra
re q̃los enplaze q̃ parezca ante nos enla nra corte doquier q̃
nos seamos del dia q̃los enplazare a quinze dias prime
ros siguientes Sola dha pena Sola qual mandamos a qual
quier escrivano publico q̃ para esto fuere llamado q̃ de ende
al q̃ gela mostrare testimonjo signado con su signo por q̃
nos Sepamos en como se cumple nro mandado. dada en la nra
cibdad de granada a treynta dias del mes de Abril Año del
nascim̃ o de nro Salvador ihu xpo de mjll e quatrocientos e
noventa e dos Años · yo el Rey · yo la Reyna · yo Juan de
Coloma secretario del Rey e dela Reyna nros señores la fize es
crevir por su mandado · Reverendada en forma · Roderiz doctor
Registrada Sabastian olano · fernando de madrid chanciller / E a
gora por q̃ vos el nro Almirante señor vos hallastes muchas dellas
e otras yslas e esperamos con la ayuda enla q̃ hallareys e
descubrireys otras yslas e tierra firme en el dho mar océano
ala dha parte delas yndias. Nos Suplicastes e pedistes por
m̃ d q̃ vos confirmasemos la dha nra carta que de suso va encor
porada e la m̃ d en ella contenjda para q̃ vos e vros fijos e desce
dientes vno en pos de otro despues de vros dias ayades e ten
gades de tener y tengades los dhos oficios de almyrante e viso
Rey e governador del dho mar océano e yslas e tierra firme
q̃ asy aveys descubierto e hallado e descubrierdes e hallardes
dagora delante con todas aquellas facultades e premyne
cias e perrogativas de q̃lango gozan e gozan los nros almy
rantes e viso Reys e governadores q̃ han sido e Son de los
dhos nros Reynos de castilla e de leon · Vos sea acudido con to dos
los derechos e Salarios a los dhos oficios Anexos e pertenescientes
vsados e guardados a los dhos nros almyrantes visorreyes e go
vernadores · e vos mandasemos proveer Sobre ello como la nra
m̃ d fuese · Et nos Acatando el Riesgo e peligro en q̃ por
nro servicio os pusistes en yr a buscar e descubrir las yslas q̃
las e en el q̃ Agora vos poneys en yr abuscar e descubrir las
otras yslas e tierra firme de q̃ avemos Seydo y esperamos
Ser de vos muy Servidos et por vos fazer bien e mrd por la

presente vos confirmamos d vos e a los dhos vros fijos e desce
dientes vno en pos de otro para agora e para sie
pre jamas los dhos oficios de almjrante del dho mar oceano e viso
rey e governador dllas dhas yslas e trra firme q aveys hallado e
descubierto e dllas otras yslas e trra firme q por vos e por vra
yndustria se hallaren e descubrieren daqui adelante e la dha pte
dllas yndias - y es nra md e volmtad q ayades e tengades vos
y despues de vros dhos vros fijos e descendientes e herederos
vno en pos de otro el dho oficio de nro almjrante del dho mar oceano
q es nro q comjença por vna raya e linea q nos avemos fecho mar
car q passa des de las yslas de los Açores alas yslas de
cabo verde de setentrion en austro y dl polo a polo por ma
nera q to do lo q es allende de la dha linea al ocidente es nro
e nos pertenece e la ley vos fizieremos e criamos nro almjrante d
vros fijos e suos sores vno en pos de otro de todo ello para siep
jamas e asy mismo vos fazemos nro visorrey e governador
e despues de vros dhos vros fijos e descendientes e herede
ros vno en pos de otro dllas dhas yslas e trra firme descu
biertas e por descubrir enl dho mar oceano ala parte de las yn
dias como dho es e vos damos la posession e la sei possesion de todos
los dhos oficios d almjrante e visorrey e governador para siempre
jamas e poder e facultad pa q dllas dhas mares podades vsar e
exercer e vse d el dho oficio de nro almjrante en todas las co
sas y en la forma e manera e con las prerogativas e prehemjne
cias e derechos e salarios segud e como lo vsaron e vsan e go
zaron e gozan los nros almjrantes delos mares de castilla e de
leon e para en la dha trra e dlas yslas e trra firme q son descu
biertas e se descubrieren de aqui adelante en la dha mar oceana
e la dha parte dlas yndias por q los pobladores de todo ello
sean mejor governados vos damos tal poder e facultad para
e poda des como nro visorrey e governador vsar por vos e por
vros lugares tenientes e almdes e alguaziles e otros oficiales
e para ello pusieredes la juridicion civile e crimjnal alta e baxa
mero mjxto ymperio los quales dhos oficiales podades amover
e qtar e poner otros en su lugar cada e quando q quisieredes
vieredes q cumple a nro servicio los quales puedan oyr e
librar e determjnar todos los pleytos e causas civiles e cri
mjnales e en las dhas yslas e trra firme dnes caeçeren e se movie
ren e aver e llevar los derechos e salarios acostumbrados d
nros reynos de castilla e de leon a los dhos oficios anexos

es pertenescientes. e vos el dho nro visorrey e gouernador po
days oyr e conoçer de todas las dhas cabsas e de cada vna dellas
cada e vos que vez de primera ynstançia e por via de apella
çon o por simple qrella e las ver e determjnar e librar como
nro visorey e gouernador e poda de fazer e faga de vos e
los dhos vros offiçiales qualesquier pes qui sas alos casos de
derecho premjssas e todas las otras cosas alos dhos offiçios
de visorrey e gouernador pertenesçientes e que vos vros lu
gares tenjentes e offiçiales q' pa ello pusierdes y entendie
des q' cumple a nro serviçio y execuçion de nra justiçia. lo
qual todo yo da e puedan ha ser como si por nos fuese
los dhos offiçiales puestos. pero es nra mrçed e volumtad q' la
tas y provisiones q' diez de sean e se espidan e libren en nro
nonbre. disiendo don fernando et doña ysabel por la gra de dios
Rey e Reyna de castilla deleo etc. e sean selladas co nro sello
e nos vos mandamos dar para las dhas yslas e tierra firme. et ma
damos eto de los vesinos e moradores e otras psonas q' estan
y estovieren en las dhas yslas e tierra firme q' vos obedezca como
a nro visorrey e gouernador dellas e alos q' andovieren e las
dhas mares en so declaradas e vos obedezcan como a nro al
mjrant del dho mar oceano e to dos ellos cumplan vras cartas e
mandamjs e se junten con vos e con vros offiçiales pa execu
tar la nra justiçia e vos den e faga dar todo el favor e ayuda
q' les pidier des e menester ovier des e las penas q' les pusier
des las quales nos por la presente les pone mos e avemos por
puestas e vos damos poder pa las executar en sus personas e
bienes. et otro es nra mrçed e volumtad q' oy vos e vres diez des ser
an plidero a nro serviçio e la execuçion de nra justiçia q' quales
quier psonas q' estan y estovieren e las dhas yn slas e tierra
firme e algun dellas e q' no entre nj esten e ellas e q' venga
o se presenten ante nos e lo po days mandar de nra parte e les
fagades saliz dellas alos quales nos por la presente mandamos
q' lo fagan e cumplan e pongan en obra sin nos Requerir nj
consultar e ello nj esperar nj aver otra nra carta nj mandami
no enbargante qualquier apellaçio o suplicaçio q' dello tal tu
vro mandami hisieren e ynter pusieren para lo qual todo
e dho es e para las otras cosas devidas e pertenesçientes alos
dhos offiçios de nro almjrant visorey e gouernador vos da
mos todo poder cumplido con todas ms ynçidençias e depen
dençias emergençias anexidades e conexidades. Sobre lo ql

to de que ellos siquisieren de mandamos al nro chanceller e notarios e a los otros officiales q estan a la tabla de los nros sellos que vos den e libren e pasen e sellen nra carta de preujlegio dada la mas fuerte e firme e bastante que les pidieredes e menester ovieredes. E los unos nj los otros non fagan en deal por alguna maña so pena de diez mjll mrs para la nra camara a cada uno que lo contrario fiziere. E demas mandamos al ome que vos esta nra carta mostrare que vos enplase que parezcades ante nos en la nra corte do quier que nos seamos del dia que vos enplasare fasta qujnse dias primeros siguj entes so la dha pena so la qual mandamos a qual quier escriuano publico que para esto fuere llamado que de ende al que gela mostrare testimonjo sygnado con su signo por que nos sepamos en como se cunple nro mandado. Dada en la cibdad de barcelona a veynte e ocho dias del mes de mayo año del nascim° de nro salua dor ihu xpo de mjll e quatrocientos e noventa e tres años. yo el rey e yo la reyna. yo fernand aluarez de toledo secretario del rey e de la reyna nros señores la fize escreujr por su mandado. pero gutierres chanceller. derechos al sello e de registro nichil. y en las espaldas aguarda da. roderic doctor. registrada al cira. E agora por quanto vos el dho don xpoual colon nro almjrante del mar oceano e nro viso rrey e gouernador de la trra firme e yslas nos suplirastes e pedistes por merced que para guarda e mejor e mas anplidamente vos fuese guardada la merced a vos fecha e a vros fijos e descendientes vos la confirmasemos e aprouasemos e vos mandasemos dar nra carta de preuj ollā o como la nra merced fuese e nos acatando lo suso dho e los muchos e buenos e leales e grandes e continos seruic° que vos el dho don xpoual colon nro almjrante visorrey e gouernador de las yndias e tra firme descubiertas e por descubrir al mar oceano en la pte de las yndias nos ave des fecho e esperamos que nos ha reydes especial mente en descubrir e traer a nro poder e so nro señorio las dhas yslas y las e trra firme mayor mente por que esperamos que con ayuda de dios nro señor se dende dara en mucho seruj° suyo e honrra nra e pro de nros reynos por que espera mos que los pobladores e indios de las otras yndias se convertiran a nra santa fe catholica tovimos lo por bien e por esta dha a nra carta de preuj o por el dho entre la do signada como dho es del nro proprio motuo e cierta ciencia e poderio real absoluto de que en esta parte queremos usar e usamos confirmamos e apro uamos para agora e para siempre jamas a vos el dho don xpoual

Colon e a los dhos vros hijos e nietos e descendientes e vos
e de vros herederos la sobre dha nra carta suso encorporada
e la md enella contenjda e queremos e mandamos y es nra md e
voluntad que vos vala e sea guardada a vos e a los dhos vros fi
jos e descendientes agora e de aquj adelante jnviolable mente
para agora e para siempre jamas en todo e por todo bien
e cunplida mente segud e por la forma e manera que enella se
tiene e por que necessario es agora de nuevo vos faremos la dha md
e defendemos firme mente que njnguna nj algunas personas no
sean osados de vos yr nj venjr cotra ella nj contra parte della por
vos la quebrantar nj menguar en tpo alguno nj por alguna manera
sobre lo qual mandamos al prinçipe don juan nro muy caro e muy
amado hijo e a los ynfantes duques perlados marqueses condes ricos
omes maestres delas ordenes priores e comendadores e a los del
nro conseio oydores dela nra abdiençia alcaldes alguasiles e otras
justiçias quales quier dela nra casa e corte e chançilleria e a los alcay
des delos castillos e casas fuertes e llanas e a todos los conçe
los e asystentes corregidores e alldes e alguasiles prebostes e
otras justiçias de todas las çibdades villas e lugares dellos nros
reynos e señorios e a cada vno dellos que vos guarden e fagan
guardar esta dha nra carta de prev e confirmaçio e la carta
de md ella contenjda e contra el thenor e forma della no vos va
yan nj pasen nj consientan yr njn pasar en tpo alguno nj por
alguna manera so las penas enellas contenjdas de lo qual
vos mandamos dar esta dha carta de prevjllejo e confirmado
escripta en pargamjno de cuero e firmada de nros nonbres e se
llada con nro sello de plomo pendiente en filos de seda a colores
la qual mandamos al dho nro chançiller mayor e notario e a los
otros ofiçiales que estan ala tabla delos nros sellos que sellen e
libren e passen. e los vnos nj los otros no fagades njn fagan ende
al por alguna manera so pena dela nra md e de diez mjll
mrs para la nra camara a cada vno que lo contrario fiziere e
demas mandamos al ome que vos esta nra carta mostrare que vos en
plaze que parezcades ante nos en la nra corte do quier que nos sea
mos del dia que vos en plazare fasta qujnse dias primeros si
gujentes so la dha pena so la qual mandamos a qual quier escriua
no publico que para esto fuere llamado que de ende al que gela mostra
re testimonjo signado con su signo por que nos sepamos en como
se cunple nro mandado. dada en la çibdad de burgos a veynte e
tres dias del mes de abril año del nasçimj de nro salvador

çihu xpo de mill e quatrocientos e noventa e syete años. yo
el rey. yo la reyna. yo ferna dalvarez de toledo secretario del
Rey e dla reyna nros señores la fize escrevir por su ma dado -
roderico doctor. Antonio doctor. ferna dalvarez. Juan velaz
quez. Antonio doctor concertado. y leylas espaldas del dho priui
legio ria. Registrada. Doctor.

El Rey E la Reyna

Merced para q
por tres años se
saq el ochauo pa
el almi ron xual
antes quelas costa
fecha en xv. de
Junio de xcvij.

Por quanto enla capitulacion e asiento q por nro ma
dado seliso e tomo con vos don xpoual colon nro al
mirante dl mar o ceano enla parte delas yndias. se con
tiene que vos ayays de aver cierta parte delo q se diere
e traxere dlas dhas yndias sacado primera ment las cos
tas e gastos q enello se diere fecho e fizieren como mas
larga mente enla dha capitula çion se contiene. e por q
fasta agora vos aveys trabajado mucho en descobrir tierra
en la dha parte delas yndias de cuya cavsa no seha avido
mucho ynteresse dellas. avnq seha fecho algunas costas
y gastos y por q nra md e voluntad es q vos fase md. por
la presente queremos e mandamos q las costas e gastos q fasta
Aqui sehan fecho en los nego cios tocantes alas dhas yndias
fasta q sean llegados ala ysla ysabela española y no se
os demande cosa alguna dellas ni vos seays obligado a cotri
buyr en ellas cosa alguna de mas delo q posistes al tpo del pri
mer viaje con tanto q vos no pidays ni lleveys cosa al
guna dello q fasta Aqui seha traydo dlas dhas yslas por
ta son del diezmo ni del ochavo que vos el dho Almirante
Aveys de aver delas cosas muebles dlas dhas yslas ni por
otra razon alguna delo q aveys avido fasta aqui vos fa
semos md e por q vos el dho Almirante desis q de lo que se
diere daqui adelant delas dhas yslas seha de sacar
primera mente el ochavo. y delo que restare sehan de
sacar las costas e despues el diezmo. e por que por la
orden e tenor dela dha capitulacion parece q se deven
primero sacar las costas y despues el diezmo y despues
el ochavo y no esta por Agora Averiguado como se esto

se ha de faser. Es nra (md) por haser (md) a vos el dho Almyra
te que por tres años se saque primero el ochauo para vos sin
costa alguna E despus se saquen las costas (et) de lo q(ue) restare
q(ue) se saque el diezmo para vos el dho Almyzant. pero pa sa do el
dho tpo q(ue) se aya de sacar el dho diezmo de las costas e ochauo
segund en la dha capitulacio se o(n) tiene. (et) que por esta (md) q(ue)
vos fasemos por el dho tpo no seos de ni qui te mas derecho al q(ue)
teneys por virtud de la dha capitulacion antes aq(ue)lla q(ue)d confu
fuerça e vigor para adelante passado el dho tpo. fecha en la
villa de me dina del campo a doze dias del mes de junio de noveta
siete años. yo el Rey. y ola Reyna. por mandado del Rey e de la
Reyna. fernand aluarez. y en las espaldas desta carta de
zia. acordada.

Para que el
almi. ponga
vna persona q(ue)
entienda en la
cõtratacion de
las yndias cõ
los oficiales de
su alteza. fecha
a xxx. de ma
yo xxxvij. a(ño)s

Don fernando e doña ysabel
por la gra de dios Rey et Reyna de castilla de leon de
Aragon de Secilia de granada de tole do de valencia de galisia
de mallorcas de sevilla et cerd(eñ)a de cordoua de corcega de mur
cia de jaen delos algarues de algesira de gibraltar e de las ys
las de Canaria Conde e condesa de barcelona señors de vis caya
et de molyna duq(ue)s de Athenas e de neopatria Condes de Ruy se
llon e de cerdanja marqueses de Oristan e de gociano. Por
quanto al tpo q(ue) don Xpoual colon nro Almyrante del mar oce
ano. fue a descobrir las yslas e tierra firme q(ue) por gra de dios
nro señor el hallo o se le descubrieron en el dho mar oceano
a la parte delas Indias se asento q(ue) el q(ue) oviese e llevase en
si cierta parte de aq(ue)llo q(ue) se hallase. E agora por su parte
nos es suplicado q(ue) porq(ue) mejor e mas cumplida mente lo
suso dho se guardase e cumpliese q(ue) a nra (md) pluguiese ma
dar q(ue) to da la negociacion e cosas q(ue) se oviessen de haser
E proveer en estos nros Reynos to cantes a la dha negociacio
delas Indias q(ue) se oviesen de hazer e hisiesen por vna persona
o personas nras con nro poder e en ello ce y te diesen e por el
o por q(ui)en su poder oviese juntamente. porq(ue) asy se podria
mejor saber lo que Resultava delos dhos gastos e pro cuti
lidad dela dha negociacion para q(ue) se te pu diese del a ued iz
con de aq(ue)lla parte e por los dhos asientos le perteneçe e de
q(ue) nos le hesimos (md) o sobre ello proveyesemos como la nra
(md) fuese (et) nos tovimos lo por bi(en) e por esta nra carta

mandamos alas personas q por nro mandado tienen o tovie
ren cargo de entender en los fusos dhos daqui adelante q lo fa
gan e negocien juntamente con la persona o personas ql dho al
mjrante o quien en poder oviere y viere o nonbrare pa ello
otro en otra manera. lo qual se entienda teniendo el dho al
mjrante delas yndias diputada o nonbrada persona o per
sonas q por su parte o a su poder en ello entiendan. a lo ye bo
nos fecho salbeis como las tales personas estan diputadas e
nonbradas por el dho almjrante para q entiendan con su poder
en la dha negociacion. delo qual vos mandamos dar la psente
firmada de nros nonbres e sellada con nro sello. dada en la
villa de medina del campo a treinta dias del mes de mayo año
del nascimj de nro salbador ihu xpo de mill e quatro cientos
e noventa e syete años. yo el Rey. yo la Reyna. yo fer
nand alvares de toledo secretario del Rey e dela Reyna nros
senores la fiz escreuir por su mandado. y en las espaldas
desta dha carta desia. en la forma acordada. Roderi
doctor. Registrada alonso perez. frn dias chanciller.

El Rey e la Reyna

Instrucion pa
el almj y obpo
de badajos pa
la poblacion
delas yndias.

Don xpoual

Colon nro dalmjrante
visorrey e governador del mar oceano las cosas
q nos parecen que con ayuda de dios nro senor se deve e han
de faser e cumplir para la poblacion delas yslas e tierra firme
descubiertas e por descubrir en nro senorio e delas q estan por
descubrir ala parte delas yndias en el mar oceano e dela
gente q por nro mandado alla esta e ha de yr e estar dagui
adelante demas q allen de lo q por otra ynstracion nra vos
y el obpo de badajos aveys de proveer es lo siguiente.

Primeramente

Que como seays en las dhas yndias dios queriendo pro
veays con toda diligencia de animar e traer a los naturales

delas dhas yndias dl todla paz e quietud e que nos dya de ser
vir e estar so nro señorio e subjection benigna mente e prin
cipal mente que se conviertan a nra santa fe catholica e que sa
ellos e a los que han de yr e estar enlas dhas yndias sean admi
nistrados los santos sacramentos por los religiosos e
clerigos que alla fueren y estan por manera que dios nro señor
sea servido e sus conciencias se seguren.

Yten que por esta vez en tanto que nos mandamos mas proveer
aya de yr e vaya con vos el numero delas trezientas e trey
ta personas quales vos eligierdes e la calidad e con sus cabos
segund se contiene enla dha ynstrucion. pero si a vos pa
reciere que algunos de aquellos se deven mudar aquese tribu
e menguando de unos oficios en otros e la calidad de
unas personas en otras que vos o quien vro poder oviere lo podi
ys fazer e fagays segund e enla manera e forma y el tpo
que a vos e a los dichos que entendierdes que cumple a nro servi e al
bien e utilidad e la governacad delas dhas yndias

Yten que quando seays enlas dhas yndias dios queriendo
ayays de mandar hazer e que se faga enla ysla española
otra poblacion e fortaleza allen de ella que esta fecha de
la otra parte delas ysla cercana al minero del oro segund e
en el lugar que a vos bien visto fuere

Yten que cerca de la dha poblacion o delas agora esta fecha o en
otra parte que a vos parezca dispuesto que aya de hazer e asenta
alguna labranca para que mejor e a menos costa se puedan
sostener las personas que estan enla dha ysla y que por esto se
pueda mejor hazer e se aya de dar e de a los labradores que
agora van a las dhas yndias del pan que alla se enbiase fasta can
quenta cahises de trigo e cevada prestado e a los sembrar
hazer veynte yuntas de bacas e de yeguas e otras bestias pa
labrar. e que los tales labradores que asi se sembraren el dho pa
lo labren e siembren e se ayan de obligar de lo bolver a la co
secha e pagar el diezmo de lo que cogeren e lo restante se lo pue
dan vender a los xpianos dl como mejor pudiere tanto que los
precios no excedan en agranjo delos e lo compraren porque en
tal caso vos e el dho almirante o quien vro poder o
viere lo ayeys de tassar e moderar.

Yten quel dho numero delas dhas tresientas y treynta p
sonas que han de yr alas dhas yndias se les aya de pagar
ot pague el sueldo delos precios segud esta aqui se los
han pagado / y en lugar del mantenjmjeto q se les suele dar
se les aya de dar o de del pan q mandamos alla enbiar a cada
persona una fanega de trigo cada mes e dos mrs cada dia para q
ellos copren los otros mantenjmjes nesesarios. los quales se les
ayan de librar por vos el dho nro almjrante o vro lugar tenjete e
por los oficiales denros contadores mayores q en las dhas yndias
estan y estoviere ot q por vras nominas y bramos e cuentas cey
la forma suso dha les aya de pagar e pague nro tesorero que
estoviere en las dhas yndias

Yten q si vos el dho nro almjrate ey ten diezdes que cumple
a nro servjq allende delas dhas tresientas e treynta perso
nas se deve acecer el numero dellas lo podays ha se hasta
llegar a numero d quynjetas personas por todas con tanto el
sueldo e mantenjmj delas tales personas acrecentadas ovieren
de aver se pague de quales qwer mercaderias e cosas de valor
q se hallaren o oviere en las dhas yndias sin q nos hayamos pro
veer para ello de otra parte.

Yten q alas personas q han estado / o estan en las dhas yndias
se les aya de pagar ot pague el sueldo q les es e fuere devido
por nominas ot segud y en la manera q de suso se contiene
ot algunos q no llevaron sueldo se les pague su servjçio se
gud que a vos de bien visto fuere ot alos q han servido por otros
asy mjsmo

Yten q los alcaydes ot otras personas principales q alla han
estado e servido e sirven se les aya d acrecentar e pagar
ot se acecienten ot pague sus tendecias e salarios ot eneldos q
ovieren de aver segud q a vos el dho nro almjrate parescere
q se deve haser avida consideracion ala qlidad dlas perso
nas e aloque cada uno ha servido ot servjere porq dmas de
esto quado a dios plega q aya de q ha se les merced delas
dhas yndias nos avremos memoria para q se les ha ser. lo
qual se aya de asentar ante los dhos nros ofiçiales
e que se les aya delybrar ot pagar en la forma suso
dicha

Iten paresciendo herederos del abad gallego ✝ Andrs de Sa
lamanca ✝ murieron en las dhas yndias ✝ seles deve pagz
el valor de los toneles e pipas ✝ seles gastaron e tomaron po
aver ydo a las dhas Indias Contra nro defendimj̃

Iten en lo q toca dl descargo de las Anjmas de los q en las dhas
yndias han fallescido e fallescieren Nos parece q̃ se deve gu̅a
dar la forma q̃esta en el capitulo de oro memorial q̃ sobr̃
esto nos distes e es el siguiente

Muchos estranjeros e naturales son muertos en las yndias
y yo mando por virtud delos poderes ✝ de v. al. tengo q̃
diesen los testamentos y se cumpliesen y dello dj cargo a esco
bar vesino de sevilla y a Jua̅ de leon vesino d̃ella y sabela q̃
bien e fielmente procurasen todo esto e q̃ Asi en pagar lo q̃ de
vria si sus albaceas no lo oviesen pag̃do Como en recabr̃
dar todos sus bienes e q̃ el ✝ otg̅ esto todo pasase por Ante
Justicia y escri̅ano publico y q̃ todo lo q̃ se recab̃dasen fuese pu
esto en una arca q̃ toviese tres llaves ✝ q̃ ellos toviesen una lla
ve ✝ un Religioso otra otg̃ o otra otg̃ estos dhos ✝ sus dineros
fuesen puestos en la dha arca y esto toviesen alla fasta tres años
por q̃ entre tanto oviesen lugar sus herederos de lo venir e
enbiar a requerir otg̃ y en este tpo no se quisiesen q̃ se destribu
yese en cosas por sus Anjmas

De si mismo nos paresce q̃ el oro q̃ oviere en las otras yndias
✝ se acuñe e fagan dello moneda de excelentes dela granada
Segund nos avemos ordenado q̃ se hagan en estos nros revnos
por q̃ en esto se evitan de haz̃ fraudes e cautelas dl dho oro
e y las dhas Indias ot para labrar la dha moneda ma̅damos q̃
llevevs las personas e aparejos q̃ ovier̃ menester e
para ello vos damos poder cumplid̃ con tanto q̃ la moneda q̃ se hi
ziere en las dhas Indias sea conforme a las ordenanzas q̃ nos a
gora ma̅damos haz̃ sobre la labor dela moneda e los oficiales
q̃ la ovier̃ de labrar guarden las dhas ordenanzas so las penas
e ellas contenidas

Iten nos parece q̃ los Indios con quien esta co̅certado q̃ dlla̅

de pagar el tributo ordenado se les aya de poner una pieça o
señal de moneda de laton o de plomo q̃ trayã al pescueço y esta
tal moneda se le mude la figura o señal que toviere cada ã vez q̃
pagare porq̃ se sepa el que no viniere a pagar. Ot q̃ cada y quãdo
se ballare por la ysla personas personas q̃ no truxeren la dha
señal al pescueço q̃ sean presos y se les de alguna pena h via
na

Item q̃ porq̃ enl coger y recaudança d̃l dho tributo sera
menester proveer de persona diligente e fiable q̃ en ello entie
da y es nra md e mandamos q̃   tenga el dho car
go e q̃ el tributo e mercadurias q̃ asi recaudaren e co
gieren l̃ pagare aya elle be para si cãco pesos e medidas o li
bras por ciento q̃ es la ventena parte delo q̃ asi recavdaren
e si cieren e ficieren coger e recabdar. Yo el rey. Yo la reyna
p̃ or mãdada do d̃l rey e de la reyna fernad alvarez de tole d̃.
Acordada

E L ○ onfernamedo e doña ysabel por
la grã de dios rey ot reyna de castilla de leon de a
ragon de Sicilia de granada de toledo de valencia
de galisia de mallorcas d̃ Sevilla de cerdeña de cordoua de
Corcega de murcia de jahen de los Algarbes de algesira de gibral
tar e delas yslas de canaria con de e con desa de barcelona
ot señores de bizcaya e de molina. Duq̃s de Atenas e d̃ neopa
tria Cond̃s de ruysellon e de Çerdania marq̃ses de oristan e
de gociano. al nro justicia mayor e a los d̃l nro conseso e oydo
res de la nra abdiencia alcaldes e alguasiles de la nra casa
e corte e chancilleria e a t̃p dos los corregidores asistentes e
alldes e alguasiles e otras justicias qualesquier de todas las
cibdades villas e logares delos nros reynos e señorios e a cada
uno e qual quier de vos en vros lugares e jurisdiciones a quien
esta nra carta fuere mostrada o su traslado d̃lla signado
de escrivano publico Salud e grã sepades q̃ para la poblaciõ
delas yslas e tierra firme descubiertas ot p̃ q̃se descubrieren de nro se
ñorio ala parte de las Indias e y l mar oceano Sera menester
comprar enestos dhos nros reynos para llenar dellas algunas
mercaderias e mantenimientos e provisiones e aparejos y herra
mientas e toneles e vasijas e otras cosas. lo qual l̃ ha de

Para q̃ se den z
vendan las co
sas que fueren me
nester para las
yndias por los
precios que suele
valer fecha a
xxiiij de abril
de xc vij.

conprar la persona q̃ por nos ot por don xp̃oual colon n̄ro almyra
te del mar oceano tiene / o diere cargo dello · E porq̃ nos es fecha
Relaçio delas personas q̃ tiene las dhas mercaderias co otras
cosas Se escusan dlas vender porlo enparecer mas · loqual se
ria en n̄ro deseruj̃ · n̄ra (md̃) voluntad es solo q̃ delo en so dh̃o se
conprare Sea por los preçios ot segnd snele valer · por ende
nos vos mandamos q̃ alas personas n̄ras e al dh̃o n̄ro Almte
dlas cosas en so dh̃as e otras quales q̃er Co conprare pala abi
ta Caon e prover m̃ delas dhas jndias e para el navegar d̃
ellas gelo fagays dar por preçios razonables ot segnd snele
valer en esas dh̃as Cabdad de e villas elogares q̃ieclos vos llas
sin encarecer mas · e no fagades end al por alguna manera
So pena dla n̄ra (md̃) ot de diez mjll m̃rs a cadavno devos q̃lo cō
trario fiziere para la n̄ra camara ot demas porq̃ual Ser cō
guales q̃ier devos las dh̃as justiçias por gen fintare ello nõ
fazer e cumplir mandamos al ome Ce esta n̄ra carta mostraze
q̃ vos enplaze q̃ parezcade anf nos enla n̄ra Corte do doq̃er
q̃ nos Seamos del dia q̃vos enplazare fasta qujnze dias pri
meros sigujente Sola dh̃a plena Sola qual mandamos a El
q̃ier escrivano publico que para esto fuere llamado q̃ de ende
al q̃ vos la mostraze testimonjo Signado con signo porq̃ nos
Sepamos en cōmo Se cunple n̄ro mandado · dada en la Cabdad
de burgos adeynt e tres dias almes de abril Año del nasçamj
d n̄ro Senor ih̃u xp̃o de mjll e q̃tro Çentos eno ueta e quete
Años · yo el rey · yo la reyna · po fernad aluard de tole do
Se q̃ al rey e ala reyna n̄os Señoras la fise escrevir por
Su mandado · Acordada Roderic dottor · Registrada aloso
perez · fran̄ co de Cruz chanciller ·

El Rey· e la Reyna

Don xp̃oual colon n̄ro Almyrante del mar ocea
no· visorrey ot gouernador dla tr̃ra firme e ys las
delas yndias · ô antonjo de torrs continto d̃ n̄ra casa las
cosas que nos parece q̃ con ayuda de n̄ro Señor dios se deve
proueer ot enbiar alas jndias para la gouernaço e mate mj

de las personas que alla estan o han de yr para las cosas que alla se han
de haser cumplideras a seruiçio de dios nuestro son las siguientes

Primeramente

En este primer viaje en tanto que nos mandamos proveer
aya de yr y estar en las dhas Indias numero de tresientas e treyn
ta personas dela suerte e calidad e ofiçios que adelante sera don
tenidos contando enel dho numero de las dhas tresientas e treynta per
sonas delas que agora estan e queda en las dhas Indias las quales
dhas tresientas e treynta personas han de ser elegidas por vos
el dho nuestro almirante o por quien vuestro poder oviere o han de ser repar
tidas en esta manera quarenta escuderos çient peones de guerra
treynta marineros treynta grumetes veynte labradores de oro
çinquenta labradores e ortelanos veynte ofiçiales de todos ofi
çios e treynta mugeres asi que son el numero de las dhas tresientas
e treynta personas los quales ayan de yr a estar en las dhas Indias
quanto en vuestra voluntad fuere por manera que si algunas delas per
sonas que estan en las dhas Indias se quisieren o oviere de venir aya
de que dar que que den ellas ny allas que agora estan como dellas que agora
fueren el dho numero delas dhas tresientas e treynta personas
pero si a vos el dho almirante paresçere ser bien e provecho de la ne
goçiaçion de mudar el dho numero de personas quitado de los vnos
ofiçiales e proueyendo de otros en su lugar lo podades fazer tanto
que no pase del numero delas personas que en las dhas Indias ha de estar
de tresientas e treynta personas e no mas

Iten para mantenimiento de vos el dho almirante e de vuestros her
manos e otros ofiçiales e personas prinçipales que con vos han de
yr e estar en las dhas Indias e para las dhas tresientas e treynta
personas e para labrar e sembrar e para el gouierno delas bestias
que alla llevaren se aya de llevar o lleven quinientos cahises de
cahises de trigo e mas çinquenta cahises de çevada los quales
se aya de proueer e provean del pan a nos pertenesçiente delas
terçias del arçobispado de Seuilla e obispado de Cadiz del año pa
sado de noventa e seys años segund se contiene en las cartas de libra
miento que sobrello mandamos dar

Iten que se ayan de enbiar a las dhas Indias las ferramientas e
aparejos que paresçere a vos el dho almirante para labrar en las

dhas Jndias. Otrosy mysmo dlcabones e açadas e picos e almadanas e palancas e asadijnes e açadas dlas dhas Jndias.

Otrosy mysmo que Sobre las vacas e yeguas que estan en las dhas Jndias se ayan de cumplir el numero de veynt e çinco de vacas e yeguas e asnos con que puedan labrar en las dhas Jndias Segund a vos el dho almyrante paresçiere.

Otrosy mysmo nos pareçe que serabien que se çiempre vna nao vieja en que vayan los mantenymjos e cosas que las dhas que supieren ella por que la tablazon e madera e clavason della se podria aprovechar en la poblacion que agora nuevamente se ha de fazer en la otra parte della ysla española çerca de las mjnas pero si a vos el dho almyrante paresçiere que no es bien llevarse la dha nao que no se lleve.

Otrosy se deue llenar a las dhas Jndias çinquenta caizes de harina e hasta mill quintales de vizcocho para en tanto que se provee de fazer molinos e atahonas et para lo fazer se deuen llevar de aca algunas piedras e otros aparejos de molinos

Ytem se deuen llenar a las dhas Jndias dos stiendas de campo que cuesten fasta veynt mill mrs

Ytem en lo que toca a los otros mantenymjos e proueymjos que Sean neçesarios llevarse a las dhas Jndias para el mantenymjento de estos dhos que alla han de yr e estar nos pareçe que se deue tener la forma siguiente.

Que busquen algunas personas llanas e abonadas las que vos el dho almyrante dixere que teneys las si conçertadas que ayan de cargar e llevar a las dhas Jndias los dhos mantenymjos e otras cosas alla neçesarias para lo qual se les aya de dar y de de los mrs que nos mandamos librar para esto lo que a vos paresçiere et que ellos se Seguridad por los mrs que ello reçibieren los quales ayan de emplear en los dhos mantenymjos e cargar los e llevar los sin costa a las dhas Jndias e que vaya a nro riesgo e aventura de la mar e que llegando alla dios queriendo ayan de vender e de dar los dhos mantenymjos el vino a onze mrs el açumbre e la libra de toçino e las carne salada a ocho mrs e los otros mantenymjos

ate segund bro a los precios q vos el dho almyrante o vro lugar
teniente les pusierdes. De manera q ellos ayan alguna ganacia e no
pierdan en ello. E a la gente no se les faga agravio. E q de los mrs q la
tal persona o personas se abieren a los dhos mantenimjos q el Rey ve diere
ayan de dar o pagar e lo que pague alla a nro tesorero q esto estoviere en las dhas yndias los dhos mrs q les diere de los q el Rey se les ha de
dar e pagar pa comprar los dhos mantenimjos para q ellos pague el
sueldo a la gente. E q si la dha gente tomaren los dhos mantenimjos pa
en cuenta de su sueldo. Sean les Rescibidos en cuenta mostrando co-
noscimj de lo q Rescibieron por donde el dho tesorero e los oficiales de la
cuenta se lo cargue en cuenta de su sueldo. E las dhas personas
en seguridad q obligan de se lo q por facer e cumplir segun dho es
e se les aya de dar e den las dhas contias de mrs q al Rey vos paresciere.

Iten se deve procurar q vayan a las dhas yndias algunos
Religiosos e cligos buenas personas pa q alla admynjstren los
santos sacramentos a los q alla estaran e pro curen de convertir
a nra sancta fe catholica a los dhos yndios naturales de las dhas
yndias e lleven pa ello los aparejos e cosas q se Requiera para
el servjcio del culto divyno e para la admynistracion de los stos
sacramentos.

El Rey mesmo que vr un fisico e un boticario e un erbolario e algunos ynstrumentos e musicas para pasatpo de las gentes q
alla han de estar.

E por q agora mandamos librar cierta quantia de mrs para estobia-
te q agora aveys de hacer vos el dho almyrate. noz vos mandamos
q aquellos se gasten segun va por una fela con firmada del
comendador mayor de leon nro contador mayor e del doctor fdgo
mal donado del nro consejo e de fernandalvarez nro secretario.

Por q vos mandamos q lo asy fagays guardar e cu plyr e pone
en obra segun q de suso se contiene. E qual plaga e servcio nos
fareys. E para ello vos damos poder cumplido con todas sus in
sidencias e dependencias anexidades e conexidades. fecha en
la villa de medina del campo a quinze dias del mes de junio año del
nascimjo de nro salvador ihuxpo de mill e quatroçientos e noventa
e syette años. yo el Rey. y yo la Reyna. por mandado del Rey e de la
Reyna fernandalvarez. Acordada. foderici doctor.

Don fernando e doña ysabel por
la gracia de dios Rey e Reyna de castilla e leon de Aragon e Seci
lia de granada de Toledo de valencia de galisia e mallorcas e sevi
lla de cerdeña de cordoua e murcia de Jahen de los Algarbes de alge zi
ra e gibraltar e las yslas de Canaria Conde e Condesa de bar çelona
Senores de vizcaya e de molyna duques de Athenas e de neopatria
condes de Rosellon e de cerdanja marqueses de oristan e de goçeano
porquanto al tpo que don xpoual colon nro almjrante mayor del mar
oceano fue al descobrir tierra a la dcha mar oceana por nro mandado e a
se tomo conel cierto asiento e despues quando el primer viaje vino
de descobrir e fallar Segund que por la gracia e ayuda de dios nro señor fa
llo las dichas Indias e tierra firme le confirmamos e aprovamos el
dcho Asiento e lo que con el por nro mandado tomo e de nuevo le
fezimos e mandamos dar ciertos preuillejos e mercedes Segund que
en el dcho Asiento e preuillejos se contiene. E Agora el dcho don xpoual
nro almjrante del dcho mar oceano nos fizo relacion e despues
aca nos mandamos dar una carta nra para provision en cierta for
ma en ella ciertos capitulos el thenor de la qual es este que se sigue. Don
fernando e doña ysabel por la gracia de dios Rey e Reyna de castilla
de leon de Aragon de Secilia de granada de Toledo de valencia de ga
lisia de mallorcas e Sevilla de cerdeña de cordoua de orce gra
de murcia de Jahen de los Algarbes de algezira de gibraltar e las ys
las de canaria Conde e Condesa de barçelona Señores de vizcaya e
de molyna duques de Athenas e de neopatria condes de Rosellon e
de cerdanja marqueses de oristan e de goçeano. Porquanto a nos
es fecha Relacion que Algunas personas vesinos e moradores en
algunas cibdades villas e lugares e puertos de nros Reynos e
Señorios nros Subditos e naturales querrian por el descobrir otras
yslas e tierra firme a la parte de las Indias en el mar oceano demas
de las yslas e tierra firme que por nro mandado Sehan descobierto
en la dcha parte del mar oceano. E asimesmo otros querrian yr a
bivir e morar a la ysla española que esta descobierta e fallada
por nro mandado e por nos les fuese dada licencia para ello. E fue
sen Ayudados de mantenimientos por cierto tpo. E que el xa de Se
sello por el de dañj e por nro mandado fue puesto para que njnguna
persona fuese a las yndias syn nra licencia e mandado so cier
tas penas. E loqual por nos visto e acatando que si descubriesen
las dchas tierras e yslas e fuesen a estar en ellas e poblar se amos la
dcha ysla española que esta descubierta que es servicio de dios nro
Señor por que la convertacion dellos podria Atraer a los que Abitan

en la dha trra en conoscimiento de dios nro Senõr e se duzir
los a nra sancta fe catholica otrosi q es servicio nro e bien
e pro avn̄ de nros reynos et senorios e a nros subditos e natu
rales acordamos de ma dar dar et por la present damos e acordamos
la dha licencia a los dhos nros subditos e naturales para q vaya
a las dhas yslas e trra firme e a descobrirlas e a tratar en
ellas con las condiciones et seguid e en la manera q en esta nra ca
sera conteni das e declaradas en esta guysa

Primera mente q todos los navios q quisieren de yr a la dꝑ
las dhas yslas de qual ser de las maneras q de yuso en esta nra
carta seran conteni das ayan de partir de la cibdad de cadiz
y no de otra part alguna . e que antes q partan se presenten
alli ante los officiales q estovieren puestos por nos o por quien nro
poder oviere para q sepan los q van a las dhas yndias et ayan de
cumplir et guar dar cada uno en su caso lo q de yuso en esta nra carta se
ra conteni do.

Que quales quier personas q quisieren yr a bivir e morar e en la
dha ysla espanola sin sueldo puedan yr e vaya libre mente
e q alla seran francos e libres e no paguen derecho alguno e tener
para sy e por suyo propio et para sus here deros e para quien de llos
oviere casa las casas q hisieren e las tierras q labraren e las
here dades q plantaren seguid q alla en la dha ysla le sera senala
das trras e logares para ello por las personas q por nos tienen et
vieren cargo de que las tales personas q ay bivieren e moraren
en la dha ysla espanola et no lleuaren sueldo nro como dicho es se
les dara mantenimi ento por un año et de mas q remos e es nra md q
vendo diligencia a los q nro poder tovieren e ovieren para ello a la
dha ysla espanola ayan para sy la tercia part del oro q ha
llaren e cogieren en la dha ysla tanto q no sea por tesorero et
las otras dos tercias partes sean para nos con las quales
ffar an asi el oficial q por nos estoviere en la dha ysla. et de mas
de esto vendo con licencia nra para sy todas las mercaderias e otras
quales quier cosas q hallaren en la dha ysla dando el diezmo a los nros
o a quien nro poder oviere para lo tener cebir et cebir el oro de q nos
han de dar las dos partes como dicho es. lo qual todo aya de ffa
guitar en la dha ysla espanola ante los nros officiales et pa
gui a nro te cebir e q no se lo oviere de dar las dos tercias partes del
oro e la dha nra diezma parte de todas las otras cosas

que hallaren como los bienes &c

Jtem q quales quier personas nros subditos e naturales que
quisieren puedan yr adelant en quanto nra md voluntad
fuere a descubrir yslas e tierra firme fecha la dha parte dlas dhas
don dias Rey alas que estan descubiertas fasta aqui como a otras
quales quier a les gastar dellas tanto q no sea dla dha ysla espa
ñola. que puedan vn praz alos xpianos q enella estan o estouieren
quales quier cosas e merca derias contanto q nos sea oro lo qual pue
dan faser e faga con quales quier navios q quisiere. Contanto q
al tpo que partiere de nros Reynos partan desde la dha cibdad de caliz
e alla se presente ante nros oficiales e porq de alli han de lleuar
en cada vno de los tales navios vna o dos personas q sean nonbradas por
los nros oficiales ante quien asi se presentare e mas han de lleuar la
diezma parte dlas tone las q por los tales navios de carga so nra
Seña por ello les aya de ser pagado flete alguno Alo q asi lleuaren
nro lo de la carga q enla dha ysla la española lo entreguen ala persona ope
sonas q alla touieren cargo dlo officec caliz por nro mandado delo q alla
se enbie tomando vn conoscimiento suyo de como le cibe e queremos de
nra md q dlo q las dhas personas fallaren enlas dhas yslas e tierra firme
ayan para si las nueve partes e la otra desena parte q sea para nos a
la qual nos aya de ser alli dadi al tpo q boluiere a estos nros Reynos
enla dha cibdad de caliz don de han de boluer primera mente alo pa
gar alas personas q alli touiere cargo por nos dlo recebir. e despues
de este pagada segund an yr a sus casas o don de quisiere con lo que
Rey tenuiere e al tpo q partiere dela dha cibdad de caliz ayan de
dar seguridas dlo en plaza dey

Jtem q quales quier personas q quisieren lleuar quales quier man
tenimjes para la dha española la o phra otras quales quier yslas q por nro
mandado estouieren pobladas dlas dhas don dias lo pue dan lleuar
e vender alli francamente e por los precios q se ygualaren con los con
pradores. lo e q les les pagien alla en merca derias (o en otro dlo q alla
tuuiere) et q el ajunto de el dho mantenimjento o parte dello ven dieren)
a nros oficiales q alla estouieren para los bastimentos dla gente que
by nos siruen lo ayan de pagar e pagien alla como dho es o les den
cedulas para q aca se les pagien conlas quales cedulas nos les
certificamos q se les sera pagado contanto q al tpo q partiere
los dhos navios en q fueren. los dhos mantenimjes aya de partir dla
dha cibdad de caliz para q alli se presente ante los dhos nros

oficiales ellenen sin flete la decima delos tales navios ala que
son q nos mandamos lleuar para la dha ysla segud desuso dise
e se obligue de pagar la decima pte delo q de alla truxere tes
gitandose segud la capitulacio q de suso se contiene o la buel
ta sean tenudos de venir ala dha cibdad de cadiz para lo pagar
como dho es.

Otrosi porquanto nos ovimos fecho mds al don xpoual colon
nro almirante delas dhas yndias q el pudiese cargar en cada uno delos
dhos navios q fuesen alas dhas yndias la ochaua pte dellos es nra
md q en cada siete navios q fuere alas dhas yndias pueda el
dho almirante o quien en poder oviere cargar uno para faser
el dho fletgaste

Lo ql todo q dho es e cada una cosa e parte dello mandamos que
se guarde e cumpla en todo e por todo segud de suso enesta
nra carta se contiene et porq venga a noticia de todos segud desu
so se contiene mandamos q sea apregonada por las plaças e mer ca
dos e otros lugares acostunbrados de todas las cibdades villas
e lugares e puertos del andalusia e otras partes de nros reynos do
conviniere y dar el traslado della signado de escriuanas gerdono solo que
queren delo qual mandamos dar et dimos esta nra carta firmada de
nenros nobres et sellada co nro sello. dada enla villa de madrid
a diez dias del mes de abril Año del nascimyento de nro saluador
ihu xpo de mill e quatrocientos e noventa e quatro años. yo el
Rey. yo la Reyna. yo fernad aluares de toledo secretario
del Rey e dela Reyna nros señores la fize escreuir por su ma
dado. Acordada Roderic doctor. frco diaz chanceller.

La ql dha nra carta de provision e lo enella contenido al dho al
myrante don xpoual colon dise q fue dada en perjuysio delas
dhas mdes q de nos tiene e delas fran seulta dos e por ellas le di
mos e nos suplico et pidio por md q cerca dello mandasemos
proueer de remedio. Lo qual nra md fuese et porq nra md e
voluntad no fue ni es de perjudicar en cosa alguna al dho don
xpoual colon nro almirante del mar oceano ni que se vaya co
plisse con tra los dhos trecyentos e preuillejos e mdes q le fesi
mos antes por los servicios q nos ha fecho le queremos demos
de fazer mas mdes por esta nra carta si te es necesario es et fir
mamos e aprouamos los dhos trecyentos e preuis e mdes por

tos al dicho almirante fechas. Et es nuestra merçed e mandamos que en todo
e por todo le sean guardadas. Et an bien dellas segund que ellas se contiene. Et se sean demos firmemente e alguna ni algunas personas
no sean osadas de yr contra ellas ni contra parte dellas en tiempo
alguno ni por alguna manera so las penas dellas contenidas. Et por
el thenor e forma dellas parte dello que algo perjudica la dicha provisio
que oy mandamos dar que dello va encorporada por la presente la re-
vocamos e queremos e mandamos que no aya fuerça ni effecto alguno en tiempo alguno ni por alguna manera en quanto toca es perju-
dizio al dicho almirante e dello que asi tenemos otorgado e afir-
mado. Lo qual mandamos dar la presente firmada de nuestros nombres et sellada con nuestro sello. Dada en la villa de medina del campo
a dies e ocho dias del mes de junio año del nasçimiento de nuestro Salvador
jhesu xpo de mill e quatrocientos e noventa e seys años. Yo el
Rey. Yo la Reyna. E yo fernand alvarez de toledo secretario del Rey
e de la Reyna nuestros señores la fize escrevir por su mandado. A-
cordada. Roderico doctor. Registrada alonso perez. fernand dias
chançeller.

Don fernando e doña ysabel por la

graçia de dios Rey e Reyna de castilla de leon de aragon de Sicilia
de granada de toledo de valençia de galizia de mallorcas de Sevilla de çerdeña de cordoua de corçega de murçia de jahen de los
Algarbes de algezira de gibraltar e de las yslas de canaria e condes de barçelona Señores de vizcaya e de molina Duques de A-
thenas e de neopatria condes de Rossellon e de çerdania marqueses
de oristan e de goçiano A vos los nuestros almoxarifes e arrendadores e
arrendadores e fieles e cogedores e otras personas que teneys e ovier-
des cargo de coger o de recabdar en renta o en fieldad o en otra qualquier manera las rentas e almoxarifadgo e alcaualas dellas çibdades
de Sevilla e cadiz este presente año de la data desta nuestra carta e
los otros venideros tanto quanto nuestra voluntad fuere A cada uno
e qualquier de vos Salud e graçia sepades que nuestra merçed e voluntad es que
todo los mantenimientos e otras cosas que por nuestro mandado e de os qual
Colon nuestro almirante de la mar oçeano en las yndias se ha-
gare para llevar dellas. Et otrosi dello que se truxere de las
dichas yndias. desas dichas çibdades e sus puertos no se aya de pagar e pague por la entrada e venta dello almoxarifadgo ni alcauala
ni otro derecho alguno este presente año en los de aqui adelante
quanto nuestra merçed e voluntad fuere. Por que vos mandamos a todos de

vt a cada vno de vos q asi lo guardeys e cumplays como d' vso en
esta nra carta se contiene e guardandolo e cumpliendolo nos no vi
dades nin de mandeys q lleveys almoxarifadgo ni alcauala ni otros
derechos algunos por la pmera venta e carga e descarga de quales
qer mercaderias e mantenimis e otras cosas q paresciere po
los d nros oficiales q al dho almjrante o personas q tienen oto
 vieren cargo dela dha arga e dscarga para las dhas yndias o se
descarga trayedolo dellas en esas dhas cabdas e puertos e en q
vna dellas toviere dho and e de aqui adelante quatro nps como vo
luntad fuere. E sy asy no lo fizierdes e cumplierdes por esta dha
nra carta mandamos a qualesqer nras justicias q vos costrin
gan e apremien a lo asy fazer e conplir. E los vnos e los otros no
fagades nin fagan ende al por alguna maña so pena dela nra
merced e de diez myll mrs a cada vno por qen fincare delo asy fazer
e cunplir e demas mandamos al ome q vos esta nra carta mostrare
q vos enplaze q parezcades Ante nos enla nra corte do qer q nos
seamos del dia q vos enplazare fasta quinze dias pmeros sy
guientes so la dha pena. So la qual mandamos a qual qer escriuano
publico q para esto fuere llamado q de ende al q la mostrare testimonio
signado con su signo por q nos sepamos en como se cumple nro
mandado. Dada en la muy noble cibdad de burgos veynte e
tres dias del mes de abril año del nasçimiento de nro senor ihu xpo de
mjll e quatroçientos e noventa e siete años. Yo el Rey. Yo
la Reyna. yo fernad aluares d toledo secretario del Rey e dela Rey
na nros senores la fize escriuir por su mandado. Acordada
Rodericus doctor. Registrada alonso gz. fran dias chanceller

Don fernando e doña ysabel
Por la graçia de dios Rey e Reyna de castilla de leon d
Aragon de siçilia de granada de toledo de valencia de ga
lisia de mallorcas de seuilla de çerdeña de cordoua de corçega
de murçia de jahen delos algarbes de algezira de gibraltar e delas
yslas de canaria e de condesa de barçelona señores de vizca
ya e de molina duques de athenas e de neopatria condes de ro se
llon e de çerdania marqses de oristan e de goçiano. Alos corr.
Alcaldes alguaziles regidores Caualleros escuderos oficiales e
omes buenos delas cibdades de seuilla e caliz e delas villas e
logares e puertos de su arçobispado de cobdad e a vos los arrenda
dores e recabdadores almoxarifes e portadgueros e aduaneros

et dezmeros et otras personas q̃ teneys et tovierdes cargo de coger
e de recabdar en rrenta o en fieldad o en otra qual q̃er manera
las rrentas delas alcaualas e almoxarifadgos e portadgos e al
mirantadgo delas dhas çibdades e villas e a cada vno de vos Sa
lud e gr̃a sepades q̃ para la poblaçio dellas yslas e tr̃ra firme des
cubiertas e puestas so nr̃o señorio e por descubrir enla parte delas
Indias sera menester traher a ver dellas
a estos nr̃os reynos algunas mercadrias y otras cosas y llevar a
ellas de nr̃a mantenimj̃os e otras provisions et cosas e para el res
gate delas dhas yndias e para otras cosas q̃ alla so e sera me
nester p̃a sustetaçio e mantenimj̃e to delas p̃sonas q̃ alla estan
e avran de estar e para su biuje das labranças e porq̃ nr̃a
m̃d e voluntad es q̃ de las cosas que agy se traxere a estos nr̃os
reynos delas dhas yndias no se pague derecho alguno antes se des
cargue libremente . e q̃ al descargo dellas no se pague derecho alguno
de almoxarifadgo nj̃ aduana nj̃ portadgo nj̃ almj̃ratadgo nj̃ otro
derecho alguno nj̃ al caual̃a dela primera vẽta q̃ dellas se hiziere
e asy mesmo de los q̃ compraren quales q̃er cosas p̃a embiar o llevar
alas dhas Indias para proveymj̃o e mantenimj̃ento dellas e de las gen
tes q̃ enellas estovieren no paguen derecho de almoxarifadgo nj̃ a
duana nj̃ portadgo nj̃ almj̃ratadgo nj̃ otro derecho por el mar q̃
dellas mãdamos dar esta nr̃a carta para vos e la dha razon por
la qual vos mãdamos a todos e cada vno de vos en q̃ cosa q̃ se
truxere y descargare alas dhas yndias quales q̃er cosas a estos
nr̃os reynos q̃ en quãto nr̃a m̃d e voluntad fuere los dexeys e con
sintays descargar las dhas cosas q̃ agy truxeren libremente sin
les llevar almoxarifadgo mayor nj̃ menor nj̃ aduana nj̃ almj̃
ratadgo nj̃ portadgo nj̃ otros derechos algunos nj̃ al caual̃a
dela primera venta que se hiziere delas tales cosas q̃ agy truxe
ren delas dhas yndias mostrãdo vos carta firmada de don xpoual colo
nr̃o almjrante delas dhas yndias o dela persona q̃ toviere para
ello en poder dela persona o personas q̃ por nos o por nr̃os con ta
dores mayors en nr̃o nombre estoviere e las dhas yndias como
aq̃llas cosas se cargaro en las dhas yndias para estos nr̃os reynos
et asy mismo dexeys libremente cargar en quãto nr̃a m̃d e volun
tad fuere quales q̃er cosas q̃ se llevare alas dhas yndias p̃a
proveymj̃ e sostenimj̃ dellas e delas gẽtes q̃ enellas estovieren
sin les demãdar nj̃ llevar derechos algunos de almoxarifadgo
mayor nj̃ menor nj̃ aduana nj̃ almj̃ratadgo nj̃ portadgo nj̃ otros
derechos algunos . lo qual fazede e cumplid asy mostrãdo vos

Carta firmada del dicho don Xpoual colon Almyrante delas dichas
yndias o del quien en su poder oviere Et ala persona e personas que
por nos e por nros contadores mayores en nro nobre estovieren enla
dicha çibdad de Sevilla para que en razon delas cosas delas dichas yndias Si
algunas personas Algo troxeren las dichas cosas e vinyeren delas dichas
yndias Syn mostrar la dicha carta del dicho almyrante o del quien en poder
oviere e dela persona o personas que por nos o por los nros contadores
mayores que estovieren enlas dichas yndias como a aquellas cosas Se Algo
traxeren e llevaren para estos dichos reynos o traxeren destos nros reynos para
las dichas yndias Syn llevar carta del dicho almyrante o de quien en
poder oviere e dela persona o personas que por nos e por los dichos nros
contadores mayores que estovieren enla dicha çibdad de Sevilla como a aquellas
cosas Se Algo e hepan para las dichas yndias e las Aya perdido e
pierdan Et por la presente damos poder e facultad ala persona o per
sonas que por nos o por los dichos nros contadores mayores estan e esto
vieren nonbradas para lo suso dicho enla dicha çibdad de Sevilla o ala
persona El dicho almyrante Rey mismo alli tiene o toviere e les
tome las tales mercaderias e otras cosas que asy troxeren delas
dichas yndias o Algo traxeren para ellas. Syn mostrar las dichas carta
firmadas enla manera que dicha es Et las tengan en deposito fasta
que nos mandemos fazer dellas lo que fuere Justicia e nra merced e
voluntad fuere. Et otrosi mandamos que los dichos tenyentes
e ofiçiales tome Seguridad de lo que Asy traxeren enlas dichas
yndias Se descargara enestos nros reynos e no en otra parte al
guna y se presentara con ello enla dicha çibdad de Sevilla Ante
los ofiçiales que alli estovieren por nos e por el dicho almyrante
delas yndias porque no pueda intervenir fraude ni cabtela alguna
Et mandamos a vos las dichas nras Justiçias que asy lo fagays e cun
plays e se faga e cunpla lo en esta nra carta contenido e que
quanto nra merced e voluntad fuere como dicho es. Et por que lo su
so dicho venga A notiçia de todos e dello no pueda ninguno pre
tender ynorançia. mandamos que esta nra carta Sea pregon
nada por las plaças e mercados e otros lugares Acostunbra
dos de sas dichas çibdades de Sevilla e Caliz e alos puertos
desa comarca. Et mandamos alos nros contadores mayores
que tome el traslado desta nra carta e lo pongan e Asyenten en
los nros libros e Sobre escripta esta carta original en las espaldas
e la tornen al dicho don Xpoual colon nro almyrante delas yndias
e a los a ffendamys que fisieren daga dela ante en quanto nra
merced e voluntad fuere e los nros almoxarifadgos e el almaxalas

alt portadgos alt de aduanas e otros nros derechos pagan por
saluado lo contenjdo enesta nra carta E los vnos nj los otros
non fagades nj fagan ende al por alguna manera so pena dela nra
md de diez mjll mrs para la nra camara a cada vno q lo contrario
fisiere Et demas mandamos al ome q esta nra carta mostrare q vos
enplase q parezcades ante nos en la nra cort do quier q nos sea
mos del dia q vos enplasare fasta qnse dias pmeros sjgujentes
sola dha pena sola qual mandamos a qual quier escriuano publi
co q para esto fuere llamado q de ende al q vos la mostrare testimonjo
sygnado con su sygno porq nos sepamos en como se cunple nro man
dado. Dada en la cibdad de burgos seys dias del mes de mayo año
del nascimjento de nro saluador ihu xpo de mjll e quatroçientos e no
venta e syete años. yo el rey. yo la reyna. y yo fernad aluarez
de toledo secretario del rey e dela reyna nros señores la fiz escriujr
por su mandado. Enla forma acordada. Rodericus doctor. Re
gistrada alonso xxx. frad dias chançiller.

Corregidores allcaldes alguasiles Regidores caualleros escuderos
oficiales e omes buenos delas cibdades de seuilla e cadiz e delas
villas e lugares e delos puertos de su mar e obispados cobrados e arren
dadores e recabdadores almoxarifes e portadgueros aduane
ros e dezmeros e las otras personas en esta nra del rey e dela reyna
nros señores desta pte es gipta contenjdas. ved esta dha carta
de sus altesas e conplidla e fazedla conplir e guardar segnd e por la for
ma e manera q ella se contiene e dis altesas por ella lo mandan
e sea entendido q todas las mercaderias q fueren del andalu
sia o de otros qualesquier puertos q son desta dha franque
za para las dhas yndias han de dar seguridad e fazer testi
monjo e fe al dho almjrante o de quien su poder oviere e ala
persona q por sus altesas o los dhos sus contadores mayores
para ello oviere señalado eso mesmo las licencias e fees q se
han de lleuar a las yndias e traer dellas delas cosas q se lleua
ren o truxieren han de ser firmadas del dho almjrante o de quien
su poder oviere e dela persona q sus altesas e sus contadores
mayores nonbraren de anbos e no del vno syn el otro Rey mes
mo se entienda e por lo en esta dha carta contenjdo no se ha
de tener cabiz en qta de mrs nj otras cosas algunas a los arren
dadores e recabdadores mayores e almoxarifes e otras personas
q tienen o tovieren cargo de coger e recabdar las Rentas
años pertenescentes al dho nro cobrado de seuilla e obispados

de caliz este dicho año mjll en de en adelant en njn gud año que[n]
fuere la voluntad d sus altesas q dure otsegua[r] d lo enesta
dhã gu̅ã contenjd Et vno geral q dise q esta dhã frã guesa
se ha de guardar tes de este dho present año sea enten didot
ba de ser guardada des de primero dia dl mes de enero del año ve
nj dero de noventa e ocho años e ende en adelant Segud dho
es eno dns mayor d mo. Jua lopes. fernad gomes. Jua fr̃
tado. mo toro. Lnys ẽs. y d azbola sha

Don fernando e doña ysabel

por la grã de dios Rey e Reyna de castilla de leõ de ara
gõ d cecilia de granada de tole d de valencia d galisia d
mallorcas d Sewlla de cordoua d murcia de sahe dlos
algrbes d algesira d gibraltar e dlas yslas d canaria. d les
de barcelona e senors de viscaya e d moslina dnqs d athenas
e de neo patria codes d tosello e d cardanja maz q̃ ses d o
ristã e d egoaano dlos dl nr̃o conseo otoy dores dla nr̃a abdi
ça allos calgua ziles dla nr̃a casa e cort e chã callia d dito
dos los d casas d nsti aas Regi dores Caualleros e sudios ofi
ales et omes buenos de todas las cabdas d villas e lugares d
los nr̃os Reynos et senorios Asy Realengos omo dbadengos cor
dne e be tetrias otras quales qer personas nr̃os va sallos Sub
ditos e naturales d qyen tp̃ra atane lo en esta nr̃a carta cotenjd
e d cada vno e qual qyer de vos A qyen esta nr̃a cã fuere mostrada
o el trasla do dla signad de escriuano publico Salud e grã
Sepad q nos avemos ma da d Albn xp̃onal colon nr̃o al mj̃
dl mj̃ oceano abnel vna dla ye la espano la e alas otras yslas
e tfã firme e son e las dhas jndias e e y tienda en la vn versio
e poblacio dllas. porq̃ desto e que nr̃o senor es seruid e e En
santa fe acre ctndia e nr̃os Reynos en gansd a dos. et para
ello avemos ma da d Armar çaertos navios e caravelas e en
ba çaerta gete pa gada por çaerto tp̃o e bastimetos e ma tenj
mjẽts pã ella. et por quãto d ello no puede Abastar pã ase faga
como cũple A seruis de dios e nr̃o Si no vã otras getes q̃ne
en ellas esten e bivan e yrũa Asus costas. e nos querien do
proveer Sobre ello A sy por lo q̃ cũple ala dhã cõversiõ e pobl
açon como por vsar de clemẽcia e piadad con nr̃os Sub ditos
e naturales. ma damos dar esta nr̃a carta e la dhã faso
por la qual e de nr̃o propo motiuo e çaerta çiencia q̃remos.

It ordenamos q̃ todas e quales quier personas varones e mugeres nros
subditos e naturales q̃ oujesen cometido fasta el dia dela publi
caçion desta nra carta quales ser muertes e feridas e otras quales
quier dlictos de qual ser natura e calidad o sea eçebto la heregia o
lese magestatis o per dulionjs o traycio o aleve o muert segura o
fecha con fuego o do caeta o crimen de falsa moneda o el sodomja o
oujere sacado moneda o oro o plata o otras cosas por nos ve dadas
fuera d nros reynos e fuere a servir en persona ala ysla española
e estuviere en ella a sus propias costas e sirviere e las cosas q̃ el dho
almirant les dixere e ma dare d nra pte los q̃ mereçcieren pena d
muerte por dos años. E los q̃ mereçcieren otra pena menor q̃ no sea
muerte von q̃ sea per dimjento d mjenbro por vn año. Sean per
donados de quales quier crimjnes e dlictos de qual quier natura o ca
lidad o gravedad q̃ sea e oujere fecho o cometido fasta el dia dla
publicaçion desta nra carta. eçebto los casos suso dhos. presenta
dos ante el dho don xpoual colon nro almirante dl mar oçeano sant
e roman o vn dl oy dia dla datta desta nra carta fasta e fin dl
mes d setiembre primero vienes e q̃ pueda el dho almi
rante ala dha ysla española e alas otras yslas e tierra firme de
las dhas indias et servir e ellas por todo el dho tpo en lo q̃ el dho al
mirante les ma dare a mjn deras al nro servj como dho es. et muy
presenta de fuere alas dhas yslas e tierra firme e estoviere el
dho servj co tinuamete por todo el dho tpo trayé la carta pa
tente firmada dl dho almyrate e signada dl escrivano publj e q̃
q̃ en fee como syr vieren los tales alnque tes e las dhas yslas e
en qual ser dlas por todo el dho tpo sea per donados no dla pre
sente d nro proprio motuo e çierta çiençia los per donamos de todos
los dhos dlictos q̃ oy oujeren fecho e cometido fasta el dia dla
publicaçion desta dha nra carta como dho es e q̃ dnde en dllante
no pue dan ser acusados por los dhos dlittos nj por njnguno dllos
nj se proçeda nj pueda ser proçedido a cta ellos nj a tra sus biens
por nras justicias njgimen nj pena alguna e vil nj crimjnal nj pe
dimj dptes nj dl or o ficio nj dl otra manera alguna nj pue dan
ser executadas en ellos nj en sus biens las gente caas q̃ ellos
son o fuere dadas. las q̃les nos por esta nra carta ñe vo camos e damos
por njngunas e de njngud efecto e valor conplido el dho servjçio
e mandamos al dho almjrante alas yndias et notras quales ser
per personas q̃ por nos estovieren en las dhas indias q̃ dexen lybre mete
servir alos q̃ oy oujeren servido el tpo q̃ son oblygados d
servjr segud el thenor desta nra carta e q̃ ne los detengan

en manera alguna. E por esta nra carta mandamos a los del nro
Conseio e oydores dela nra abdiençia e alos dela nra cort e chan
çillia e a todos los corregidores e otras justiçias quales quier
de todas las çibdades e villas e logares de los nros Reynos e se
norios e esta nra carta de perdon e ffuere mostrada e tenida
e la dada vna cosa parte della guarde e cunplan e fagan guardar e cun
plir en todo e por todo segund que ella se la tiene e en guardando lo
non proçedan contra los tales que al Rey ovieren servido en las Indias
por ningund delicto que ovieren fecho en cometido e arbto en las cosas
en so dichas a pedimj de parte nin de su ofiçio nin de otra manera alguna
nin las executen e sus personas e bienes por ffasta a los alcaldes dellos
los Reyes algunos pro çessos contra ellos estan fechos o sentençias
dadas lo tenemos o den por ningunas e nos por la presente las da
nra carta çiençia desde agora para esto Reuoco e tenemos e las
mos e annulamos e damos por ningunos. E testimonios a los dichos
delinquentes en buena forma e el punto estado en questa va antes
que lo oviesen fecho e cometido los dichos delictos. E por que lo en so dicho
sea notorio e ninguno dello pueda pretender ygnora las mandamos
que sea pregonado publica mente por las plaças e mercados e otros
lugares acostunbrados. E los vnos nin los otros non fagades nin fagan
ende al por alguna manera so pena dela nra mrd e de diez mjll mrs
para la nra camara acada vno que lo contrario fiziere. E demas man
damos al ome que esta nra carta mostrare que vos enplaze que parez
cades ante nos en la nra cort do quier que nos seamos del dia que vos en
plazare fasta qunze dias primeros siguientes so la dicha pena so
la qual mandamos a qual quier escriuano publico que para esto fuere
llamado que de ende al que gela mostrare testimonio signado con su
signo por que nos sepamos en como se conple nro mandado. Da
da en la villa de medina del campo a veynte e dos dias del mes de
Junio anno del nasçimj de nro Saluador ihu xpo de mjll e quatro
çientos e noventa e syete annos. yo el Rey. yo la Reyna. yo
fernand aluarez de toledo secretario del Rey e dela Reyna nros sennores
la fiz escreuir por su mandado. Acordada. toderic doctor. re
gistrada. doctor. frn diaz. chançiller.

Don fernando e dona ysabel. por la
graçia de dios Rey e Reyna de Castilla de leon de aragon de Seçilia
de granada de toledo de valençia de galizia de mallorcas de se
villa de cordoua de murçia de jahen de los algarbes de algezira

de gibraltar et delas yslas de canaria Conde e condesa de bar celo
na Señores de viscaya e demolina Duqs de Athenas e deneopatria co
des de ffosellon e de cerdania · marqses de oristan e de goçiano · Atodos
los corregidores asystentes Alldes alguasiles e otras justiçias quales
qer de todas las cibdades villas e logares delos nros reynos et
señorios aqen esta nra carta fuere mostrada o su traslado signado
de escriuano publico · salud e gra sepades qnos avemos mandado a
Don xpoual colon nro almyrante delas Indias qbuelua Ala ysla
española e Alas otras yslas e trra firme qes enlas dhas Indias Nen
tender enla poblaçio dellas et para ello nos le mandamos dar çiertas naos
e carauelas enq vaya çierta gente pagada por çierto tpo e bastimentos
et manten mjs pa ella e porque dallá no puede bastar para qse faga
la dha poblaçion Como mas le aserujçio de dios enro sino va otras gen
tes q dellas esten e biua de sus costas. A vor damos de mandar dar esta
nra carta enla dha razon por do vos mandamos
mos q fasta equando Alguna o Algunas personas Asy varones como
mugeres de nros reynos obiere cometido e cometieren qual quer dli
to o dlitos porq merezca o deua ser desterrados segud derecho e leyes
de nros reynos para Alguna ysla o para labrar e serujr çertos me tales
e los tales qlos desterreys q vayan a estar e servir enla dha ysla española elas
cosas qel dho almyrante delas Indias les dixere e mandare por el tpo
q avian de estar eyla dha ysla e labor demetales · Et esso mysmo to
das las otras personas q fuere culpantes en delittos q no merezca pe
na demuert Salvo q tales los dlittos q justamete seles puedan
desterrio yalas dhas Indias Segud la qlidad delos dlittos los que deneys
de desterreys pa la dha ysla españolca pa q esten Ally e faga lo q
por el dho almyrante les fuere mandado por el tpo q a vos tres pareç
çere · Et Alos q fasta Aqui teneys condenados o condenar deueys Agora ga dllos
te pa yr alas dhas yslas elos tuyer desos presos. los qerys presos
a buen recabdo de vna delas nras carçeles dellas nras Abdien cías de
vallid o Cibdad Real · o Ala chançellería de seuilla e los entreguen los
q los llevare Alas dhas dha caçerrias Alos nros Alcaldes dellas e
los q se llevare Ala carçel de seuilla Se entregue Alnro Asystente
e costa Alos tales condenados Si tuvier bienes Asy bienes non tuviere
Se pague Acosta delos mrs delas penas de nra camara Et mandamos A
las dhas nras justiçias q Asy lo ffaga e cumplan Segud de suso
se contiene e dlos conçejos de todas las cibdades villas e lugares
de nros reynos q vos den pa ello todo el fauor e ayuda q menes
ter ovier des · Et y otras Algunas personas oviere cometido e come
tiere delitos porq deuan ser desterrados fuera destos dhos nros

reynos los desterreys para la dicha ysla en la manera siguiente. los que
ovieren de ser desterrados perpetua mente delos dichos nros reynos. los des
terreys para la dicha ysla por diez años a los que ovieren de ser desterrados
por çierto tpo fuera delos dichos nros reynos sean desterrados pa la dicha
ysla por la mytad del dicho tpo que avian de ser fuera destos nros reynos
e los vnos e los otros no fagan ny fagan en ello por alguna maña
so pena dela nra mrd e de diez mill mrs pa la nra camara a cada vno que lo
contrario fiziere. e demas mandamos al ome que vos esta nra carta mos
trare que vos emplaze que parezcades ante nos en la nra corte do quier que nos
seamos del dia que vos emplazare fasta quynze dias primeros siguien
tes so la dicha pena so la qual mandamos a qual quier escriuano publico que
para esto fuere llamado que de ende al que vos la mostrare testimonio signa
do con su signo por que nos sepamos en como se cumple nro mandado. dada
en la villa de medina del campo veynt e dos dias del mes de Junio año
del nascimiento de nro señor ihu xpo de mill e quatrocientos e noventa e
siete años. yo el rey. yo la reyna. yo fernand aluarez de toledo
secretario del rey e dela reyna nros señores la fiz escreuir por su mandado
don aluaro. acordada. roderici doctor. registrada. doctor
francisco diaz chançeller

Al Rey e la Reyna

Conde de cifuentes nro alferez mayor e asystente dela
cibdad de seuilla Nos enbiamos mandar a las Justiçias
de nros reynos e to das las personas que ovieren de desterrar e desterra
ren pa yslas o para fuera delos dichos nros reynos que los destierren pa la
ysla española e los enbien a esa nra carçel de seuilla. por ende nos
vos mandamos que cada e quando vos fueren enbiados los tales ordena
dos por los presidente e oydores e alcaldes delas nras chançillerias
de valladolid o cibdad real o por quales quier otros corregidores o
Justiçias delos dichos nros reynos que los resçibays e los tengays pre
sos a buen recabdo fasta que los entreguedes al nro almirante delas
yndias del mar oceano. o en su absençia a la persona que por nos tovie
re cargo del proveymiento delas cosas delas dichas yndias e a la persona que
para ello estoviere puesta por el dicho almirante. los quales vos los
ordenara por ellos al tpo que estoviere prestos los nauios pa partir e
fazer enbiarse alas dichas yndias. al qual dicho tpo vos gelos dad
e entregad dentro en los dichos nauios en la dicha cibdad de seuilla

o enla abda d e calis don de ser q̃ los dhōs navios estoviere prestos
para partir presos e abue ffe cabo . por ant̃ escriuano e testigos
e sobie de conoschmie e seguridad dlos maestros dlos tales navios q̃
los lleuara con prestos e abuē recabdo fasta los q̃ tregu dl dhō almy
rate o dla persona q̃l nōbrare q̃ los fecibiz dentro dla dhā ysla
española . e q̃ traera fe e testimonjo vmd los lleno e entrego e q̃ dado en
la dhā ysla española dla vsta e se hiziere fasta los entregue en los
dhōs navios . ffaçed acplir e pagar dlos bienes delos tales ordenados
e sy non toviezen bienes fased lo cumplir e pagar delos mrs dlas penas
de nrā camara . e no fagn̄ de endeal . fecha en la villa de medina del
campo a veynte e dos dias dl mes de Junio de noventa e syete años . yo
el Rey . yo la Reyna . por mā dado del Rey e dela Reyna . fernand
Aluarez .

el Rey e la Reyna

. para la poblaçon dlas yslas e tiē rrā fir
me descubiertas en el mar oceano e q̃ a lleuar man teny miē dlas perso
nas q̃ alla estan e ovieren destar e para descobriz otras tiē rras e tra
er de alla quales q̃er mercaderias q̃ se fallare sera menester
freytar algunas naos o carauelas e otros navios e por q̃ los ma
estres o dueños dellas por aventura se escusara delos fleytar . o de
mandaria mayores fleytes delos q̃ de costumbra lleuaz e se deven aver
justament . lo qual seria en deservicio nrō e daño e estorno dlos
viajes q̃ se han de fazer alas dhās Jndias . por ende nos vos encargamos
e mandamos q̃ quado el nrō almyzant dlas Jndias no fallare los na
vios q̃ oviere menester . o fallan dolos no los quisiere yr con el vos de
mandare quales q̃er navios o carauelas con otras fustas q̃ p̃a los dhos
viajes e vos vea dlos navios e fustas q̃ oviere menester . e de q̃ se for
ma con los dueños dellos dlos fleyte a p̃recios razonables se
gud que a vos parescaere e Justa mente q̃ los deveis fleytar e ten
gays manera q̃ los dueños e maestres dellos vayan dlos
dhōs navios . lo mas sin agrauio e perjuysio delas partes q̃ ser
pueda q̃ por la present vos damos p̃a ello poder complido . fe
cha en la villa de medina del campo a veynte e dos dias
del mes de Junio de mjll e quatro çientos e noventa e
siete años . yo el Rey . yo la Reyna . por man
dado del Rey e dela Reyna . fernan daluarez .

Alcaldes de sacas e cosas vedadas dezmeros e portad
gueros e guardas del arçobispado de Sevilla e obispado de Calis e a
cada uno de vos. Nos vos mandamos que del pan que nos tenemos e se
cogiere en el dicho arçobispado delas terçias a nos pertenesçientes. dexedes
con vuestra liçençia libremente sacar e cargar por la mar a don Xpoual
Colon nuestro Almirante delas yndias o ala persona que el enbiare con su
firma de su nombre quinientos e çinquenta cahizes de trigo e çin
quenta cahizes de çevada para el bastimento e provymiento delas yslas
delas yndias. Al qual dicho Juan le dexad sacar dentro de çinco me
ses primeros siguientes contando desde oy dia dela fecha desta
nuestra çedula en quantos caminos el quisiere e dentro del dicho ter
mino. tanto que en cada camino aya de registrar e registre por
ante un alcalde e dos de vosotros con escrivano e las espaldas desta
nuestra çedula lo que sacare porque no pueda sacar mas delos dichos caniçes
e çinquenta cahizes de trigo e çinquenta cahizes de çevada. del qual
dicho pan vos mandamos que no le demandedes ni lleve de derechos algunos
de saca ni otros derechos algunos por quanto nuestra merçed e voluntad es
que los no pague por el dicho pan es nuestro e lo mandamos llevar para cosas
de nuestro servyçio. lo qual vos mandamos que lo fagades e cunplades oy sin
le poner enbargo ni contrario alguno e non fagades ende al so pena
dela nuestra merçed e de diez mill maravedis para la nuestra camara a cada uno
que lo contrario fiziere. fecha en la villa de medina del campo overde
a dos dias del mes de Junio de noventa e siete años. yo el Rey.
yo la Reyna. por mandado del Rey e dela Reyna fernand alvares
acordada

fran de Soria lugar tenyente de nuestro Almirante mayor de Castilla
nos vos mandamos que dedes e fagades dar a don Xpoual Colon
nuestro Almirante del mar oçeano un traslado su autorizado en
manera que faga fe de qualesquier cartas de merçedes preveillejos e confirma
çiones que el dicho Almirante mayor de Castilla tiene del dicho cargo
del ofiçio del almirante por donde el e otros por el lleve e se aprovechan

los drechos e cosas del pertenesçientes coñl dicho cargo. por
que avemos fecho mrd al dho don xpoual colon q aya ego se d
las mds e honrras e perrogatiuas e libertades e derechos e
salarios enel almirantadgo dlas yndias cha tiene e gosa
el dho nro almirante mayor ceyl almiraãtadgo de castilla. lo
qual fazed cumplid luego como fueredes requerido destã ntã nã
sin ello põgays escusa ni dilaçion alguna. e si asy no lo fi
sierdes e cumplierdes mandamos al nro aysystete e otras justs
dela çibdad d sevilla e vos e delã e apremie a lo asy fazer
e cumplir. e no fagades nin fagã ende al. fecha dla çibdad de bur
gos a veynt e tres dias dl mes de abril de noventa e siet años
yo el rey. yo la reyna. por mãdado del rey e dela reyna. fer
nad alvareç. Acordada

El Rey e la Reyna

Por la presente damos liçençia e facultad dl vos don xpoual
colon nro almirant dl mar oçeano qu q podays tomar e to
meys a Sueldo fasta en numero destresientas e treynta pe
sonas para q esten enlas yndias delos ofiçios e fama siguys
quarenta escuderos çient peones de guerra e de trabajo treynta ma
rineros treynta grumetes veynte labradores de oro e anguera
labradores diez ortelanos. veynt ofiçiales de todos ofiçios
treynta mugeres. e son todas las dhas tresientas e treynta pe
sonas. las quales pagays de dl Sueldo se contiene
enla ynstruçion que çerca dello mandamos dar. e sy alguno delos
dhos ofiçios o gente fuere neçesario mudarse o çeçar el nu
mero delos unos abaxar de e dlos otros lo podays fazer segid
vierdes e entendierdes ser cumplidero al nuestro serviçio
tanto q no sea mas por todos delas dhas tresientas e treynta
personas. fecha dla çibdad de burgos a veynt e tres dias dl mes de
abril de myll e quatro çientos e noventa e siete años. yo el rey
yo la reyna. por mandado del rey e dela ffeyna. fernad alvares.
cordada

Al Rey e la Reyna

Nro thesorero dla hasienda e cosas d nos pertenesçientes

delas yslas e tierra firme descubiertas e puestas so nro Señorio
enl mar oceano e yla parte delas yndias. Nos vos mandamos que
del oro e mercaderias e otras cosas q se oviere enlas dhas yndias
de dar pagues alas personas que oviere de aver de nos qual quier
Salario e Sueldo e otros mrs q ayan de aver flete de navios e
marineros e para las otras cosas q sean necesarias para la habita
cion e poblacion dela gente q esta o viere de yr alas dhas yndias
por sueldo e Salario e la gente q nos oviere servido el tpo pa
sado lo q les oviere de aver e les fuere devido seguid se vos
diere por nominas e cedulas e libramtos firmadas de sus nombres
de don xpoual colon nro Almirante visorrey e governador de
las dhas yndias o su lugar teniente e los oficiales de nros con
tadores mayores q enlas dhas yndias estan e estoviere Con los
quales ffe cabdad e nominas e cuentas el pago delas otras ma de
tvos Sea rescibidos en cuenta los dhos mrs q asy librare el
dho almirate con ffiaales e diez dos e paguos como dho es cno
fuga de Abril. fecha enla cibdad de burgos a veynte e tres dias
del mes de Abril de mill e quatrocientos e noventa e siete Años
Yo el Rey. yo la Reyna. por mandado del Rey e dela Reyna
fernand aluares. Non dada

El Rey e la Reyna

Nros Contadores mayores e vros lugares thenjentes e oficia
les don xpoual colon nro Almirante del mar oceano. nos hiso
Relacion quel ha prestado y presta a algunas delas personas
q estan enlas yndias algunas quantias de mrs. las quales
diz le han de ser pagadas del sueldo e mantenimj dha de
Avez de nos las dhas personas. nos suplico vos man dasemos
q gelas librasedes en los mrs q las tales personas ovieren
de aver de nos. por ende nos vos mandamos e mostra do vos el
dho Almirate o quien su poder oviere ce y forma bastante de de
recho como los dhos mrs le son devidos por las tales personas
q los libreys el nro thesorero/o en su lugar tenjente delas
dhas yndias para q se los pague alo que oviere de dar
de pagar alas tales personas q asy las denjeren al dho al
mirante. fho en burgos nueve dias de mayo de noventa e sie
te Años. yo el Rey. yo la Reyna. por mandado del

Rey Et dela Reyna · fernand aluares · dl por da da ·

El Rey Et la Reyna

Por la presente damos liçençia Et facultad Dl vos Cristoual
Colon nro almyrate dl mar oçeano · para q̃ vbierdes q̃ con
viene Anro serviçio Et se tome el sueldo mas numero de personas
delas q̃ agora mandamos yr Alas yn dias Et estar en ellas y pays
tomar Et tener fasta llegar Al numero de quinientas personas por
todas porel tpo Et segud q̃ a vos bien visto ffuere Contanto Aquel
Et se mantenimy Et las tales personas q̃ Açeptar Et oviere de a vez
Se les pague de qual quier mercaderia Et otras cosas de valor q̃ se
oviere enlas dhas yn dias Sin q̃ nos ma dmos proveer para ello Se otra
parte · fecha enla çibdad dl burgos a veynte Et dos dias dl mes de
Abril / de mjll Et quatro cientos Et noventa Et syete Años · yo el Rey
yo la Reyna · por ma dado dl Rey e dela Reyna · fernad aluares
Acor da da.

Don fernande e dona ysabel

por la graçia de dios Rey Et Reyna de castilla Aleo de Aragon
de Siçilia dl grana da dl tole do dl valençia dl guliçia dl mallor cas dl
Sevilla de cerdeña de cordoua de corçega Et murcia de jahen delos Al
garves de algesira dl gibraltar e las yslas de canaria e de e de
ha de barçelona Et señors de vizcaya e dl molyna Duq̃ dl Athenas
Et dneopatria e dos de ffosello e el ter dama marq̃ses de oristan Et
de goçiano · Por quanto por parte de algunas personas q̃ estan Aveçin
da das en la ysla española e de otras q̃se çere Avezindar Ellos
Nos fue Suplicado les ma dasemos dar Et señalar e la dha y dela ysla
en q̃ ellos pu diesen Senbrar y an otras semyllas e plantar huertas
e algo donde e hazer viñas e Arboles e caña verales de Açucar
e otras plantas e fazer e dificios casas e molynos e engenios q̃
el dho Açucar e otros he dificios proverhosos e neçesarios q̃ an Son
bivir · lo qual es serviçio nro e bien Et feliçidad como dlos morad
res dla dha ysla · Por ende por la presente damos liçençia e facultad
A vos don Cristoual Colon nro Almyrate dl mar oçeano e nro viso Rey
Et governador dla dha ysla para q̃ Atodos los terminos della poda des
dar e ffepartir e de des e ffeparta des Alas A les personas e A rada

vno dellos que agora biuen e mora en la dicha ysla de los que de aqui
adelant fueren a biuir e morar en ella las tierras e montes e aguas que vos
vieredes que a cada vno dellos se debe dar e repartir segund que fuere e lo que nos dieredes por nuestra carta e obligacion e qual dia el primer sona
obiuir a la mitad e a media a cada vno los que vos le dieredes e repartieredes para que dello aya e tenga el posea por suyo e como suyo e
lo vse e ylant e labre e se aproueche dello e a final todo de lo poder vender e dar e donar e trocar e cambiar e enajenar e empeñar e fazer dello
e en ello todo lo que quisiere e por bien touieren como de cosa suya propia e
vnida de justo derecho tittulo obligandose las tales personas de tener
e matener vezindad con su casa poblada en la dicha ysla española por quatro
años primeros siguientes contados desde el dia que les dieredes e se repar-
tieren de las tales tierras e haziendas algunas fazer en las dichas e poblas labores e plantaran las dichas viñas e huertas en la manera e cantidad que
a vos bien visto fuere con tanto que en las tales tierras e montes e a-
guas que ansy dieredes e repartieredes las tales personas no pueda tener
ni tengan hizieredes algunas ceviles ni criminal en cosa e dotada cuyo se ha
dada en termino redondo mas de aquello que tuuiere cercado de vna ta-
pia en alto e que todo lo otro de cerca de cogidos los frutos e esquilmos
dellos sea pasto comun e baldio e sito de. otro mismo reseruamos para nos el brasil e qualquier metal de oro e plata e otro metal que en las
tales tierras se hallare e otro mismo que las tales personas a quien
dieredes e repartieredes las dichas tierras no pueda fazer en fin de ellas
ni en parte dellas algo ni descargo alguno de metal ni de brasil ni de
otra cosa alguna que a nos pertenezca el deja por nuestro ma dado de la de
fazer algo e descargo e que solamente ellos pueda sembrar e coger e lleuar e gastar los frutos e pan e semillas e arboles e viñas e algodo-
nales e que en las dichas tierras sembraren e cogieren vno dichos es exgremos
e mandamos que las tierras que les vos dieredes e repartieredes en la manera
que dicha es ningunas ni algunas personas no gelas tomen ni ocupen ni les
pongan en ellas ni en parte dellas embargo ni impedimento alguno mas
libremente gelas dexen tener e poseer de esto e los en ellas segund que
en esta nuestra carta se contiene. e los vnos ni los otros no fagan ende al
por alguna manera so pena de la nuestra merced e de diez mill mrs a cada vno
que lo contrario fiziere para la nuestra camara. dada en la villa del medina
del campo a veynte e dos dias del mes de jullio año del nascimiento del
nuestro Saluador jhu xpo de mill e quatrocientos e noventa e tres años
yo el Rey. yo la Reyna. yo juan de la parra secretario del Rey e
de la Reyna nuestros señores la fiz escreuir por su mandado. e a las espaldas de la dicha
carta dezia Rodericus dottor fernandus ortis por chançiller registrada dottor

Don fernando e doña

ysabel por la gra de dios rey e reyna de castilla de leon de aragõ de si
cilia de granada de toledo de valecia de galisia de mallorcas de seuilla
de cerdeña de cordoua de corcega de murcia de jahen delos algarbes de al
gesira e gibraltar et delas yslas de canaria Conde e do de la e barçelo
na et senors de viscaya e de molina duqs de athenas e de neopatri
Con de de rosellon e de cerdania marqses de oristan e de goçiano. por q̃
alos reyes e principes es propria cosa e honrraz e publicar e faz̃ m̃ds
e gras a los q̃ subditos e naturales especial ment a aq̃llos q̃ bien
e leal ment los siruen. loqual por nos visto e considerado los muchos
et buenos e leales serus̃ q̃ vos don barto lome colon hermano de don xpo
val colon nro almyrante del mar oçeano e visorrey e gouernador
delas yslas nueua ment falladas en las indias nos aveys fecho
e fasedes de cada dia et esperamos q̃ nos fareys de aqui adlante
tenemos por bien e es nra merçed e voluntad q̃ agora adlante vos llameys
e yntituleys adlantado delas dhas yslas nueua mete falladas en
las dhas yndias e podades vsar e exerçer e faz̃ e las dhas yslas
et en cada vna dllas todas las cosas q̃ los otros adlantados de los dhos
nros reynos pueden e deuen faz̃ e q̃ ayades e gozedes e vos sea guar dadas
todas las honrras e gras e mds e preheminençias e prerrogatiuas
q̃ son deuidas e se deuen faz̃ e guardar segud les leyes por nos
fechas e q̃las cortes de toledo et las otras leyes de nros reynos alos
otros nros adlantados de los dhos nros reynos Ay en sus adla
tamys como fuera dellos Et porque esta nra cã o por su traslado signado de es
criuano publico mandamos al Illustrissimo prinçipe don Jua̅ nro muy
caro e muy amado fijo e alos Infantes duq̃s marq̃ses e condes
e adlantados e ricos omes maestres de las ordenes priores comendadors
et subcomendadors e a los del nro consejo e oydores de la nra abdiençia alos
alguasiles e otras justiçias qualesquier dela nra casa e corte e chançelle
ria et a todos los conçejos Justiçias Regidores caualleros escuderos
ofiçiales e omes buenos de todas las çibdades villas et lugares delos dhos
nros reynos et senorios et al dho nro almyrante visorrey e gouer
nador delas dhas yslas et a los vezinos e moradores e a la otra gen
te q̃ en ellas esta e estouiere de oy en adelante o en otra qual q̃r manera
q̃ de aqui adlante vos yntitulen e llame et vos ayan e tengan por
adlantado de las dhas yslas e trra firme et vos guarden e fagan
guardar todas las dhas honrras e preheminençias prerrogatiuas
ynmunidades que segud las dhas leyes vos deue ser guardadas
e vos sea dada e fagan bien a dir con los derechos e salarios al dho
offiçio de nro adlantado anexos et pertenesçientes bien e ayud̃

mente en guysa q̃ vos no mengue cosa alguna ea nos por esta nra
carta vos q̃amos e fa semos adelantado alas dhas ys las otra
firme q̃ nuevamente sela fallado e descubierto enlas yn
dias de vos ffescabimos e avemos por ff̃ e ebido al dho ofiçio e al
vso de exerçicio del ma damos e enello ni e parte dillo embargo
ni ynpedimento alguno vos no poga ni ansi e ta poner ca
desto q̃ dho es e sier de nra carta de pñ ni ma damos al nro ch̃acillr
e notarios e alos otros ofiçiales q̃ estan ala tabla de los nros se
llos e vos lo de ra pagen e sellen e los vnos en los otros no fa
gan ende al por alguna manera sopena ala nra m̃d e de diez
mill mrs ã cada vno e lo ã trario hisiere para la nra camara e
demas ma damos al ome q̃les esta nra carta mostraze q̃los enplase
e parezean ant̃ nos e en la nra corte doquier q̃ nos sepamos al dia
e los enplase fasta q̃ se dias primeros siguientes sola dicha
pena sola qual ma damos a qual q̃er escriuano publico q̃ para
esto fuere llamado q̃ de ende al q̃ gelo mostraze testimonio sig
nado con su signo porq̃ nos sepamos en como se cumple nro ma
dado. dada enla villa de medina del campo a veynt e dos dias del
mes de jullio año del nasçimiento de nro salua dor ihu xpo de mill
e quatroçientos e noventa e siete años. yo el rey. yo la
reyna. yo juan dela parra secretario del rey e dela reyna nros
señores la fis escriuir por su ma dado. e enlas esp̃al das dela
dha ca de sia acordada. roderic doctor. fernad ortis por
chancillr. ff̃registrada doctor

El Rey e la Reyna

Por la presente damos licencia e facultad a vos don xpoual
colon nro almyrante del mar oceano e al nro e sejo para q̃ poda
des pagar e pague a las personas q̃ ha estado e esta e estouiere
daqui adelante conforme ala ynstriçion q̃ de nos teneys del nu
mero dela gente q̃ ha de estar enlas dhas yndias e a las personas
e dueños de nauios q̃ han lleuado e lleuare mantenimientos e otras
cosas alas dhas yn dias e de todos los mrs q̃ geles deue e deue
zen daqui adelante de quales q̃er muel dos e mantenimientos de fle
tes de nauios e de el sello primera mente aberiguan dos lo q̃
ca se ouiere de pagar. por el obispo de badajoz e por vos e
lo q̃ ouiere de pagar enlas yn dias por vos e por el q̃ g̃ teniete

de nros contadors mayores que alla residen dando de cada uno
lo que justamente se le deue e deuiere. lo qual les ayays de pagar et
pagueys de qualesquier mercadurias e otras cosas que en las dichas yn
dias se ovieren con tanto que la paga o obra ça que les hizieres sea se
ñalada del dicho lugarteniente de nros contadores mayores e asenta
da en los nros libros parа lo qual vos damos poder cumplido. fecha
en la villa de alcala de henares a veynte e tres dias del mes de diziembre
de noventa e siete años. yo el rey yo la reyna. por mandado del
rey et de la reyna fernad aluares decorada.

Al rey et la reyna

Reuerendo en xpo padre obispo de badajoz et don xpoual colo
almirante del mar oceano anbos del nro consejo. vimos una vra
letra y cerca de lo que dezis que no se ha proveydo cosa alguna fasta a
gora en lo de los mantenimientos que han de yr a las yndias aunque ya no fa
llays persona que lo tome encargo por los precios que desian fueron
tasados en las ynstruciones e vos el dicho almyrante lleuastes por
que dis que valen los dichos mantenimientos a mayores precios que alla se ta
saron. y pues avn es nos vos mandamos y encargamos que anbos de
dos juntamente lo veays e busqueys personas fieles que lo tomen
y hazeys el precio que justo fuere e vos paresciere que fuese devdo
aviendo respecto al valor de los dichos mantenimientos et si no fallar
des tales personas lo proveays como a vosotros mejor paresciere
por manera que no se detenga la partida de vos el dicho almyrante. Ca
para ello vos damos poder auylbo. fecho en la villa de alcala de he
nares a veynte et tres dias del mes de diziembre de noventa et siye
te años. yo el rey. yo la reyna. por mandado del rey e de la
reyna. fernad aluares et en las espaldas decia. Acordada.

Don fernande e doña
ysabel por la graçia de dios rey et reyna de castilla
de leon de aragon de sicilia de granada de toledo de
valencia de galisia de mallorcas de sevilla de cerdeña de cor
doua de corcega de murcia de jahen de los algarues de algezira de
gibraltar e de las yslas de canaria conde e conde de barçelona
et señores de viscaya et de molina duques de athenas e de neopatria

condes de Rosellon et de Cerdanya Marqueses de Oristan et
de Goçiano A vos los Cavalleros e escuderos oficiales e omes
buenos et otras qualesquier personas de qualquier estado o con
diçion que soys e por nro mandado fuystes e estays e estuvierdes
daqui adelant en las yslas por nro mandado descubiertas e por
descobrir en el mar oçeano en la provinçia de las Indias e a cada vno e
qualquier de vos Salud e graçia sabeys Como don xpoual co
lon nro Almirante de las dhas yndias del dho mar oçeano es nro
visorrey e governador dellas por virtud de nras cartas e poderes
e para ello le mandamos dar et dimos e porque nra merçed e volutad
es quel dho Almirante tenga el dho cargo de nro visorrey e gover
nador e el vse e exerçite en las dhas yslas e que todos fagays e
cumplays todo lo quel de nra parte vos mandare e en tendieyre ser
a nro serviçio Nos vos mandamos a todos e a cada vno de vos
que le obedescays e cumplays e executeys e que todos vos conformeys con el e fa
gays e cumplays todo lo quel de nra part vos mandare Como si nos
en persona vos lo mandasemos Solas penas que vos pusiere et mandare
poner de nra parte las quales de nra parte vos ponemos e avemos por
puestas por las quales execuar en los que lo contrario fisierdes damos poder
cumplido al dho Almirante don xpoual colon o al que su poder
oviere e los vnos ni los otros no fagades ni fagan ende al por
alguna maña So pena de la nra merçed e de diez mill mrs para la nra
Camara a cada vno de los que lo contrario fisierdes Dada en la
çibdad de Segovia a diez e seys dias del mes de Agosto Año del
nasçimiento de nro senor Jhu xpo de mill e quatroçientos e noventa e
quatro Años yo el Rey yo la Reyna yo fernand alvares de to
ledo secretario del Rey e de la Reyna nros senores la fiz escrevir por
su mandado e en las espaldas de la dha carta estava escrito esto
que se sigue Registrada Alonso perez por chançeller

Don fernando e Doña
ysabel por la graçia de dios Rey et Reyna de castilla
de leon de aragon de Seçilia de granada de toledo de valençia
de galisia de mallorcas de sevilla de Cerdena de cordova de cor
çega de murçia de Jahen de los algarbes de algesira de gibraltar
e de las yslas de canaria conde e condesa de barçelona e senores
de viscaya e de molina duques de Athenas e de neopatria condes
de Rosellon e de Cerdania marqueses de oristan e de goçiano

sto dos e quales quier Capitanes maestres e patrones e contra
maestres e marineros de naos e caravelas e otras fustas. E otras
quales eser personas de qual quier condiçion que sea nros vasallos subdi
tos e naturales algunos de vos en esta nra ca ... quien o atanner
puede e a cada vno e qual eser de vos a quien esta nra carta fuere mos
trada o el traslado della signada de escrivano publico Salud e
gra sepades que nos avemos mandado a don xpoual colon nro Almyrante
del mar oçeano e nro visorrey e governador delas yslas e tierra fir
me del dho mar oçeano dela parte delas Indias que con çiertas naos e ca
ravelas e otras fustas como nro capitan vaya alas dhas Indias
e tierra firme que son enla dha parte delas Indias descubiertas e por
descubrir. Por ende por la present mandamos a todos e a cada
vno de vos los dhos maestres e capitanes e patrones e contramaestres
e compañas delas dhas naos e caravelas e otras fustas e a todas las com
pañas e enellas e en cada vna dellas navegaren e estan e esten por
nro capitan general delas dhas naos e fustas e caravelas del dho
don xpoual colon nro Almyrante e visorrey e governador del dho mar
oçeano e le obedezcades e tengays por nro capitan general. e fagades
e cumplades e pongades en obra todo lo que por el de nra parte vos fuere
dho e mandado e a cada cosa dello. Segund e como e la forma
e maña e alos plazos e so las penas que de nra parte vos mandare. Syn
poner ello escusa ni dilaçion alguna. bien asy e a tan cumplidamente
como a nos esa persona vos lo mandasemos ca nos por la present le fazemos
nro capitan general delos dhos navios e caravelas e otras fustas e le
damos poder e facultad para las mandar e governar como nro capitan ge
neral. E para executar enla compaña dellos quales eser penas en que caye
ren e incurrieren por no complir e obedeçer en se mandamos como dho
es nra merced e voluntad que el dho nro capitan general don xpoual colo
nro Almyrante e visorrey e governador con vosotros con alguno de vos
no vaya de ala ... ni al trato della que tiene el serenissimo rey de
portugal nro hermano porque nra voluntad es de guardar e que se
guarde por vos nros subditos e naturales lo que çerca dela dha con na
tenemos capitulado e asentado con el dho rey de portugal. Lo
qual vos mandamos que guardeys asy so pena dela nra merced e de çis
da çion de vros bienes para la nra Camara e fisco. Dada enla çib
dad de barcelona a veinte e ocho dias del mes de mayo año
del nasçim de nro Salvador jhu xpo de mill e quatroçientos
e noventa e tres años · yo el rey · yo la reyna · yo fernand alvares
de toledo secretario del rey e dela reyna nros señores la fiz escrivir por su
mandado · e enlas espaldas dela dha Carta estava escripto

Lo que ſe ſigue. dvz dada. Rodericus. Regiſtrada. alo
Go perez. pero gõſ chanceller

El Rey A la Reyna

Por quãto en el poder que mãdamos dar ⁊ dimos A vos don xpõual
Colon nõ almyrãte ſe las Indias ⁊ trra firme que ha deſcubierto
o ſe ha de deſcobrir en el mar occano A la pte de las yndias en nõ
ſo rrey ⁊ gonernador de las dhas yslas ⁊ trra firme ſe cõtiene
que vos ayays de librar las cãs ⁊ prouyſiones patentes que ſe ouiere de
librar ⁊ expedir en las dhas Indias ⁊ trra firme en nõ nõbre pr
don fernãdo ⁊ doña ysabel etc̃ las quales hã de yr ſelladas del
nõ Sello que para ello vos mãdamos ſellar aſſe de lo que podria aduẽ
eſcer que vos non eſtouieſſe de en las dhas Indias ⁊ trra firme por que
an verna que fueſſe dd ⁊ deſcobriz otras yslas ⁊ trra firme ⁊ fazẽ
otras coſas en ꝑ de las A nõ ſeruyꝗ de aya ꝑſa aue ꝑe de de ꝑr
en vro lugar alguña perſona que entiẽda ⁊ ꝑuea en las coſas de las
dhas Indias ⁊ trra firme en vra abſencia el qual no podria en
tender ⁊ proueer ⁊ ello dando las dhas nras cãs ⁊ prõyſiones en
nro nonbre ⁊ ſyn aver para ello nro poder ⁊ authoridad. Por ende
por la pſente damos poder ⁊ faꝗtad A la perſona que en vra abſen
cia vos nõbrares para que dar en las dhas yslas ⁊ trra firme pa
que pueda librar ⁊ expedir los negocios ⁊ cõſas que alli oꝗrie
ten. dando las dhas cartas ⁊ prõyſiones en nro nõbre ⁊ ſellã do
las cõ nro Sello ſegũd que vos lo podriades hazer ſeyẽdo pſente
en las dhas yslas ⁊ trra firme por virtud de los dhos nros pode
res que teneys. de lo qual mãdamos dar la pſente firmada de
de nros nõbres. fecha en barcelona A veynte ⁊ ocho dias de
mayo de noventa ⁊ tres años. yo el rey. yo la ffeyna. por
mãdado del rey ⁊ de la ffeyna. Fernã aluarez. ⁊ en las eſpaldas
de dia ⁊ vz dada

Al Rey ⁊ la Reyna

Por quanto ſegũd el aſiento que nos mã damos fazer con vos
don xpõual colon nro almyrãte del mar occano ⁊ nro

visorrey e gouernador delas yslas e tᵃrra firme del dᵒ mar oce
ano q son dla parte dlas jndias entre otras se cõtiene q pa
los oficios dgouernaaçõ que oviere dhaver enlas dhas yslas e
tᵃrra firme vos nõbrays de nõbrar tres perzonas pa cada ofiçio or q
nos nõbremos e proueamos dll vno dllos al tal ofiçio. y al pre
sent nose pue de guardar el dhᵒ asyento por la brevedad de vᵃa
partida para las dhas yslas. confiaado de vos el dhᵒ nrᵒ vi sᵒ mi
visorry e gouernador qᵉ lo prouereys fiablemᵉte cõmo cũple
a nrᵒ servᵒ. e ala buena gouernaaçõ dlas dhas yslas. por la pre
sent vos damos licençia poder e facultad para q entanto que
fuere nᵃa merçed e volũntad vo days proveer alos dhos oficios e
gouernaçiõ dlas dhas yslas e tᵃrra firme alas perzonas e por
el tpᵒ en la forma e mᵃña q a vos bie visto fuere. alos quales e
a cada vno por vos fuere proveydos les damos poder e facultad q usen
vsen dllos dhos oficios segũ e por la forma e mᵃña q en vᵃas
prouysiones q alos dhos oficios les dieredes sera cõtenido. ferha
enla çibdad dbarçelona a veynte ocho dias d mayo de mjll e
quᵒ çientos e noventa e tres dude. yo el rey. yo la reyna
por mandado del rey e dla reyna. fernadalvarez. dᵉ vᵃa dada.

Don fernando e doña
ysabel por la graçia de dios rey e reyna de castilla
de leon de aragon de seçilia de granada de toledo de valençia
e galiçia de mallorcas de sevilla de cerdeña de cordova de cor
cega de murçia de jahẽ de los algarbes de algesira degibraltar
e dlas yslas de canaria conde e condesa de barçelona e señores
devizcaya e demolina. duqs de athenas e deneopatria. cõ
des de rosellõ e de çerdania. marqses de oristã e de goçiano.
por qᵃnto vos don xpoval colõ nrᵒ almirante viso rey
e gouernador del mar oceano nos suplicastes e pedistes por
mᵈ vos diesemos nrᵒ poder e facultad para faz e establesçer
de vros bienes e vasallos e eredamᵒs e fijos pᵃz rᵉtenos vno o dos
mayoradgos por q dl epetᵃa memorja de vos e de vᵃa casa
e linaje e por q los q de vos vinieᵉ sean honrrados. lo qual
por nos visto e cõsiderado q a los reys e prinçipes es propia cosa
honrrar e sublimar a sus subditos e naturales e cada lmᵉte
a aqllos q bie e leal mᵉte nos sirvẽ. e por q en sᵉ fuᵃ si los
tales mayoradgos es honrra dela corona real destos nros reynos

e pro e bien dellos e acatando los muchos buenos e leales e grandes
seruiçios que vos el dicho don xpoual colon nuestro almirante aueis fecho e fazeis de cada dia e especialmente en descubrir e traer a nuestro poder e señorio las yslas e tierra firme que des-
cobristes en el dicho mar oçeano. mayormente por que esperamos que con
ayuda de dios nuestro señor se nos dara en mucho seruiçio en nuestro seruiçio e pro e autoridad de nuestros reynos e por que se espera que los
pobladores delas dichas yndias se conuertiran a nuestra santa fe catholica touimoslo por bien. E por esta nuestra carta de nuestro proprio motu
e çierta çiençia e poderio real absoluto de que en esta parte queremos vsar
e vsamos como rey e reyna e señores no reconosçientes superior
en lo tenporal. vos damos liçençia e facultad para que quando vos
quisierdes e por bien touierdes asy en vuestra vida por que le contrato e
manda como por donaçion entre biuos como por vuestro testamento e
postrimera voluntad e por do de calo o en otra manera qual quier que
quisierdes e por bien touierdes podades fazer e fagades mayorazgo
o mayorazgos por vna o dos o tres escripturas o por muchas tantas
quantas veses en la manera que quisierdes e bien visto vos fuere e
el o los o qual quier cosa o parte dellos podades defazer tornar
e emendar e añadir e quitar e menguar e acreçentar vna o dos o tres
veses e quantas mas veses e como e en la manera que quisierdes e bien
visto vos fuere e el dicho mayorazgo o mayorazgos podades fazer
e fagades en don diego colon vuestro fijo mayor legitimo o en qual quier de
vuestros fijos herederos que oy dia teneis o touierdes de aqui adelante e
en defecto e falta destos en vno o dos de vuestros parientes o otras personas que vos quisierdes e bien visto vos fuere e lo podays fazer
e fagays de qualesquier vasallos e juridiçiones e casas e tierras e
heredamientos e molinos e dehesas e otros quales quier heredamientos e bienes e de quales quier que vos de nos tengays señorio e de her-
dad e que de todo lo suso dicho e en cada cosa e parte dello que oy dia teneis
e poseeis e vos perteneçe aver e tener fasta aqui e touierdes e po-
seyerdes de aqui adelante asy por merçed e donaçion como por defunda-
çiones e conpras e trueques e canbios e permutaçiones o por otros quales
quier titulos onerosos o lucratiuos o en otra qual quier manera
o por qual quier causa o ffaso o sea el qual dicho mayorazgo o mayorazgos podades fazer e fagades asy a vuestra voluntad e beze
queredes e disponiades e sy ellos dichos vuestros bienes e vuestra cosa enteramente cumplidamente sin diminuçion alguna como de qual quier parte
o partes dellos para que ynviolablemente que en los dichos vuestros bienes
e qual quier cosa e parte dellos por mayorazgo el dicho don diego

Colon vro fijo e en los dhos vros fijos e descendientes en gen qu
sier dn fazer sugades el dho mayoradgo o mayoradgos a las con
diciones e limytaçiones cargos vinculos e firmezas Instituçiones e
Sostituçiones modos e Reglas e penas el sibmysiones que vos qysier
des e por bien tovier des e con quales qer hordenan ças e mandas e pa
ctos e convenençias Uehegnos e por la forma e manera q vos vin en
lar des e mandar des e disponsier des e otorgar des por vna o por muchas es
cripturas como dho es. lo qual todo e cada cosa e part dello avie do a
qy por expresado e declarado como sy de palabra a palabra aq fue
se puesto e especificado nos asy de agora para estonçes dela dha nra çier
ta çiençia e propio motuo e poderio Real absoluto de q enesta pte
qremos vsar e vsamos lo loamos e aprovamos confirmamos e Inter
ponemos a ello e a cada cosa e pte dello nro decreto e abtoridad
Real e mandamos q vos vala e sea guardado todo e cada cosa e pte
dello Inviolable mente para agora e para siempre jamas avn que
a ello e cada cosa e parte dello sea la dicta expreso derecho e contra
to da forma e orden del e sea tal e de tal maña q dene neçessario se
oviesse hazer expressa y especial minçion enesta nra carta e q no
un diese ser contra prehen dido sola generalidad della e que sea guar
dada bien asy e tan cumplida mente como sy sobre cada cosa e pte e ar
ti culo dello diese nra provança e graçia e mandado como e fegnd e por
la forma q ela devra disponsiçion o disponsiçiones se contuviere
lo qual todo es nra mrd q se faga asy no enbargant e los otros
vros fijos herederos e los otros vros parientes e deb dos e desçe
dietes e transversales sean agraujados en su legitima e alimen
tos o les perteneçer e al dho don diego colon vro fijo e a los o a q
llos a qyen fiziere des el dho mayoradgo o mayoradgos o ma dalome
joria lleve o lieva muy grande e notable demajoria de los q segnd de
recho e leyes de fuero les podys e par en vro testamento o postrimera
voluntad e dar por donaçion entre bivos o en otra qual qer manera
los quales dhos donbienos q a vos yn Anyer des e vn bier des el dho vro ma
yoradgo o mayoradgos queremos e es nra mrd q sean vin prestibles
e inpartibles para siempre jamas de la persona o personas en qen
fizier des el dho mayoradgo o mayoradgos o q segnd vra dispusiçio
lo diere o los oviere. no los pueda vender ni daz ni donar ni enajenaz
ni diviydiz ni apartar ni los pueda peder ni pierda por ni nguna deba
te de una ni por otra ffasa ni suhsa ni por ningnd delicto ni crime q
comertan. Salno qien lepd ma lestatis o perdulionis o trayçio
o qime de heregia. lo qual qremos q es nra mrd q sequir de no
enbargante las leyes q se contienen q los mayoradgos no ayan lngar

Albñ se fagan por virtud de quales quier cãs e tes çiptos q̃ sobre
ello se den. E otro sy no enbargant quales qer leys e fueros e dre
chos ordenamẽs vsos e costunbres estilos e fasañas asy comunes
e municipales delos Reys nros antecessores q̃ en cõtrario dllo en lo
susodcho sean o ser puedan. nylas leys e derechos q̃ disen q̃ cosa fecha en
perjuysio de tercero / o contra los buenos vsos e costunbres en que la
parte ey tiende ser lesa e dañificada en no vale. nila ley q̃ dise q̃ los
derechos proybitiuos no pueden ser renocados e las leys q̃ disen q̃
las merced dadas cõtra ley fuero e derecho deuen ser obedescidas
e no conpli das aun q̃ contenga en sy quales qer clausulas derogatiuas
e otras firmesas e non obstancias e la ley q̃ dise q̃ la defensa dela
parte es prometida de derecho natural. otq̃ a ella no puede ser
quitada ny renocada ni q̃ las leys fueros e derechos valederos no
pueden ser renocados saluo por cortes e otra qual ser cosa e
effecto calidad vigor ministerio q̃ en contrario dllo en lo susodcho sea o ser
puede a aun q̃ sea urgente e necessario o nyxto o en otra qual ser
maña. Ca dlla cõ nra çierta sçiençia e proprio mutuo e poderio
real absoluto de q̃ en esta pte queremos vsar e vsamos como Reyes
e soberanos señores no Reconosçentes superior en lo tporal
noviendo aqui por expressado y declarado como sy de palabra a pa
labra aqui fuese puesto e expressado dispesamos con ello e lo abro
gamos e derogamos e casamos e anulamos en quanto a esto toca
e atañe e puede atañer puede destra manera cã e dllo e lla cõ toda
el q̃to de obrepçion e subrrepçion e todo otro obstaculo en perjuysio. e
suplimos quales ser defectos cõ tres quales ser cosas q̃ de fecho
e de derecho subtancia e solepnidad sean nescesarias e pro
vechosas de suplir cã valida ad e corroboraçion dello. e mã damos
al sereníssimo prinçipe don Jhoan nro muy caro e muy amado fijo e alos
ynfantes perlados duqs condes marqses ricos omes maestres dlas
ordenes priores comendadores e subcomendadores e alos alcaydes
delos castillos e casas fuertes e llanas e alos del nro consejo e oydores
de la nra abdiençia e chançelleria e alcaldes e alguasiles dela nra casa
e corte e chançelleria e a todos los corregidores e assistentes dllos alguasiles
merinos prebostes regidores caualleros escuderos oficiales e omes
buenos de todas las çibdades e villas e lugares destos nros Reynos
e señorios q̃ agora son e seran daqui adelant e vos guarden esta
merced q̃ vos fasemos en todo e por todo segund q̃ en ella se contiene
e q̃ vos non vayan nin passen contra ella ni contra parte dello en tpo alguno
nin por alguna manera e por qual qer cosa en ffraçion que
sea o ser pueda. e q̃ manden e guarden e lleven o deuen

execuçion con efetto. la dispusicion o dispusiçiones q̃ fi
zieredes al dho mayoradgo o mayoradgos criada o mejoria
segund e porla forma e manera q̃ enellas e en cada vna dellas se
contega e as tuviere sin atender ni esperar para ello otra nra
carta ni mandamiento ni segunda ni terçera jusion delo qual todo
mandamos al nro chançeller mayor e notarios e otros ofiçiales q̃
estan ala tabla delos nros sellos q̃ vos libren e passen e sellen
nra carta depremj̃ la mas firme e bastante q̃ para ello menester
ovieredes. e los vnos ni los otros no fagades ni fagan ende al por al
guna manera so pena ala nra mrçed e de diez mill mrs para la nra
camara a cada vno por qen fincare delo asy fazer e complir. e
demas mandamos al ome q̃ vos esta carta mostrare q̃ vos enplaze
q̃ parezcades ante nos en la nra corte do quier q̃ nos seamos del
dia q̃ vos enplazare fasta quinze dias primeros siguientes so la
dha pena so la qual mandamos aqual quier escriuano publico q̃ pa
esto fuere llamado q̃ de ende al q̃ vos la mostrare testimonio
signado con su signo por q̃ nos sepamos en como se cumple nro manda
do. Dada en la çibdad de burgos a veynte e tres dias del mes de
abrill año del nasçimiento de nro señor ihu xpo de mill e quatro çie̅
noventa e siete años. yo el Rey. yo la Reyna. e yo fer
nand alvarez de toledo segretario del Rey e dela Reyna nros señores
la fize escriuir por su mandado. e las espaldas de la dha
carta estava escripto lo siguiente. en forma Rodericus
Doctor. Registrada Alonso perez e sellada

Al Rey e ala Reyna

Don xpoual colon nro Almirante del mar oçeano
viso Rey e governador delas yslas q̃ se han descubierto
en las Indias. vimos vras letras e ovimos mucho plazer en
saber lo q̃ por ellas nos escriuis. y de averos dios dado tan
buen fin en vro trabajo y encaminado bien en lo q̃ començ astes
en el. sera mucho servido e nos otros Rey e muy mucho e nros
Reynos se de aver tanto provecho. plazera a dios q̃ demas
de lo q̃ en esto le seruis. por ello e sera servido de vos mucho hazer de

las quales creed que se vos faran como vros previllejos y traba
jos lo merece y por que queremos que lo que aveys començado con la
ayuda de dios se continue y se leve adelante y deseamos que vra
venida fuese luego. porende por serui nro que de os la mayor
priessa que podieredes en vra venida porque con tpo se prouea
todo lo que es menester. y porque como ves el verano es venido
y no se pase el tpo para la yda alla ved si algo se puede de
adereçar en sevilla o en otra pte para vra tornada alla que
que aveys fallado. y escreuidnoslo luego con este correo que ha de bol
ver presto porque luego se prouea como se haga. en tanto que
vos bolveys y tornays. de mana que quando bolvier de seдça
este todo aparejado. de barçelona a viij dias de mayo de no
venta e tres años. yo el rey. yo la reyna. por mandado del rey
e de la reyna. fernand alvares. e en las espaldas de Sria. y del rey
e la reyna. A don xpoual colon nro almyrante del mar oceano
et visorrey e gouernador de las yslas que se ha descubierto en las
yndias.

La Reyna

Don xpoual colon nro almyrante del mar oceano vi
rey et gouernador de las yslas nuevamente falladas en las
yndias. con este correo vos enbio un traslado del libro que nos de
xastes el qual ha tardado tanto porque se escriviese secreta
mente para que estos que estan aqui de por tugal ni otro alguno no
lo supiese y ha seydo y no se ha acabado desto. y porque mas presto se hiziese va
de dos letras segun vereys. ciertamente segun lo que en este
negocio aca se ha platicado y visto cada dia se conoce ser
muy mayor y de grand calidad e sustancia. y que vos nos aveys en ello
mucho servido y tenemos de vos grand cargo. y asy esperamos
en dios que demas de lo asentado con vos que se ha de fazer cumplir
muy enteramente como vos nos escriveys de nos mucha merced. por
ende y de cierta mj como es razon. y lo aveys de vros seruicios
enteramente. la carta del almazur que avia de se fazer y es
acabada nos la enbiad luego. y por ser nro como el es grand priessa
a vra partida para que allá con la gra de nro senor depose
y obra sin dilacion alguna pues vedes quanto cumple al

bien el negocio y de todo lo q̃ alla nos escrivis e fazed siem
pre saber q̃ de aca de todo lo q̃ oviere vos avisaremos e vos
lo faremos saber. Enl negocio de portogal nose ha tomado cõ
estos q̃ aqui estan determinaçion alguna yo creo q̃l Rey se llegara
a Razon enello. qrria q pensase de lo contrario porq̃ yo e ello no
vos desayudare cu lo q̃ veys devir sobre aviso al q̃ cabo q̃ ay le
para q̃ en manera alguna no podays ser cabiz engaño. de bar
celona a can̄ dias del mes de setiembre de noventa e tres años
yo la Reyna. por mãdado de la Reyna. Jua alaparra e las
espaldas de sia lo siguient. por la Reyna a Don Xpoval colo
su almirate del mar oceano e viso Rey e governador delas
yslas meva mente falladas enlas jndias.

El Ry e la Reyna

Don Xpoual colon. nro almirãte del mar
oceano y nro visoRey e governador delas ys
las nueva mente falladas en las ⟨parte⟩ delas yndias
vimos las cartas q̃ nos enbiastes cõ Antonjo de torres cõ las q̃ lo
ovimos mucho plazer y damos muchas graçias a nro Senõr dios q̃
tambien lo ha fecho. y en averos en todo tã bien gujado. En mucho
cargo y servjçio vos tenemos lo q̃ alla aveys fecho e trabajado cõ
tan buena orden y proveymj̃ q̃ no pudo ser mejor. y asy esso mjs
mo oymos al dicho antonjo de torres y fue q̃ escrivimos todo lo q̃ cõ el
nos enbiastes y no se espera menos de vos segud la mucha volun
tad y afiçad q̃ de vos se ha conosçid y conoçe enlas cosas de nro
serviçio. sed çierto q̃ nos tenemos de vos por mucho servidos
y en cargados enello q̃ a vos faremos mucha mrçed y honrra y a los q̃ sã ta
mjento como vos gra aveys servjs lo te qujere p̃a deb ser. y por
q̃l dicho antonjo de torres tardo en venjr aqui fasta agora
y no aviamos visto vras cartas. las q̃les nos avia enbiado por las
traer el almes forte q̃ lo y p̃ la priessa dela partid destos na
vios q̃ agora va. los quales alla orã çlo e aquj copimos los mã
damos despachar cõ todo fecabd delas cosas q̃ se alla cõ bi
astes por memorial. q̃ quanto mas ayna dam̃ent se pu
diesse fazer sin destorperlos. y Rey se faza y abxe a los

to de lo otro el trabajo del cargo al tpo y a mj el lo dixere. no ha
lugar de vos responder como esperamos yo qua del el vaya pla
ziendo a dios vos responderemos y mandaremos proveer en todo
ello como es le. nos lo avemos avido enojo delas cosas q della se
han fecho fuera de vra voluntad las quales mandaremos bie reme
diar e castigar enl primer viaje q della se fiziere enbiad abez
nal de pisa al qual nos enbiamos a mandar q ponga en obra con venir
y enl cargo q llevo entie da ello la persona de vos y al padre
frey buyl pareciere con tanto q la dcha deprovee e por la pssa
a la partida dlos dhos navios no se pueda en algo pveer lo en ello. de el
primero viaje q si plaze a dios se proveera de tal persona qual
conviene para el dho ofiçio. de medina del campo a xxviij. de abril
de noventa e siete años. yo el Rey. e yo la Reyna. por mandado
del Rey e dela Reyna. Jua de la parra. e alas espaldas desia lo
siguiente. por el Rey e por la Reyna a don xpoual colon su al
mjrante del mar oçeano e su visorrey e governador en las yslas
nuevamente falladas enlas tras delas yndias.

El Rey e la Reyna

Don xpoual colon Almjrante mayor delas yslas delas
yndias. vimos vras letras e memoriales q nos enbiastes
con torres y avemos avido mucho plazer de sabir todo lo q por ellos
nos escreviste y damos muchas graças a nro señor por todo ello por
q con su ayuda este negocio vro sera causa q nra sancta fee
catholica sea mucho mas acreçentada. e vna delas principa
les cosas por q esto nos ha plazido tanto es por ser vra invençion
prinçipio da cabida por vra mano trabajo e yndustria e pa
reçe q de lo q al prinçipio nos dexistes q se podia alca
çar por la mayor parte todo ha salido çierto como si lo ovierads
visto antes q nos lo dixesedes. esperança tenemos en dios
que en lo q adelante se ha de continuar se hara por el modo q vos
q damos en mucho cargo para vos hazer mds lo veremos q vos
ser a vos muy bien contento. y visto todo lo q nos escrevistes
como sera q a dezir largamente veris todas las cosas de q es
muy grande alegria leerlas. pero algo mas q rriamos q nos
escriviesedes de. es en q sepamos quantas yslas fasta

las q̃ aveys fallado y d̃las q̃ aveys puesto nonbres q̃ nõbre
tiene cada vna porq̃ avn q̃ nõbrays algunas en vr̃as cãs no con
todas y alas otras llos nõbres q̃les llama los Indios e quãto ny
se b̃na a otra Ento do lo q̃ aveys fallado en cada vna dellas y lo q̃ diezen
q̃ ay enellas. y enlo q̃ de ha enbiado despues q̃ alla fuystes q̃se ha
avido pues ya es passado el tp̃o q̃ todas las cosas senbradas
sehan de coger. y principalmente deseamos saber todos los tpos
d̃l año q̃ tales son alla encada mes por si porq̃ anos pareçe
q̃ enlo q̃ dezis q̃ ay alla ay mucha difereçia enlos tpos d̃los d̃aca
algunos q̃ren dezir q̃ en vn año ay alla dos ynviernos. to
do noslo escrevid por nr̃o servicio. y enbiadnos todos los mas hal
cones q̃ de alla se pudiere enbiar y de todas las aves q̃ alla ay
y se pudiere aver porq̃ q̃rriamos las ver todas. y quãto d̃las co
sas q̃ nos enbiastes por memorial q̃ se proveyese y enbiase d̃aca
todas las mãdamos proveer Como d̃ d̃s̃ torres sabreys y vereys
porlo q̃ el lleva. q̃rriamos saber si os pareçe q̃ ay ya senti d̃vos y
de toda la gente q̃ alla esta Como ya q̃ cada dia pudiese dos ser pro
veydos d̃lo q̃ fuese menester q̃ cada mes viniese vna cara vela de
alla y de d̃n fuese otra. pues q̃ las carave̅s de portogal estan
d̃sentadas q̃ los navios podra yr y venir segura mente vel
do d̃ vos os pareçe esto q̃ se deve hazer. hazeldo d̃vos y escrevidnos
la manera q̃ os pareçe esto q̃ se deve enbiar de d̃ca. y esto q̃ to̅
d̃la forma q̃ alla deveys tener con la gente q̃ alla teneys bien
nos pareçe lo q̃ fasta agora aveys principiado ya si lo deveys
Cõtinuar. dando les el mas contentami̅ q̃ ser pueda. y no
dando les lugar q̃ ex... dan en cosa alguna enlas cosas q̃ de
viere haser. y vos les mãdardes d̃ nr̃a p̃te. y quãto ala
poblaçion q̃ le dezistes end̃ d̃llo no ay q̃ en pueda dar regla çier
ta ny entendar cosa alguna d̃ d̃l d̃ca. porq̃ alla estaria
mos presentes. y tomariamos v̅r̃ consejo y pareçer enello quã
to mas en avsençia por esto voslo remjtimos. si todas las
otras cosas contenjdas enel memorial q̃ traxo el d̃s̃ torres enlos
margenes del va r̃espõdido lo q̃ conviene q̃ vos sepiese d̃ la
res puesta d̃ d̃llo vos la remjtimos. y quãto d̃las cosas t̅portogal
d̃ m̃ q̃ tomo çierto d̃ eyto con sus enbaxadores q̃ nos pareçia q̃
hera mas d̃ fin y moviment. y porq̃ d̃llo seays bien infor
mado largame̅te vos enbiamos el traslado d̃los capitulos q̃
sobrello se fisiero y por eso d̃ q̃ no conviene d̃las q̃ d̃llo y no
q̃ vos mãdamos y encargamos q̃ a d̃llo quã d̃ys enteramente
e fagnys q̃ por todos sea guardado ansy como q̃ los capitlos

se contiene y en lo dela raya o limite q se ha dela z por q nos
pareçe cosa muy dificultosa y de mucho peligro y confiança. querriamos
si ser puдiese q vos os hallase de enello y la hisiese q o los otros
q por parte del rey de portogal enello han de entender y si ay
muchos dificultad en vra yda nesto o podria haer algud yncon
viniente en lo q ende estays. ved q vro hermano o otro alguno te
 reys q sea de lo sepa. y en formalдos muy bien por escripto y pd pala
bra y aun por pintura. y por todas las maneras q mejor pudieren
ser ynformados. y enbiadnos los лca luego delas primeras ca
ravelas q vinieren porq con ellas enbiaremos otros dellos para
el tpo q esta лsentado. y en q ayays vos de yr nesto o no es q bido
nos muy larga mente todo lo q en esto supierдes q a vos pareçiere
q se deve haser para nra ynformacion y para q en todo se provea
como cumple лnro serviçı. y hazed de manera q vras cartas y los que
aveys de enbiar vengan presto porq pueda bolver adonde q ha de
ha ser la raya Antes q se cumpla el tpo q tenemos лsentado con el
rey de portogal como vereys p dla capitulaciд. De segovia
л pby de лgosto de. xciiij. años. yo el rey. yo la reyna.
por mandado del rey e dela reyna. fernaд лluarez. e en las
espaldas desia. por el rey e la reyna. A don xpoval colon
su almirate mayor delas yslas delas yndias.

Don fernanдo e doña ysabel

por la graa de dios rey e reyna de castilla de leon de ara
gon de seçilia de granada de toledo de valençıa de galisia de
mallorcas de sevilla de cerdeña de cordoua de corcega de murçia
de jahen de los algarues de algesira de gibraltar e de las yslas de
canaria condes e condesa de barçelona e señores de bizcaya e de mo
lina duques de athenas e de neo patria condes de rosellon e de
cerdania marqueses de oristan e de goçiano. A vos лon xpoval
colon nro almirante delas nras yslas e tierra firme q por nro
mandado se han descubierto e se han de descubrir en la mar oçeano
en la parte delas yndias e a vos don juan de fonseca ardedıano de
sevilla del nro conseso. salud e graa sepades q nos avemos a
cordado de mandar q se faga çıerta armada de algunos navios
e fustas para enbiar a las dhas yndias Asi para governar e
poseer las dhas yslas e tierra firme de q en nro nombre esta toma
da posesion como para descubrir otras y por q para faser y pel
trechar la dha armada y la proveer de todas las cosas a ella

neçesarias e cumplideras q̃ neçessario q̃ nos nõbremos e dipu-
temos personas q̃ enello entiendan e lo põgan en obra. cõ fiãnd
de vosotros q̃ soys tales q̃ guar de reys nr̃o serviçio e bie e fiel
e dilligent mẽte fareys lo q̃ por nos vos fuere mãdado e encomen-
dado mã damos dar estanra c̃a para vosotros en la d̃ha taso por la
qual vos mã damos q̃ vades a las çibdades de Sevilla e caliz e otros
q̃les q̃r çibdades e villas e lugares e puertos de mar d̃ gu d̃ho
obispado e cõdado donde entẽ dier d̃ q̃ cumple e fagays fletar e cõ-
prar e en preçis e fleteys q̃les q̃r navios e naos e caravelas e
fustas q̃ bien d̃ e entẽ dier d̃ q̃ q̃ylen e cõ convenẽtes para
la d̃ha Armada de q̃les q̃r personas/o personas. E q̃l q̃ destaui-
no las pudier d̃ aver las po d̃ es tomar e tome d̃ dõ q̃ estẽ fle-
tados a q̃les q̃r personas lo mas sin daño q̃ ser pud̃iere. Ot
mã damos a los dueños de las d̃has naos e navios e fustas e caravelas q̃ vos los den e entreguen o en dan o flete pagãdoles el flã
q̃ por vosotros fuere apraados o fletadas. lo q̃ oviere de aver. Se q̃ñ
los os tratos e açuetos q̃ con vosotros hizieren e disentare ut usus pra-
das e fletadas las d̃has naos e navios e fustas e caravelas las po d̃a-
des Armar e pertrechar e bastecer de armas e p̃trechos e bastiz cru-
ya de las Armas e p̃trechos e bastimẽtos e tiros de p̃ e n ot da e gẽtes e marineros e apareso de marar e oficiales q̃ menester fueren e
vosotros vier d̃ e entẽ dier d̃ q̃ cumple. lo qual po d̃a d̃ tomar e
tome d̃ a q̃les q̃r lugares e p̃tes e puertos don de los fallar d̃
paga d̃ al dueñs dellos los preços razonables q̃ por ellos se d̃
aver. Ot muy mismo po d̃a d̃ costreñir e apremiar a q̃les q̃r oficiã-
a les e q̃ q̃les q̃r oficios q̃ son convinientes q̃yor en la d̃ha
armada e entẽ dier d̃ q̃ cumple q̃ vaya en ella a los q̃les q̃r a po
ga do el suelso o salario razonable q̃ por ello se van a ver. Otra para q̃ açerca dello po d̃a d̃ otorgar e otorgue d̃ qual q̃r seguridad
en nr̃o nõbre q̃ convenga e menester sea para lo q̃l to do que ofrez
e para q̃ q̃r en ello po d̃a d̃ faser e faga d̃ todas las prẽ das
y prẽ das prisions e exe n caones e ffemate e vẽ caones de bienes
e convenga e menester sean con todas fus n ci den cias e de-
penden caas Anexi dades e conexi dade vos damos poder cumplido por esta nr̃a carta. pero es nr̃a mẽ e mã damos q̃ de todo lo q̃
en so d̃h p̃ teng̃a razõ e cueta para q̃ d̃ nos la q̃ siere-
mos mã dar ver e de al siente en los nr̃os libros q̃ tien en los
nr̃os contadores mayores e q̃ q̃les q̃r cosas de las en so d̃h
to cate a la d̃ha Armada se fagã ot p̃ ase ante nra de sori
segun del prinçipe d̃ sua nr̃o muy caro e muy amado fiso d̃ va

por lugar teniente de los dchos nros contadores mayores e con su poder e no en otra manera alguna. Otrosí es nra mrd e mandamos que todo lo que toca a las obras de armadas e pellos tchos e mantenimientos e otras cosas e flete de navíos e otros gastos de la dcha armada se faga e passen dante el lugarteniente de nro visorrey que de agora nombramos para esta armada juntamente con el dcho Juan de Soria teniente de nros contadores mayores. Et así mismo por que en el sueldo que se oviere de pagar de la gente e fuerça de la dcha armada no aya fraude ni encubierta alguna es nra mrd que las presentaciones e alardes de la gente que se faga dante el teniente del dcho nro escrivano Et que por fee suya firmada de su nombre se faga el libramiento dello e lo qual dcho los dchos almirante e don Juan de Fonseca e el dcho teniente de nros contadores mayores firmen los dchos libramientos por que el tenga la razón e cuenta dellos por manera que el que oviere de pagar no pague cosa alguna sin carta o nómina de los dchos almirante e don Juan de Fonseca e firmada del dcho teniente de nros contadores mayores. E muy para fazer e cumplir e poner en obra lo suso dcho lo qual ser que de ello menester oviere des favor e ayuda por esta dcha nra carta mandamos a quales quier juez e corregidores asistentes corregidores alcaldes alguaciles regidores cavalleros escuderos oficiales ommes buenos e maestres de navíos e fustas e otras quales quier personas que para ello fueren requeridos que lo dhos vos lo den e fagan dar bien e complidamente e que en ello ni en parte dello enbargo ni contrario alguno vos no pongan ni consientan poner so pena de la nra mrd e de privación de los oficios e de confiscación de todos sus bienes al que lo contrario fiziere e de más mandamos al ome que vos esta nra carta mostrare que vos enplaze que parezcades ante nos en la nra corte do quier que nos seamos del día que vos enplazare fasta quinze días primeros siguientes so la dcha pena so la qual mandamos a qual quier escrivano público que para esto fuere llamado que de ende al que vos la mostrare testimonio signado con su signo por que nos sepamos como se cumple nro mandado. Dada en la cibdad de Barcelona a veinte e quatro días del mes de mayo año del nascimiento de nro señor ihu xpo de mill e quatrocientos e noventa e tres años. Yo el rey. Yo la reyna. Yo Fernand Alvares de Toledo secretario del rey e de la reyna nros señores la fiz escrevir por su mandado. E en las espaldas de ella registrada en forma. Roderico Doctor. Pedro Gutierrez chanciller e sellada.

E así presentadas ante los dchos sus altezas en la manera

e dha es dixo alos dhos all de el dho señor almyra te enso dho
q por qua te el ha menester de llevar e presentar los dhos preuys e
çedulas e cãs originales d enso encorporadas d muchas partes e
lugares d dn derecho convenja e q se tenja e te e lleva d llas
o presenta d llas q se le perderia o las guria o d meterria e llas o en
alguna d llas algund caso fortituyto e q por evitar los dhos in c
vinjentes pedia d pi dio alos dhos all de e d ca da vno dellos q amos d
dos juntament viesen et exeminasen los dhos pruys e cãs e çedulas
q ante ellos presentava e manda sen a mj el dho escrivano q sa
case ofisiese sacar vn tras lado o dos lomas los q menester oviese e
q ental dho tras lado o otras lados ellos pusiesen su actoridad e de
creto jndicial pa q faga entera fe e crujeza parescieze ley como va
len e fa sen fee los dhos pruys e cãs e çedulas o riginales enso dhos
all firmados d sus nobres e otrosi firmados signados de mj el dho
escrivano y los mandase dar para guarda d su derecho. Sobre lo qual
dixo q era necesario hera yn plorava e yn ploro el noble ofiçio delos
dhos all de. E luego los dhos all de visto el dho pediny tomaro
las dhas cãs e preuillejos e çedulas originales en sus manos e leye
ron por ellas ellos e cada vno dllos e por q las viero sanas e no
rotas nj en selladas nj en alguna pte sospechosas por q de derecho
no deviesen valer antes caresçente de todo viçio e ynspiçion
e pero anbos junta mente q mandava e mandaro amj el dho escr
q sacase ofisiese sacar dlas dhas cãs e pruys e çedulas vn tras
lado e dos o mas los q el dho señor almjzant me pidiese e viese
menester e gelos diese e entregase firmados d sus nobres e fir
mados o signados de mj el dho escrivano d los quales e d cada vno
dllos yn terponja e inter pusiero su actoridad e decreto
pa q valiesen e fisiesen fee en juysio e fuera dl en todo tpo e
lugar do paresciesen bie asy e atan en pli da mente como valdria
e faria e fee las dhas cãs e pruys e çedulas original mente pa
resçied e de todo esto en como paso el dho señor almyzante dixo
q gelo diese por fee e testimonjo pa guarda de su derecho e yo
dile en d este el qual va firmado e signado d los dhos all de
e de mj el dho escrivano pu. q fue fecho e saca d e corregid e d cer
ta dlos dhos originales e con cada vno dllos en la çibdad de
de sevilla en el d dia e mes e d año enso dho — pero luys
all de. escreva dela toca all de. e d u gomez njeto çibd de se
villa fuy psent ala actoridad e manda m dlos dhos all de
djo testigo. yo alfonso lunes qu dize m esc fuy present
ala abtoridad e manda m delos dhos all de e so testigo.

Yo mjn Rodrigues escrivano publico de Sevilla fiz es qz viz
estas escripturas e fuy presente ala dha abtoridad y ma
danyento delos dhos alldes e fiz aqui mjo signo que estaly

Ferdinando Bucharoni Portiere di Casa di,
Duca di Albanecchi

Sig.ᵃ Luigi Cacciatore

A portrait of Christopher Columbus attributed to Ridolfo Ghirlandaio (1483–1561), painted after Columbus's death.

Discovery

Daniel De Simone

Columbus: A Bibliographic Journey

olumbus's *Book of Privileges*, part of the Americana collections at the Library of Congress, is now commonly referred to as the Washington Codex[1] but was also called the Columbus Codex by Herbert Putnam, who served as Librarian of Congress from 1899 to 1939. According to Putnam and the numerous bibliographical references that describe the *Privileges*, four copies of the original documents were produced for Columbus, three on vellum (the Genoa, Paris, and Washington copies) and one on paper. Two copies plus the original were to be given to Columbus's descendants. The remaining two copies were to be given to the Ambassador of the Genoa Republic. Over the years, one of the Genoa copies would disappear and finally be discovered in 1880 by the London bookseller B. F. Stevens in a Paris archive, where it still resides.

The paper copy was also thought to be lost, but it has been argued[2] that a manuscript purchased in Spain by Maggs Bros. (Catalogue 442, N. 1724) and sold to Otto Vollbehr was the missing paper copy; it contains no signatures or notarial markings, but does have some marginal notations. This incomplete paper copy was then sold by Vollbehr to Henry Huntington, and today resides in the collections of the Huntington Library in San Marino, California.

Putnam maintains that the copy in the collections at the Library of Congress is one of the two that were given to the descendants of the Columbus family. It was lost for more than three hundred years, until it surfaced in Florence in 1818, and was then purchased by an American named Edward Everett. Everett referenced his copy of the *Book of Privileges* in a speech delivered in Plymouth, Massachusetts, and printed in 1824. That same year, Caleb Cushing mentioned it in *The North American Review*, in an article he published that discussed the publication of the text of the surviving Genoa Codex, which was published for the first time in London in 1823. It was from this publication that Everett learned that the manuscript pages he purchased in Florence "coincide precisely with the text of the first thirty-seven documents contained in the 240 pages of the Genoese volume."[3] For the next sixty-five years this manuscript remained in the library of Edward Everett, unknown to anyone until Justin Winsor, the noted Americanist who was working on a biography of Columbus, found the citation that mentioned the manuscript and contacted Edward Everett's son, Dr. William Everett. Dr. Everett inherited the library after his father's death but claimed to have no recollection of the manuscript being in his father's collection. He sent his regrets to Winsor.

> The copy at the Library of Congress is one of two given to the Columbus family. It was lost for more than three hundred years.

In 1898, eight years after Winsor's request and eighty years after the *Book of Privileges* came into Edward Everett's library, Dr. Everett's secretary found the manuscript while looking for another document that had gone missing. In a statement written by Dr. Everett and quoted by Putnam, he states that the manuscript was found in a locked bookcase in the library, where it had most likely sat for seven decades. The manuscript, ". . .a thin folio, bound in Russia, elaborately tooled, but with no lettering, giving the secretary no indication of its nature, was handed by him to Mr. Everett with a word of enquiry. A moment's examination showed it to be the Columbus MS., concerning which Mr. Winsor's phrase, that it was not at all accessible, proved to be literally true. It had never left the possession of Mr.

Everett or his son; had been moved from house to house a score of times, through a period of seventy years, during the last thirty of which its existence was unknown to its owner." Dr. Everett took the manuscript to England for authentication, and it was returned to him by mail in September of 1898. Three years later, in 1901, fire ruined much of Dr. Everett's home and library, but the manuscript, still in its wrapping from England, was rescued. Later that year it was sold to Herbert Putman and became part of the collections of the Library of Congress.[4]

This manuscript of Columbus's *Book of Privileges*, one of the Library of Congress's treasures, has an important relationship to two significant collections of the Library's that focus on Columbus and the bibliographical record that was spawned by his discovery. One is the Henry Harrisse Collection, which is housed in the Rare Book Division and contains sixty years of research by one of the great bibliographers of the nineteenth century. The other is the John Boyd Thacher Collection, which contains not only a library of incunables and fifteenth- and sixteenth-century editions of Ptolemy's *Geographia*, but also a collection of early Americana.

When I worked as a clerk at J. N. Bartfield Books in New York in my early days in the book trade, one of the first works of bibliography the owner gave me to read was Henry Harrisse's *Bibliotheca Americana Vetustissima* (*BAV*).[5] It was Harrisse's Introduction, which outlined his bibliographical method, that Bartfield wanted me to read. Having studied it, Harrisse's essay became one of the foundations upon which I built my bibliographical career.

Where Harrisse was a historian of Columbus as well as European voyage and discovery, Thacher was a private collector who built a library reflecting the achievements of his era. Not that his first book, *The Continent of America* (1896), or his three-volume biography, *Christopher Columbus* (1903-1904), were anything but triumphs of careful research, but it is his library that survives him and is most well known. It includes a collection of nearly nine hundred early books printed before 1501 that document the development and spread of printing in the fifteenth century. He also formed an important collection of the French Revolution, in both print and manuscript, that focuses on Enlightenment ideals and the rise of Napoleon. In his quest to form a significant collection on the discovery of America and the New World, Thacher purchased thirty-four editions of Ptolemy's *Geographia* printed before 1700; an early Mexican imprints collection, one of the first of its kind formed in the United States; and a collection of early Americana that focused on Columbus's voyages and those of other explorers.[6] It is from these two men—one a driven, demanding, and prolific student of Columbus and the other a businessman, politician, and private collector dedicated to preserving the historical record—that the Library of Congress gained its preeminence in the field of Columbus studies and the history of the discovery of the New World.

> Dr. Everett took the manuscript to England for authentication, and it was returned to him by mail in September of 1898. Three years later, in 1901, fire ruined much of Dr. Everett's home and library.

Henry Harrisse's collection, housed in vaults of the Rare Book Division, was given to the Library of Congress after his death in 1910. It contained all of his published works, many of his unpublished manuscripts, and a small collection of maps. Harrisse also collected hundreds of scholarly articles on Columbus and the New World, along with newspaper clippings, reviews, and letters to and from the major Columbus scholars of the period. Many of his printed books are heavily annotated with additions and corrections in Harrisse's hand, and many contained tipped-in letters and reviews that are also annotated.[7] In all, the collections contain more than two hundred volumes of books, eighteen bound volumes of manuscripts, thirteen containers of unbound manuscript material relating to Harrisse's writings, a few rare books and maps, ephemera, Harrisse's card catalogue, and a large number of monographs by Harrisse's contemporaries.[8]

In order to gain insight into the content of Harrisse's collection, one must look to its organizing principle, which can be found in his fifty-four page Introduction to *Bibliotheca Americana Vetustissima*. Harrisse begins with a nod to the philosopher Herbert Spencer, his goal of systematizing all the sciences into a coherent whole, and the movement from the hypothetical to reliance on "well-ascertained facts." Harrisse endorses Spencer's philosophical position for the study of history. He suggests that the laws of science, based on recorded observations in the "real order of successions," is required of historians if superstition and ignorance are to be dispelled.[9] After demonstrating how this methodology is used to study chemistry, astronomy, and natural history, Harrisse outlines how the tools of the historian, thought different from those of the hard scientist, can capture meaning by establishing a chronology that accurately reflects the evolution of events over time. For Harrisse, the most important tool of the historian is "bibliography," the study of books and printing, the most basic source of recorded human knowledge.

For Harrisse, the most important tool of the historian is "bibliography," the study of books and printing, the most basic source of recorded human knowledge.

Harrisse continues his essay on bibliography by describing the tenets that govern the field and the extent to which it "assumes a encyclopaedical [sic] character, which we deem necessary to bring the science in closer connection with historical studies."[10] He then outlines the development of the field of bibliographical study, listing in chronological order the field's most famous authors and providing a critique of their most important books. To make his point, he includes both historians and bibliographers in his research, and clearly demonstrates how these fields of study depend on one another to produce a reliable and accurate account of the activities of human history. For the most part he focuses on those historians and bibliographers who studied and wrote about the discovery of America. This includes the work of Antonio de León y Pinelo, whose *Epitome de la Bibliotheca Oriental e Occidental*, published in 1629, is considered to be the first *Bibliotheca Americana*. This is followed by citations for the eighteenth-century works of White Kennett, Lenglet Du Fresnoy, Andréa Gonzalez de Barcia, Pierre F. X. de Charlevoix, William Robertson, Juan José de Eguiara, and Thomas L. Reid. For the nineteenth-century authors, Harrisse cites the work of José Mariano Beristain, Antonio de Alcedo, David B. Warden, A. Asher, E. B. O'Callahan, Obadiah Rich, Hermann E. Ludewig, H. R. Schoolcraft, and Alexander von Humbolt, to name the most prominent. In each case, Harrisse shows the progression of information as it is passed on, corrected, and added to by the next generation of bibliographer.

He concludes by weighing the relative merits of these works and determines the limitations that accompany some of the methods used by the authors to write their works. By doing so, Harrisse justifies the need for—and in fact, demands—a more scientific analysis of the field of American history. His first major work, and perhaps his most notable contribution to the field, *Bibliotheca Americana Vetustissima*, is the culmination of a decade of recording "with extreme minuteness and accuracy" every aspect of the historical record as it is applied to the study of Columbus and the New World.[11] It was his attempt to set the record straight and provide a guide to future students of the subject. It is this dedication to furnishing an accurate, evidence-based history of the discovery of America that is the foundation of this remarkable library. It is not a collection of rare books, but rather, a collection of scholarship. It is an assemblage of books, manuscripts, and articles that represent one man's passion for finding truth, and the explication of his methods on how he went about the business of historical bibliography.

Henry Harrisse (1829–1910) came to the United States from Paris in 1847 as an eighteen-year-old eager to experience the New World. To make a living, he taught French in a South Carolina school and received an honorary Master of Arts degree from the University of South Carolina. He moved north to Chapel Hill, where he studied law, and then on to Washington, where he taught French literature at Georgetown. From there he traveled to Chicago, where he practiced law for a couple of years, and in 1861 went to New York, where he was introduced to Samuel Latham Mitchill Barlow, a prosperous lawyer and collector of early Americana. It was from Barlow's collection that Harrisse based his research for his *Bibliotheca Americana Vetustissima*. Harrisse continued to practice law in New York and studied the collections of Americana in the city, both public and private, until he returned to Paris and created a profitable practice representing American interests in the French courts. His success allowed him to continue his research on early discovery by studying the collections of voyages and travel that were in the public and private collections of France, Belgium, and Spain.[12]

As Rosemary Plakas, a curator of Americana at the Library of Congress, records in her finding aid to the Harrisse Collection, his research on Columbus was extensive. In 1884 he published *Christophe Columb, son Origine, sa Vie, ses Voyages,* his first major work on Columbus. Before the appearance of *Christophe Columb,* he published eleven monographs on the subject, but it was this book that propelled him into the upper echelons of Columbus research. Harrisse's research "stimulated controversies on a number of topics relating to Columbus, including his origins, date and place of his birth, his voyages, his final burial, and the authenticity of his son Ferdinand's biography."[13] *Christophe Columb* was to be followed by thirty more publications on Columbus, as well as books and articles on the discovery of New France, the claims of John and Sebastian Cabot, and the voyages of Amerigo Vespucci, Giovanni da Verrazano, and the Portuguese mariner Gaspar Corte-Real. In total, the Harrisse Collection contains one hundred forty-one individual publications by Harrisse, many in proof format, and most with manuscript annotations, tipped-in letters, and news clippings. In addition, the collection includes hundreds of short articles and reviews of the work published by his contemporaries who were also researching and writing on Columbus and the discovery of the New World.

> *Thacher's goal was to provide an evidence-based platform for evaluating the claims of Columbus, Vespucci, Cabot, and the other explorers who set out to win wealth and fame in the New World.*

The John Boyd Thacher Collection arrived at the Library of Congress in 1915, about the same time that Harrisse's will was adjudicated and his collection sent to Washington. As mentioned earlier, Thacher's library of Americana was only part of a larger collection that included incunables and books and manuscripts on the French Revolution. But it was the collection of early Americana, formed while he was writing his three-volume biography *Christopher Columbus,* that complemented so perfectly with the Harrisse archive, and that gives the Library of Congress such depth in the field, as is fitting for a national institution.

Unlike the immigrant scholar Harrisse, who made his way in America on wit and determination, John Boyd Thacher (1847-1909) had roots reaching back to the Massachusetts Bay Colony and to his ancestor Thomas Thacher, who arrived there in 1635. Thacher was born into a family of manufacturers, studied at Williams College, stood for election in upstate New York in the 1880s, and was elected mayor of Albany twice. He was instrumental in organizing the Columbian Exposition of 1892-1893, wrote a number of scholarly histories, including a biography of Columbus, and formed one of the great libraries in nineteenth-century America.[14]

In the preface to his biography of Columbus, Thacher states the purpose for his research.[15] It was "first to print in facsimile original documents relating to the discovery as was available to the reader at the beginning of the sixteenth century; and second to give the reader of today such knowledge concerning the discovery as has come to the world since that time."[16] His reasoning was based on his understanding of the many questions and contradictions that existed in the study of early American history. His hope was that by compiling these original sources used by both the early historians of Columbus and nineteenth-century scholars, a better understanding of the positions taken by historians over five hundred years could be achieved. Thacher's goal was to provide an evidence-based platform for evaluating the claims of Columbus, Vespucci, Cabot, and the other explorers who set out to win wealth and fame in the exploration of the New World. Given his methods, it is no wonder that he dedicated his book on Columbus to Henry Harrisse.

Included in the facsimiles of original documents that appear in volumes one and two of Thacher's biography are extracts from contemporary biographical information describing Columbus's family and upbringing, written by Agostino Giustiniani and Bartolomeo Senarega, historians of Genoa and first biographers of the Admiral. With the publication of Thacher's book, these documents by the Genoese historians were translated into English for the first time. Also included is the 1474 letter supposedly written by Paolo Toscanelli that was so influential with the Spanish court, supporting reports of Marco Polo's description of Asia and suggesting a route west to the Spice Islands. Thacher also provides extracts from Peter Martyr's *Decades,* first published in 1511, documenting Columbus's voyages. In addition, he has firsthand information describing Columbus's First, Second, and Third Voyages never before translated into English; it was written by Bartolomé de las Casas and published in his book *Historia de las Indias.* Some of this information corroborates the biographical portraits provided by the Genoese historians and focuses on Columbus's appearance and character. Also included are translations of two papal bulls that outline the demarcation of the territories found in the oceans by Spanish and Portuguese explorers, and the Treaty of Tordesillas, which ratified the division of these territories. Two other documents of note that were translated into English are the letter of Dr. Diego Alvarez Chanca, physician on the *Santa Maria*, which discusses the first voyage of Columbus, and the 1494 Torres Memorandum that Columbus wrote and sent to Spain, discussing the potential trade in slaves from the newly discovered islands. All of these documents, and others not mentioned, contributed to the importance of Thacher's work and helped earn its reputation in American scholarly circles as the "most voluminous and sumptuous work devoted to Columbus that has ever been published in the United States."[17]

Volume three of Thacher's *Columbus* is devoted to an analysis of the numerous portraits of the Admiral that have appeared though the ages. No lifetime image of him has survived (except perhaps that on page ix), and those that have come down to us are by later artists who have in many cases defined Columbus's appearance to satisfy a nationalistic or political agenda. Thacher identifies forty images and provides detailed descriptions, information on the artists, and provenance details for each. He depicts some of the most contentious, but offers no personal opinion on which image he finds most accurate. The volume continues with evidence about Columbus's death, burial, and a genealogical table of his descendants, subjects that Harrisse also examined.

To facilitate his research process, Thacher added to his already extensive library a collection of early Americana and bibliography that supported his biographical study of Columbus. In fact, he collected many books that Henry Harrisse listed in his *Bibliotheca Americana Vetustissima.* Thacher's library of Americana created continuity between Harrisse's research on Columbus and the original printed books that would support Columbus studies in the future. Thacher purchased five sixteenth-century editions of the *Decades* of Peter Martyr, including the 1555 English edition published in London by Richard Eden. Three editions of *Novus orbis regionum*, printed in Paris and Basel between 1532 and 1537, are included in the collection, as is the 1508 Nuremberg edition of Francanzano da Montalboddo, a compilation of voyages that includes reports of the discoveries of Columbus. Thacher also purchased editions of the work of the Genoese historian Agostino Giustiniani, as well as a Polyglot Bible, edited by Giustiniani and published in Genoa in 1516, that "contains the first biographical account of Christopher Columbus." [18] The collection also includes the letters of Maximilianus and the works of Pedro de Medina, Mercator, Hakluyt, Hennepin, Monardes, Ramusio, and Nicolò Zeno, to name some of the prominent writers on the subject. The histories written by Columbus's son Ferdinand are included, as are the writings of Bartolomé de las Casas.

> Included are translations of two papal bulls that outline the demarcation of the territories found in the oceans by Spanish and Portuguese explorers, and the Treaty of Tordesillas, which ratified the division.

Thacher purchased and studied the works of classical authors writing on geography, astronomy, and travel, including editions of works by Pomponius Mela, Joannes de Sacro Busto, Strabo, C. Junius Solinus, and, of course, Ptolemy. It was for his study of Columbus that Thacher acquired thirty-four editions of Ptolemy's work. This vast selection includes texts based on the earliest translations from the Greek, and modern editions that offered new projections and views of the world, based on information incorporated from the discoveries of Columbus and his rivals. Complementing his collection of Ptolemy are two first editions of Martin Waldseemüller's *Cosmographia introductio*, printed in 1507, and three subsequent editions printed in 1509, 1533, and 1537. This was the publication that changed the way the world was understood.

> *The new methods of scholarship, in the form of electronic data mining, will no doubt reveal heretofore hidden secrets.*

A unique item in Thacher's Americana collection is what's known as the Trevisan Manuscript, which contains the letter written in Granada by a friend of Columbus named Angelo Trevigiano, and which was sent to Domenico Malipiero at Venice. The one hundred sixty-eight-page manuscript, written between 1501 and 1503, includes a transcription of Peter Martyr's description of Columbus's first three voyages before they were published in his *Decades,* as well as the first known description of Columbus's physical appearance.[19] It is a very rare survival that is sometimes referred to as the Sneyd manuscript, as the "ex-libris" of the Rev. William Sneyd appears on the manuscript's front endpaper. The Trevisan Manuscript has become an important primary source for Columbus scholars who have been working on the many debates that surround the exact landing of the fleet in October 1492.

The scope and content of the Harrisse and Thacher collections offer historians and bibliographers the opportunity to examine underutilized resources that could provide new insight into the historical questions regarding the discovery of the New World. It is true that today, these questions revolve around the peoples who populated the Americas and the legacy of colonization, rather than on those explorers who sailed from Europe. But without a doubt, the evidence to answer these questions is buried in the books and manuscripts that were written and collected by the Frenchman and the Yankee whose passion for the study of history and the origins of the New World consumed their lives.

With the publication of this facsimile edition of Columbus's *Book of Privileges,* a revival of research into its origins and authenticity is expected. The Harrisse archive and the Americana collection of John Boyd Thacher will be investigated anew. The new methods of scholarship, in the form of electronic data mining, will no doubt reveal heretofore hidden secrets and provide fresh insights into Columbus, his voyages, and his legacy.

EPILOGUE

Where History Begins

n the beginning of his dialogue *On Laws*, the great Roman orator Marcus Tullius Cicero (106-46 B.C.) has his characters, Quintus, Marcus, and Atticus, engage in a conversation on the true nature of history. The three debate whether in the writing of history, the standard by which everything is judged is truth, or if it is more like other forms of writing such as poetry, where the standard is the pleasure it gives. Atticus explains that for a long time he has thought it was both and he has hoped that the brilliant Marcus might write a history, but he wonders where one should begin. The answer they arrive at is with law. History, simply stated, begins with law. But why law?

Marcus explains that the history of law is both so large ("What subject indeed is so vast as the law of the state?") and so small ("But what is also so trivial as the task of those who give legal advice?"). For him it is this dual nature that makes it affect the lives of all people, that allows it to change according to their needs, and that provides the framework for people to live together in society.

Columbus's *Book of Privileges* contains law, both vast and trivial. Its documents relate what, on the one hand, appears to be a simple business deal, a writ for the distribution of profits and losses, that gave a visionary explorer the rights and grants that were deemed necessary for him to set sail across a nearly endless ocean, and instructed him to colonize the lands he found. On the other hand, this simple privilege set the stage for the destruction of indigenous empires, and changed Europe's view of its unique place on the globe.

The Washington Codex contains many unanswered questions concerning why it was copied and for whom, but in its pages, we find deeper lessons, those that so long ago Cicero also searched for, and that are important for us to take to heart today: that in history the trivial sometimes becomes the vast, and the simple sometimes the revolutionary.

Illustration depicting the house in Santo Domingo of Columbus's son Diego, from a book published in France in 1811.

Notes

Van Duzer, pp. 1 - 26

[1] Samuel Eliot Morison, *Admiral of the Ocean Sea* (Boston: Little, Brown, and Company, 1942), in the two-volume edition, vol. 1, pp. 294-313; in the one-volume edition, pp. 211-31; David Henige, "The Mutinies on Columbus' First Voyage: Fact or Fiction?" *Terrae Incognitae* 23 (1991): 29-38. The location of Columbus's first landfall is much disputed, but archaeological finds on San Salvador tend to confirm that it was on this island that Columbus first landed: see Charles A. Hoffman, "Archaeological Investigations at the Long Bay Site, San Salvador, Bahamas," in Donald T. Gerace, ed., *Columbus and His World: Proceedings, First San Salvador Conference* (Fort Lauderdale, Fla.: Bahamian Field Station, 1987), pp. 237-45; and Robert H. Brill, I. Lynus Barnes, Stephen S. C. Tong, Emile C. Joel, and Martin J. Murtaugh, "Laboratory Studies of Some European Artifacts Excavated on San Salvador Island," in the same volume, pp. 247-92.

[2] See Noble David Cook and W. George Lovell, eds., *Secret Judgments of God: Old World Disease in Colonial Spanish America* (Norman, Okla.: University of Oklahoma Press, 1991); Noble David Cook, *Born to Die: Disease and New World Conquest, 1492-1650* (Cambridge and New York: Cambridge University Press, 1998).

[3] The account of the Taíno religion is Ramón Pané's *Relación acerca de las antigüedades de los indios*, available in English as *An Account of the Antiquities of the Indians: Chronicles of the New World Encounter*, ed. José Juan Arrom, trans. Susan C. Griswold (Durham, N.C.: Duke University Press, 1999).

[4] A law passed by the Spanish Crown on October 30, 1503, allowed the enslavement of any Native peoples deemed to be cannibals: see Michael Palencia-Roth, "The Cannibal Law of 1503," in Jerry M. Williams and Robert E. Lewis, eds., *Early Images of the Americas: Transfer and Invention* (Tucson: University of Arizona Press, 1993), pp. 21-64. On the depictions of Native peoples of the New World as monsters, see Peter Mason, "Classical Ethnography and Its Influence on the European Perception of the Peoples of the New World," in W. Haase and M. Reinhold, eds., *The Classical Tradition and the Americas*, vol. 1, part l, *European Images of the Americas and the Classical Tradition* (Berlin and New York: Walter de Gruyter, 1994), pp. 135-72; and Juan Casas Rigall, "Razas humanas portentosas en las partidas remotas del mundo (de Benjamín de Tudela a Cristóbal Colón)," in Rafael Beltrán Llavador, ed., *Maravillas, peregrinaciones y utopías: literatura de viajes en el mundo románico* (Valencia: Universitat de Valencia, 2002), pp. 253-90.

[5] It is worth bearing in mind that Bartolomé de las Casas (c. 1484-1566), one of the early and most energetic defenders of Native Americans against the abuses they had suffered, generally supported Columbus.

[6] On Columbus's Second Voyage, see Samuel Eliot Morison, *The European Discovery of America*, vol. 2, *The Southern Voyages, 1492-1616* (New York: Oxford University Press, 1993), pp. 92-140; and Jesús Varela Marcos and María Montserrat León Guerrero, *El itinerario de Cristóbal Colón (1451-1506)* (Valladolid: Diputación Provincial de Valladolid, 2003), pp. 161-211.

[7] Columbus famously asked all of the officers and crew members of the ships that were with him to swear that Cuba was the mainland: see John Boyd Thacher, *Christopher Columbus: His Life, His Work, His Remains as Revealed by Original Printed and Manuscript Records* (New York and London: G. P. Putnam's Sons and The Knickerbocker Press, 1903-1904), vol. 2, pp. 321-32.

[8] On Columbus's Third Voyage, see Morison, *The European Discovery of America*, vol. 2, *The Southern Voyages, 1492-1616*, pp. 141-61; and Varela Marcos and Montserrat León Guerrero, *El itinerario de Cristóbal Colón (1451-1506)*, pp. 213-64.

[9] Bartolomé de las Casas, *Las Casas on Columbus: The Third Voyage*, ed. Geoffrey Symcox and Jesús Carrillo, trans. Michael Hammer and Blair Sullivan (Turnhout: Brepols, 2001), pp. 48-49 (English) and 179 (Spanish). The passage is Bartolomé de las Casas, *Historia de las Indias*, Book 1, chapters 2 and 139; in the standard edition of Las Casas' works, this is in his *Obras completas*, ed. Paulino Castañeda Delgado (Madrid: Alianza, 1988-1998), vol. 4, p. 1069.

[10] For discussion of Paradise on medieval maps, see Alessandro Scafi, *Mapping Paradise: A History of Heaven on Earth* (Chicago: University of Chicago Press, 2006). Columbus had indicated that he thought he was near the Terrestrial Paradise during his first voyage: see Christopher Columbus, *A Synoptic Edition of the Log of Columbus's First Voyage*, ed. Francesca Lardicci and Valeria Bertolucci Pizzorusso, trans. Cynthia L. Chamberlin and Blair Sullivan (Turnhout: Brepols, 1999), pp. 131 and 296 (English) and 421 and 615 (Spanish). These passages are in Columbus's journal of his First Voyage, as abstracted by Bartolomé de las Casas: see Christopher Columbus, *The 'Diario' of Christopher Columbus's First Voyage to America 1492-1493* (Norman, Okla., and London: University of Oklahoma Press, 1989), pp. 382-83; and Las Casas, *Historia de las Indias*, Book 1, chapter 72, in his *Obras completas*, vol. 3, p. 685.

[11] Bartolomé de las Casas gives a long discourse aimed at rendering some of Columbus's claims about the location of the Terrestrial Paradise plausible in his *Historia de las Indias*, Book 1, chapters 141-45, in his *Obras completas*, vol. 4, pp. 1082-1106; translated into English in Bartolomé de las Casas, *Las Casas on Columbus: The Third Voyage*, pp. 58-73. For discussion, see Thacher, *Christopher Columbus*, vol. 2, pp. 409-15; and Mary B. Campbell, "'The End of the East': Columbus Discovers Paradise," in her *The Witness and the Other World: Exotic European Travel Writing, 400-1600* (Ithaca: Cornell University Press, 1988), pp. 165-209.

[12] Leonard J. Hoenig, "The Arthritis of Christopher Columbus," *Archives of Internal Medicine* 152.2 (1992): 274-77.

[13] Aldo Albònico, "Bartolomeo Colombo, adelantado mayor de las Indias," in Alberto Boscolo and Bibiano Torres, eds., *La Presenza italiana in Andalusia nel basso Medioevo: atti del secondo Convegno, Roma, 25-27 maggio 1984* (Bologna: Cappelli, 1986), pp. 51-70.

[14] Amadeo Julián, "Cristóbal Colón y los inicios de la justicia en la isla Española. Nombramiento y actuación de los primeros alcaldes mayores," in Francisco Morales Padrón, ed., *XVII Coloquio de Historia Canario-Americana (2006)* (Las Palmas de Gran Canaria: Cabildo Insular de Gran Canaria, 2008), pp. 676-700; Frank Moya Pons, "Bobadilla, Francisco de," in Silvio A. Bedini, ed., *The Christopher Columbus Encyclopedia* (New York: Simon & Schuster, 1992), vol. 1, pp. 72-73.

[15] See Aldo Albònico, "Il malgoverno dei Colombo all'Hispaniola, I: Le critiche coeve," in Stefano Pittaluga, ed., *Columbeis* (Università di Genova, Facoltà di lettere, Istituto di filologia classica e medievale, 1986-1997), vol. 2, pp. 203-23; reprinted in *Presencia italiana en Andalucía, siglos XIV-XVII: actas del III Coloquio Hispano-Italiano* (Seville: Consiglio nazionale delle ricerche: Consejo Superior de Investigaciones Científicas, Escuela de Estudios Hispano-Americanos, 1989), pp. 87-108. A document discovered in the Archivo General de Simancas in 2005 gives Bobadilla's side of the story: see Isabel Aguirre and Consuelo Varela, *La caída de Cristóbal Colón: el juicio de Bobadilla* (Madrid: Marcial Pons Historia, 2006). For remarks on the biased nature of the document, see Carol Delaney, *Columbus and the Quest for Jerusalem* (New York: Free Press, 2011), pp. 182-83.

[16] Joaquín Marino Incháustegui Cabral, "En torno a uno de los más trágicos episodios de la vida de Colón," *Anuario de estudios americanos* 23 (1967), pp. 839-60. On the statue in fig. 4, see Néstor Ponce de León, *The Columbus Gallery: The 'Discoverer of the New World' as Represented in Portraits, Monuments, Statues, Medals, and Paintings* (New York: N. Ponce de León, 1893), pp. 98-99; and José Llavallol, "Colón," *El Vendrellense* 237 (April 11, 1897): 2; 238 (April 18, 1897): 1-2; and 239 (April 25, 1897): 1-2, reprinted in José Llavallol, *Colón: estatua de D. Venancio Vallmitjana; y La Víctima junto al verdugo!!* (Vendrell: Impr. Ramón hermanos, 1899).

[17] Samuel Eliot Morison, *Admiral of the Ocean Sea*, in the two-volume edition, vol. 1, pp. 418-30; in the one-volume edition, pp. 324-35. See Christopher Columbus, *A Synoptic Edition of the Log of Columbus's First Voyage*, pp. 126-27 and 290-91 (English) and 416-17 and 609 (Spanish). These passages are in Columbus's journal of his First Voyage, as abstracted by Bartolomé de las Casas: see Christopher Columbus, *The 'Diario' of Christopher Columbus's First Voyage to America 1492-1493*, pp. 370-71; and Las Casas, *Historia de las Indias*, Book 1, chapter 69, in his *Obras completas*, vol. 3, pp. 677-78.

[18] Quoted by Helen Nader and Luciano Formisano, *The Book of Privileges Issued to Christopher Columbus by King Fernando and Queen Isabel, 1492-1502* (Berkeley: University of California Press, 1996), p. 9. This document is now in Seville in the Archivo General de Indias, Patronato, legajo 295, doc. 2. There is a photograph of the document in the Library of Congress, Manuscripts Division, Collection Concerning Christopher Columbus, 1488-1515, call number Oversize 0115J, Box 1, nos. 3-4.

[19] Translation by Nader, *The Book of Privileges Issued to Christopher Columbus by King Fernando and Queen Isabel*, document 52, p. 155; Spanish text transcribed by Formisano in the same book, p. 395. This document is not included in the Library of Congress manuscript of the *Book of Privileges*.

[20] For basic discussions of the *Book of Privileges*, see Thacher, *Christopher Columbus: His Life, His Work, His Remains as Revealed by Original Printed and Manuscript Records*, vol. 2, pp. 530-65; Helen Nader, "Book of Privileges," in Silvio A. Bedini, ed., *The Christopher Columbus Encyclopedia*, pp. 73-75; and Nader, "General Introduction," in *The Book of Privileges Issued to Christopher Columbus by King Fernando and Queen Isabel*, pp. 3-16.

[21] See Christopher Columbus, *The 'Libro de las profecías' of Christopher Columbus*, trans. and ed. Delno C. West and August Kling (Gainesville: University of Florida Press, 1991), pp. 86-92, discussing Columbus's annotations to his copy of the *Historia rerum ubique gestarum* by Aneas Silvius Piccolomini. Columbus's copy of this book has been reproduced in facsimile as Pope Pius II, *Historia rerum: cuyo original se encuentra en la Biblioteca Colombina de Sevilla* (Madrid: Testimonio Compañía Editorial, 1991), with a volume of commentary by Juan Pérez de Tudela titled *La Historia rerum ubique gestarum del papa Pío II y el descubrimiento de América* (Madrid: Testimonio Compañía Editorial, 1993). West dates these annotations to 1481, but Pérez de Tudela, pp. 294-96, makes a good argument that they should be dated to 1490-1491. The missionary character of Columbus's First Voyage is also discussed by Daniel J. Woodab (who accepts the earlier date for the annotations), "Religious Motives for Columbus's First Voyage," *Primary Sources & Original Works* 2.1-2 (1993): 209-25.

[22] Christopher Columbus, *The Book of Prophecies Edited by Christopher Columbus*, ed. Roberto Rusconi, trans. Blair Sullivan (Berkeley: University of California Press, 1997), p. 75.

[23] On Columbus's signature, see Thacher, *Christopher Columbus*, vol. 3, pp. 454-58; West and Kling, *The 'Libro de las profecías' of Christopher Columbus*, pp. 71-73. Alain Milhou, in *Colón y su mentalidad mesiánica en el ambiente franciscanista español* (Valladolid: Casa-Museo de Colón: Seminario Americanista de la Universidad de Valladolid, 1983), p. 88, says that it was between his Third and Fourth Voyages that Columbus added the line "Christoferens" to his signature, but in fact he had used it a few times in 1493: see Thacher, *Christopher Columbus*, vol. 3, pp. 94-113, an undated letter by Columbus datable to late April or early May 1493; and letters dated January 4, 1493, and February 20, 1493, transcribed in Christopher Columbus, *Textos y documentos completos: relaciones de viajes, cartas y memoriales*, ed. Consuelo Varela (Madrid: Alianza, 1982), pp. 138-39 and 146-47.

[24] Delno C. West, "Wallowing in a Theological Stupor or a Steadfast and Consuming Faith: Scholarly Encounters with Columbus's Libro de las profecías," in Donald T. Gerace, ed., *Columbus and His World: Proceedings, First San Salvador Conference*, pp. 45-56.

[25] Christopher Columbus, *Christopher Columbus's Book of Prophecies: Reproduction of the Original Manuscript with English Translation*, trans. Kay Brigham (Barcelona: Editorial Clie, 1991); Christopher Columbus, *The 'Libro de las profecías' of Christopher Columbus*; and Christopher Columbus, *The Book of Prophecies Edited by Christopher Columbus*.

[26] For discussion of the attributions of different parts of the manuscript to different hands, see Christopher Columbus, *The Book of Prophecies Edited by Christopher Columbus*, pp. 35-48.

[27] The sources cited in the *Book of Prophecies* are conveniently listed by West and Kling, *The 'Libro de las profecías' of Christopher Columbus*, p. 23.

[28] See the passage on the precursors of the Apocalypse that begins on f. 26v of the Book of the Prophecies, which is supplied by West and Kling, *The 'Libro de las profecías' of Christopher Columbus*, pp. 160-65; and by Rusconi and Sullivan, *The Book of Prophecies*, pp. 170-75. For discussion of and bibliography regarding the global scope of the evangelical mission, see Chet Van Duzer and Ilya Dines, "The Only *Mappamundi* in a Bestiary Context: Cambridge, MS Fitzwilliam 254," *Imago Mundi* 58.1 (2006): 7-22, at 13-15.

[29] For discussion of Columbus's beliefs about his role in bringing about the Second Coming, see Adriano Prosperi, "America e Apocalisse. Note sulla 'conquista spirituale' del Nuovo Mondo," *Critica Storica: rivista trimestrale* 13.1 (1976): 1-61; reprinted in his *America e apocalisse e altri saggi* (Pisa: Istituti editoriali e poligrafici internazionali, 1999), pp. 15-63; Abbas Hamdani, "Columbus and the Recovery of Jerusalem," *Journal of the American Oriental Society* 99 (1979): 39-48; Alain Milhou, *Colón y su mentalidad mesiánica en el ambiente franciscanista español* (Valladolid: Casa-Museo de Colón: Seminario Americanista de la Universidad de Valladolid, 1983); Pauline Moffitt Watts, "Prophecy and Discovery: On the Spiritual Origins of Christopher Columbus's 'Enterprise of the Indies'," *American Historical Review* 90.1 (1985): 73-102; Kay Brigham, *Christopher Columbus: His Life and Discovery in the Light of His Prophecies* (Barcelona: Editorial Clie, 1990); and Carol Delaney, *Columbus and the Quest for Jerusalem* (New York: Free Press, 2011). On Columbus's chronology of the end of the world, see West and Kling, *The 'Libro de las profecías' of Christopher Columbus*, pp. 108-09; and Rusconi and Sullivan, *The Book of Prophecies*, pp. 70-71. From Adam to the coming of Christ was supposed to be 5343 years and 318 days; adding to this 1500 years plus one incomplete year (i.e., Columbus was writing in 1501), we get a total of 6845 years since the Creation—and the world was supposed to end 7000 years after the Creation, according to a widespread medieval belief.

[30] See Nader and Formisano, *The Book of Privileges Issued to Christopher Columbus by King Fernando and Queen Isabel*, pp. 63-66, at p. 63, with discussion of the document on pp. 17-24, with the Spanish on pp. 263-65. The Spanish text is also printed in the standard collection edited by Juan Pérez de Tudela, *Colección documental del descubrimiento (1470-1506)* (Madrid: Real Academia de la Historia 1994), vol. 1, pp. 64-70, with a very good bibliography. The Santa Fe Capitulations are on ff. 11r-11v of the Library of Congress manuscript of the Privileges, with the Spanish corresponding with the passage quoted here on f. 11r.

[31] Columbus's copy of Marco Polo, with his annotations, survives and has been published in facsimile as Marco Polo, *Libro de las maravillas del mundo: facsímil del que, usado por Cristóbal Colón, se encuentra depositado en la Biblioteca Capitular y Colombina del Cabildo Catedral de Sevilla* (Madrid: Testimonio, 1986). Columbus's annotations are transcribed in the volume accompanying the facsimile, Marco Polo, *El libro de Marco Polo (ejemplar anotado por Cristóbal Colón y que se conserva en la Biblioteca Capitular y Colombina de Sevilla)*, ed. Juan Gil (Madrid: Testimonio, 1986).

[32] In the Library of Congress manuscript of the *Book of Privileges* the bull *Dudum siquidem* is on two unnumbered paper folios bound into the manuscript preceding the parchment folios. The Latin text of the bull was first published in Juan de Solorzano Pereira, *Disputatio de Indiarum jure* (Madrid: Franciscus Martinez, 1629-1639), vol. 1, book 2, chapter 24, pp. 613-14. The Latin text together with an English translation are supplied by Thacher, *Christopher Columbus*, vol. 2, pp. 162-64; and with a good introduction in Frances G. Davenport, *European Treaties Bearing on the History of the United States and Its Dependencies* (Washington, D.C.:

Carnegie Institution of Washington, 1917-37), vol. 1, pp. 79-83. An English translation is supplied in Geoffrey Symcox and Giovanna Rabitti, eds., *Italian Reports on America, 1493-1522: Letters, Dispatches, and Papal Bulls*, trans. Peter D. Diehl (Turnhout: Brepols, 2001), pp. 41-43; and the Latin text in Nader and Formisano, *The Book of Privileges Issued to Christopher Columbus by King Fernando and Queen Isabel*, pp. 400-02.

[33] On European works about India before Columbus, see Marica Milanesi, "La percezione dell'India meridionale da parte dei viaggiatori europei del '500," in Robert Geipel et al., eds., *Ricerca geografica e percezione dell'ambiente* (Milan: Unicopli, 1980), pp. 183-90; Marcello Ciccuto, "L'India del Milione: sistemazione enciclopedica di una scoperta," in *L'immagine del testo. Episodi di cultura figurativa nella letteratura italiana* (Rome: Bonacci, 1990), pp. 63-102; and James D. Ryan, "European Travelers before Columbus: The Fourteenth Century's Discovery of India," *Catholic Historical Review* 79.4 (1993): 648-70.

[34] Carmen Manso Porto, "La *Cosmografía* de Ptolomeo de la Real Academia de la Historia y su relación con Cristóbal Colón," in *Cartografía e Historia Natural del Nuevo Mundo: Libros, grabados y manuscritos en Italia y España entre los siglos XV y XVIII: V Centenario de la muerte de Cristóbal Colón, 1506-2006, Valladolid, Sala de Exposiciones Palacio de Pimentel, 12 de abril-28 de mayo de 2006* (Valladolid: Diputación de Valladolid; Fermo: Comune di Fermo, 2006), pp. 57-65; and Carmen Manso Porto, "Cristóbal Colón y el incunable de la Cosmografía de Ptolomeo de la Real Academia de la Historia," in Jesús Varela Marcos and María Montserrat León Guerrero, eds., *Cristóbal Colón y el Descubrimiento del Nuevo Mundo: Actas del Congreso Internacional 'V Centenario de la muerte del Almirante,' Valladolid, 15 a 19 de mayo de 2006* (Valladolid: Instituto Interuniversitario de Iberoamérica, Universidad de Valladolid, and Ayuntamiento de Valladolid, 2006), vol. 1, pp. 371-83. On the maps with which Columbus was familiar, see also Roberto Almagià, "I mappamondi di Enrico Martello e alcuni concetti geografici di Cristoforo Columbo," *La Bibliofilia* 42 (1940): 288-311. A map by Henricus Martellus is illustrated in fig. 5 here.

[35] Franco Machado, "O conhecimento dos arquipélagos atlánticos no século XIV," in António Baião et al., eds., *História da expansão portuguesa no mundo* (Lisbon: Editorial Ática, 1937), vol. 1, pp. 269-73, esp. 272-73; and Samuel Eliot Morison, *Portuguese Voyages to America in the Fifteenth Century* (Cambridge: Harvard University Press, 1940), pp. 5-10. Wilcomb E. Washburn in his important article "The Meaning of 'Discovery' in the Fifteenth and Sixteenth Centuries," *The American Historical Review* 68.1 (1962):1-21, reprinted in Ursula Lamb, ed., *The Globe Encircled and the World Revealed* (Aldershot, Hampshire, and Brookfield, Vt.: Variorum, 1995), pp. 49-69, offers valuable insights on several related issues, but his discussion of the meaning of the word "discovery" (pp. 12-15) does not shed any new light on the issue.

[36] See Alexander von Humboldt, *Examen critique de l'histoire de la géographie du nouveau continent et des progrès de l'astronomie nautique aux quinzième et seizième siècles* (Paris: Gide, 1836-39), vol. 5, pp. 182-85 (note). Ilaria Luzzana Caraci discusses Columbus's use of the term "otro mundo" in her article "Columbus' *Otro mundo*: The Genesis of a Geographical Concept," *Renaissance Studies* 6 (1992): 336-51; reprinted in her *The Puzzling Hero: Studies on Christopher Columbus and the Culture of his Age* (Rome: Carocci, 2002), pp. 183-201, but gives too much credit to Vespucci in understanding the nature of the newly discovered lands.

[37] See Pietro Martire d'Anghiera, *Opus epistolarum Petri Martyris Anglerii Mediolanensis* (Amsterdam: Typis Elzevirianis; and Paris: Leonard, 1670), p. 76, letter 138, and published in Peter Martyr's *The Discovery of the New World in the Writings of Peter Martyr of Anghiera*, ed. Ernesto Lunardi et al., trans. Felix Azzola (Rome: Istituto Poligrafico e Zecca dello Stato, Libreria dello Stato, 1992), pp. 46-47.

[38] This letter is in only the Paris and Genoa manuscripts of the *Book of Privileges*. In the Paris manuscript the letter to Juana de la Torre is on ff. 70r-74v; see *Christopher Columbus, His Own Book of Privileges, 1502*, trans. George F. Barwick, introd. Henry Harrisse, ed. Benjamin Franklin Stevens (London: B. F. Stevens, Chiswick Press, 1893), pp. 246-65. The text from the Paris manuscript is also supplied and translated into English in Thacher, *Christopher Columbus*, vol. 2, pp. 423-38. In Nader and Formisano, *The Book of Privileges Issued to Christopher Columbus by King Fernando and Queen Isabel*, which has a translation and transcription of the Genoa manuscript of the *Book of Privileges*, the English translation of the letter is on pp. 161-69, and the Spanish on pp. 377-87.

[39] Las Casas, *Las Casas on Columbus: The Third Voyage*, pp. 137-44 (English) and 296-302 (Spanish). The passage is Bartolomé de las Casas, *Historia de las Indias*, Book 1, chapter 181; in the standard edition of Las Casas' works, this is in his *Obras completas*, vol. 4, pp. 1266-273.

[40] Nader and Formisano, *The Book of Privileges Issued to Christopher Columbus by King Fernando and Queen Isabel*, pp. 385 (Spanish) and 167 (English).

[41] In chapter 14 of the treatise titled *Orbis nova descriptio* that follows the Ptolemaic maps in the 1508 Rome edition of Ptolemy's *Geography*, Marcus Beneventanus writes that *Mundum novum vocant ob sui vastam quantitatem*: "They call it the New World because of its great size." A similar phrase is written in the legend on the western coast of South America on the map by Johannes Ruysch that is featured in this edition. There is no indication that the lands must be totally separate from all other known lands in order to

merit this name. But there is good evidence of the modern understanding of the term "new world" by the end of the sixteenth century, in Giuseppe Rosaccio's *Il mondo e sue parti, cioe Evropa, Affrica, Asia, et America* (Florence: Francesco Tosi, 1595), chapter 24, p. 160, who says that the newly discovered lands in the West are rightly called a new world because of their great size, many islands, and also because the people, animals, trees, and grains are different from those in Africa, Europe, and Asia.

[42] Nader and Formisano, *The Book of Privileges Issued to Christopher Columbus by King Fernando and Queen Isabel*, pp. 378 (Spanish) and 161 (English).

[43] The passage in Isaiah that Columbus refers to is 65:17, "See, I will create new heavens and a new earth. The former things will not be remembered, nor will they come to mind."

[44] Juan Gil in his article "Nuevo cielo y nueva tierra: exégesis de una idea colombina," in *Homenaje a Pedro Sáinz Rodríguez* (Madrid: Fundación Universitaria Española, 1986), vol. 2, pp. 297-309, tries to make sense of this passage, but his solution is simply to deemphasize Columbus's reference to Revelation, and emphasize his reference to Isaiah—falling back on the canard that Columbus was a Jew (see his pp. 302 and 305-06). But there is no denying the primacy of Columbus's reference to Revelation here.

[45] The translation is from Rusconi and Sullivan, *The Book of Prophecies*, p. 291; in West and Kling, *The 'Libro de las profecías' of Christopher Columbus*, the passage is on pp. 224-25.

[46] The Spanish is from Rusconi and Sullivan, *The Book of Prophecies*, p. 290, and the English, with some small changes, from their p. 291; in West and Kling, *The 'Libro de las profecías' of Christopher Columbus*, the passage is on pp. 226-27. For discussion of Columbus's interpretation of this passage in Seneca's *Medea*, see Gabriella Moretti, "Nec sit terris ultima Thule (La profezia di Seneca sulla scoperta del Nuovo Mondo)," in Stefano Pittaluga, ed., *Columbeis* (Università di Genova, Facoltà di Lettere, Istituto di Filologia Classica e Medievale, 1986-1997), vol. 1, pp. 95-106; Diskin Clay, "Columbus' Senecan Prophecy," *American Journal of Philology* 113.4 (1992): 617-20; and James Romm, "New World and 'novos orbes': Seneca in the Renaissance Debate over Ancient Knowledge of the Americas," in Wolfgang Haase and Meyer Reinhold, eds., *The Classical Tradition and the Americas*, vol. 1, part 1, *European Images of the Americas and the Classical Tradition* (Berlin and New York: De Gruyter, 1994), pp. 78-116, esp. 78-88.

[47] Columbus's use of the plural, Indies, in place of the singular, India, reflected contemporary thought that India had more than one part, including, in some accounts, a part in Africa, and this usage allowed more flexibility about where exactly the lands he discovered were located. For discussion of the different divisions of India, see the editor's note in Marco Polo, *The Book of Ser Marco Polo, the Venetian: Concerning the Kingdoms and Marvels of the East*, 3rd ed., trans. and ed. Henry Yule (London: J. Murray, 1903), vol. 2, pp. 425-27; Michael Harney, "The Geography of the Caballero Zifar," *La corónica* 11.2 (1983): 208-19; and Philip Mayerson, "A Confusion of Indias: Asian India and African India in the Byzantine Sources," *Journal of the American Oriental Society* 113.2 (1993): 169-74.

[48] On the riches from Ophir, see 1 Kings 9:28, 10:11, and 22:48; and 2 Chronicles 8:18. For discussion of claims that Ophir was located in the New World, see James Romm, "Biblical History and the Americas: The Legend of Solomon's Ophir, 1492-1591," in Paolo Bernardini and Norman Fiering, eds., *The Jews and the Expansion of Europe to the West, 1450 to 1800* (New York: Berghahn Books, 2001), pp. 27-46; Gerald Arthur Ward, "Columbus, Jerusalem, and Ophir: A Voyage to the Ends of Earth and Time," in his "Restoring the Shattered World: The Apocalyptic Mercantilism of Samuel Purchas and the Revelation of World Trade" (Ph.D. dissertation, Boston University, 2003), pp. 227-48; and Jorge Magasich-Airola and Jean-Marc de Beer, "King Solomon's Mines in America," in *America Magica: When Renaissance Europe Thought It Had Conquered Paradise*, trans. Monica Sandor (London and New York: Anthem Press, 2007), pp. 53-67.

[49] On the different versions and editions of Columbus's letter on his Third Voyage, see Miles H. Davidson, *Columbus Then and Now: A Life Reexamined* (Norman, Okla.: University of Oklahoma Press, 1997), pp. 407-10. The text of this letter, together with an English translation, is supplied in Christopher Columbus, *The Four Voyages of Columbus: A History in Eight Documents*, ed. and trans. Cecil Jane (New York: Dover Publications, 1988), vol. 2, pp. 2-47; and in Christopher Columbus, *Accounts and Letters of the Second, Third, and Fourth Voyages*, ed. Paolo Emilio Taviani, Consuelo Varela, Juan Gil, and Marina Conti (Rome: Istituto poligrafico e Zecca dello Stato, Libreria dello Stato, 1997), vol. 1, pp. 59-97. On pp. 6-7 in Jane's edition, and 64-65 in Taviani's, Columbus tells the sovereigns that Solomon had sent ships to the east to visit Mount Sopora, "which mountain Your Highnesses today possess in the island of Española," and Mount Sophora, as Jane notes, is the name given to Ophir by Pierre d'Ailly, *Imago mundi*, chapter 38. Also, Peter Martyr, in a letter dated August 21, 1495, says that Columbus believed Hispaniola was Ophir: see Pietro Martire d'Anghiera, *Opus epistolarum Petri Martyris Anglerii Mediolanensis* (Amsterdam: Typis Elzevirianis; and Paris: Leonard, 1670), pp. 92-93, letter 164; also published in Peter Martyr, *The Discovery of the New World in the Writings of Peter Martyr of Anghiera*, ed. Ernesto Lunardi et al., trans. Felix Azzola (Rome: Istituto Poligrafico e Zecca dello Stato, Libreria dello Stato, 1992), pp. 70-71.

[50] These two letters of February 3, 1500, are transcribed in the commentary accompanying the facsimile of the *Libro copiador*, in Antonio Rumeu de Armas, *Libro copiador de Cristóbal Colón: correspondencia inedita con los Reyes católicos sobre los viajes a América: estudio historico-critico y edición* (Madrid: Testimonio Compañía Editorial, 1989), vol. 2, pp. 567-68 and 571-72, with good discussion of Columbus's identification of Hispaniola with Ophir in vol. 1, pp. 317-21; the Spanish text and an English translation of the letters is supplied in Christopher Columbus, *Accounts and Letters of the Second, Third, and Fourth Voyages*, vol. 1, pp. 396-99 and 400-03.

[51] For Columbus's collection of biblical passages on Ophir, see Rusconi and Sullivan, *The Book of Prophecies*, pp. 330-33; and West and Kling, *The 'Libro de las profecías' of Christopher Columbus*, pp. 244-47.

[52] The Spanish text of the letter of February 1502 is supplied in Christopher Columbus, *Textos y documentos completos: relaciones de viajes, cartas y memoriales*, ed. Consuelo Varela (Madrid: Alianza, 1982), pp. 285-88, with the passage about Ophir on p. 286. The passage about Ophir is translated into English in Djelal Kadir, *Columbus and the Ends of the Earth: Europe's Prophetic Rhetoric as Conquering Ideology* (Berkeley: University of California Press, 1992), p. 202.

[53] The legend about Hispaniola on Waldseemüller's *Carta marina* is transcribed, translated, and discussed in Gaetano Ferro, Luisa Faldini, and Marica Milanesi, *Columbian Iconography*, trans. Luciano F. Farina and Carla Onorato Wysokinski (Rome: Istituto poligrafico e Zecca dello Stato, Libreria dello Stato, 1996), pp. 526-27.

[54] Kirkpatrick Sale, in his article "What Columbus Died Believing: The True Geographic Concepts of the Great Discoverer," *Terrae Incognitae* 21 (1989): 9-16, tries to show that Columbus believed he had discovered a new continent, placing great emphasis on these passages in the letter about the Third Voyage in which Columbus says that the lands were previously unknown. But Sale's argument is flawed by his assumption that the Spanish *tierra firme* is synonymous with the modern concept of continent, and he also ignores later evidence concerning Columbus's ideas about his discoveries.

[55] The Spanish and English are from Christopher Columbus, *The Four Voyages of Columbus: A History in Eight Documents*, vol. 2, pp. 30-33. That translation is superior to the one in Christopher Columbus, *Accounts and Letters of the Second, Third, and Fourth Voyages*, vol. 1, pp. 82-85.

[56] Christopher Columbus, *The Four Voyages of Columbus: A History in Eight Documents*, vol. 2, pp. 42-43. That translation is superior to the one in Christopher Columbus, *Accounts and Letters of the Second, Third, and Fourth Voyages*, vol. 1, pp. 92-93.

[57] See Christopher Columbus, *The Four Voyages of Columbus: A History in Eight Documents*, vol. 2, pp. 80-83; and Christopher Columbus, *Accounts and Letters of the Second, Third, and Fourth Voyages*, vol. 1, pp. 134-37.

[58] See Christopher Columbus, *The Four Voyages of Columbus: A History in Eight Documents*, vol. 2, pp. 94-95. That translation is superior to the one in Christopher Columbus, *Accounts and Letters of the Second, Third, and Fourth Voyages*, vol. 1, pp. 144-45.

[59] The quotation is from Christopher Columbus, *The Four Voyages of Columbus: A History in Eight Documents*, vol. 2, pp. 98-99; I modify the translation slightly. This same material appears in Christopher Columbus, *Accounts and Letters of the Second, Third, and Fourth Voyages*, vol. 1, pp. 148-49. The passage that Columbus refers to in Pope Pius II's *Cosmographia* is identified by Major in Columbus, Christopher, *Select Letters of Christopher Columbus, with Other Original Documents, Relating to his Four Voyages to the New World* (London: Hakluyt Society, 1847), pp. 198-99; the passage may be read in full in Pope Pius II, *Descripción de Asia, Eneas Silvio Piccolomini (Papa Pío II)*, ed. and trans. Domingo F. Sanz (Madrid: Consejo Superior de Investigaciones Científicas, 2010), pp. 126-27.

[60] The Spanish text is from Nader and Formisano, *The Book of Privileges Issued to Christopher Columbus by King Fernando and Queen Isabel*, p. 373, and the English is modified from that on pp. 176-77. The most important of these modifications is supplying a translation of the word *oçidentales*, which Nader somehow neglected to do.

[61] For the relevant passage in the Paris manuscript, see *Christopher Columbus, His Own Book of Privileges, 1502*; the passage in question is on pp. 237-38, with a facsimile of the relevant folio on p. 236.

[62] The relevant passage in the Providence manuscript, which is at the John Carter Brown Library, Spanish Codex 1, is problematic. The passage is on p. 12 of the manuscript, which Helen Nader reproduces in facsimile in her *Rights of Discovery: Christopher Columbus's Final Appeal to King Fernando; Facsimile, Transcription, Translation & Critical Edition of the John Carter Brown Library's Spanish Codex I* (Cali, Colombia: Carvajal; and Providence, R.I.: John Carter Brown Library, 1992). But her transcription of the important phrase here, *segun la calidad de las dichas yslas y adelantes a todo el mundo y notables de necesydad*, on her p. 46 is incorrect: *y adelantes* is not an accurate transcription and does not make sense, and *notables* is an incorrect transcription and conveys exactly the opposite of the intended sense. What happened is that the scribe mistakenly collapsed the words *yndias oçidentales* to *ynd tale*, and

wrote *ynotas* (meaning unknown), with an abbreviation over the "t" rather than the "n." Thus the Providence manuscript does allude to the idea of the West Indies, though the scribal error renders the reference obscure.

[63] Thacher, *Christopher Columbus*, vol. 2, pp. 560-61.

[64] Fernando Colón, *The Life of the Admiral Christopher Columbus by His Son Ferdinand*, trans. Benjamin Keen (New Brunswick, N.J.: Rutgers University Press, 1959), pp. 16-17.

[65] Thacher's discussion of the question of the West Indies is alluded to by Wilcomb E. Washburn, "The Meaning of 'Discovery' in the Fifteenth and Sixteenth Centuries," *The American Historical Review* 68.1 (1962): 1-21, at p. 16, note 43; the article is reprinted in Lamb, ed., *The Globe Encircled and the World Revealed*, pp. 49-69; and by Sale in "What Columbus Died Believing: The True Geographic Concepts of the Great Discoverer," 9-16, at 11. It is unfortunate that George E. Nunn does not address this subject, though he does discuss Thacher's other contributions to the theme, in his "Did Columbus Believe that He Reached Asia on His Fourth Voyage?" in *The Geographical Conceptions of Columbus: A Critical Consideration of Four Problems* (New York: American Geographical Society, 1924); expanded edition with an essay titled "The Test of Time" by Clinton R. Edwards (Milwaukee: American Geographical Society Collection of the Golda Meir Library, University of Wisconsin-Milwaukee; and New York: American Geographical Society, 1992), pp. 54-90.

[66] For mentions of the *fin de Oriente* or "end of the East," see Christopher Columbus, *The Four Voyages of Columbus: A History in Eight Documents*, vol. 2, pp. 4-5, 6-7, and 30-31; and Christopher Columbus, *Accounts and Letters of the Second, Third, and Fourth Voyages*, vol. 1, pp. 62-63, 64-65, and 82-83.

[67] The Spanish text is from Christopher Columbus, *The Book of Prophecies Edited by Christopher Columbus*, p. 75. The translation is from Margarita Zamora, *Reading Columbus* (Berkeley: University of California Press, 1993), pp. 114-15. This same material appears in West and Kling, *The 'Libro de las profecías' of Christopher Columbus*, pp. 104-05. For more detailed discussion of Columbus as a mapmaker, see Gaetano Ferro, "Christopher and Bartolomeo Columbus, Cartographers," in *The Genoese Cartographic Tradition and Christopher Columbus*, trans. Hann Heck and Luciano F. Farina (Rome: Istituto poligrafico e Zecca dello Stato, Libreria dello Stato, 1997), pp. 93-129.

[68] Christopher Columbus, *The Journal: Account of the First Voyage and Discovery of the Indies*, ed. Paolo Emilio Taviani and Consuelo Varela; trans. Marc A. Beckwith and Luciano F. Farina (Rome: Istituto poligrafico e Zecca dello Stato, Libreria dello Stato, 1992), p. 11.

[69] This letter by Queen Isabella is dated September 5, 1493, and appears in the Library of Congress manuscript of the *Book of Privileges* on ff. 38v-39r. See Nader and Formisano, *The Book of Privileges Issued to Christopher Columbus by King Fernando and Queen Isabel*, p. 92 (English) and 336 (Spanish).

[70] Henry Harrisse, "Cartographia Americana Vetustissima," in his *The Discovery of North America: A Critical, Documentary, and Historic Investigation, with an Essay on the Early Cartography of the New World* (London: Henry Stevens and Son; Paris: H. Welter, 1892; Amsterdam: N. Israel, 1961), pp. 363-648, at 399-437, *passim*.

[71] This letter about Columbus's Second Voyage is the second document in the *Libro copiador*; the passage in question is transcribed in Rumeu de Armas, *Libro copiador de Cristóbal Colón*, vol. 2, pp. 451-52, with discussion of the map in vol. 1, pp. 163-69. The Spanish text with an English translation is offered in Christopher Columbus, *Accounts and Letters of the Second, Third, and Fourth Voyages*, vol. 1, pp. 208-11. The translation cited here is from this latter source, with some modifications in the penultimate sentence. This passage is cited and discussed by Zamora, *Reading Columbus*, pp. 111-12; and a reconstruction of the map is supplied by Jesús Varela Marcos, "La cartografía de los descubrimientos colombinos," in Annalisa d'Ascenzo, ed., *Mundus novus: Amerigo Vespucci e i metodi della ricerca storico-geografica : atti del convegno internazionale di studi, Roma-Firenze 27-30 novembre 2002* (Rome: Società geografica italiana, 2004), pp. 177-88, at 182-83; and also in his *La cartografía colombina* (Valladolid: Diputación Provincial de Valladolid, 2006), p. 59.

[72] Rumeu de Armas, in *Libro copiador de Cristóbal Colón*, vol. 1, p. 165, suggests that the *Tin d'España* is Cabo Samana in the Dominican Republic. An extensive discussion of the term may be found in Rosa María Espinosa Elorza, "Sobre el origen de algunos términos relacionados con la dirección. Un viaje por tierra, cielo y mar," *Cuadernos del Instituto Historia de la Lengua* 1 (2008): 19-43.

[73] The chart of c. 1504 that includes a scale of latitudes was made by Pedro Reinel: see W. G. L. Randles, "De la carte-portulan Méditerranéenne à la carte marine du monde des grandes découvertes: la crise de la cartographie au XVIe siècle," in Monique Pelletier, ed., *Géographie du Monde au Moyen Age et à la Renaissance* (Éditions du C.T.H.S., Paris, 1989), pp. 125-31, at 128; and Joaquim Alves Gaspar, "The Myth of the Square Chart," *e-Perimetron* 2.2 (Spring, 2007): 66-79. Reinel's chart is reproduced in Cortesao and Teixeira da Mota, *Portugaliae monumenta cartographica*, vol. 1, plate 8.

[74] For discussion of the Casa de Contratación's continuous updating of the *padrón real*, or official state map, beginning in 1508, see Alison Sandman, "Spanish Nautical Cartography in the Renaissance," in David Woodward, ed., *The History of Cartography*, vol. 3, *Cartography in the European Renaissance* (Chicago and London: The University Chicago Press, 2007), part 1, pp. 1095-142, esp. 1107-130.

[75] Previous surveys of the early cartography of the newly discovered lands include Kenneth Nebenzahl, *Atlas of Columbus and the Great Discoveries* (Chicago: Rand McNally, 1990); Guglielmo Cavallo, ed., *Cristoforo Colombo e l'apertura degli spazi: mostra storico-cartografica* (Rome: Istituto poligrafico e Zecca dello Stato, Libreria dello Stato, 1992); Osvaldo Baldacci, ed., *Columbian Atlas of the Great Discovery*, trans. Lucio Bertolazzi and Luciano F. Farina (Rome: Istituto poligrafico e Zecca dello Stato, Libreria dello Stato, 1997); and Ilaria Luzzana Caraci, "Nascita ed evoluzione della cartografia europea dell'America," in Francesca Cantù, ed., *Scoperta e conquista di un mondo nuovo* (Rome: Viella, 2007), pp. 83-160.

[76] Columbus's map of Hispaniola is reproduced in facsimile in *Documentos colombinos en la Casa de Alba* (Seville: Diputación Provincial de Sevilla; and Madrid: Testimonio, 1987), with discussion in the accompanying volume of commentary, pp. 17-19. The map is also discussed by Thacher, *Christopher Columbus*, vol. 3, pp. 88-91; Baldacci, *Columbian Atlas of the Great Discovery*, pp. 31-32; and Ferro, "Christopher and Bartolomeo Columbus, Cartographers," in *The Genoese Cartographic Tradition and Christopher Columbus*, pp. 93-129, at 108-09.

[77] On the dissemination of information about Columbus's discoveries, see Morison, *Admiral of the Ocean Sea*, in the two-volume edition, vol. 2, pp. 32-45; in the one-volume edition, pp. 375-85; and Rudolf Hirsch, "Printed Reports on the Early Discoveries and Their Reception," in Fredi Chiappelli, Michael J. B. Allen, and Robert Louis Benson, eds., *First Images of America: The Impact of the New World on the Old* (Berkeley: University of California Press, 1976), vol. 2, pp. 537-51.

[78] The first Barcelona printing of information about Columbus's First Voyage is reproduced in facsimile and translated in Mauricio Obregón, *The Columbus Papers: The Barcelona Letter of 1493, the Landfall Controversy, and the Indian Guides: A Facsimile Edition of the Unique Copy in the New York Public Library, with a New English Translation by Lucia Graves* (New York: Macmillan, 1991), pp. 51-73.

[79] On the two Basel editions of Columbus's letter on his First Voyage, see Henry Harrisse, *Bibliotheca Americana Vetustissima: A Description of Works Relating to America Published Between the years 1492 to 1551* (New York: G. P. Philes, 1866), pp. 16-17, no. 2, and pp. 43-45, no. 15.

[80] For discussion of the illustrations in the Basel editions of Columbus's letter, see J. B. Harley, *Maps and the Columbian Encounter: An Interpretive Guide to the Travelling Exhibition* (Milwaukee: Golda Meir Library, University of Wisconsin, 1990), pp. 57-59; and Ferro et al., *Columbian Iconography*, pp. 176-79 and 294-97.

[81] On Juan de la Cosa, see J. B. Harley and David W. Tilton, "Cosa, Juan de la," in Silvio A. Bedini, *The Christopher Columbus Encyclopedia*, vol. 1, pp. 213-15. His map is in the Museo Naval in Madrid, shelfmark MN 257. For discussion of it, see Ricardo Cerezo Martínez, "Aportación al estudio de la Carta de Juan de la Cosa," in Monique Pelletier, ed., *Géographie du Monde au Moyen Age et à la Renaissance* (Paris: C.T.H.S., 1989), pp. 149-62; Sandra Sáenz-López Pérez, "La Carta de Juan de la Cosa (1500), colofón de la cartografía medieval," in Ana Ros Togores, ed., *Piezas del Mes, Museo Naval de Madrid, 2003/2005* (Madrid: Museo Naval de Madrid, 2006), pp. 10-31; and Hugo O'Donnell y Duque de Estrada, "Lo colombino en la carta de Juan de la Cosa," in *Cartografía e Historia Natural del Nuevo Mundo: Libros, grabados y manuscritos en Italia y España entre los siglos XV y XVIII: V Centenario de la muerte de Cristóbal Colón, 1506-2006, Valladolid, Sala de Exposiciones Palacio de Pimentel, 12 de abril-28 de mayo de 2006* (Valladolid: Diputación de Valladolid; Fermo: Comune di Fermo, 2006), pp. 597-614. The map has also been reproduced in facimile as *El mapa de Juan de la Cosa* (Madrid: Testimonio Compañía Editorial, 1992), accompanied by a study by José Luis Comellas; and as *Carta de Juan de la Cosa: año de 1500* (Madrid: Editorial Egeria, 1992).

[82] Hugo O'Donnell, "La Carta de Juan de la Cosa, primera representación cartográfica del Tratado de Tordesillas," in Luis Antonio Ribot García, Adolfo Carrasco Martínez, and Luís Adao da Fonseca, eds., *El Tratado de Tordesillas y su época* (Valladolid: Junta de Castilla y León, 1995), pp. 1231-244.

[83] On the image of St. Christopher, see Ferro et al., *Columbian Iconography*, pp. 166-67; Hugo O'Donnell y Duque de Estrada, "Lo colombino en la carta de Juan de la Cosa," pp. 612-14; and the same author's "La carta de Juan de la Cosa: tradición y originalidad en sus aspectos decorativos," *Jornadas de Historia Marítima* 35 (1999): 75-87, at 79-80.

[84] An early manifestation of the wish to keep the discoveries in the West secret is found in a letter of Queen Isabella's that is preserved in the *Book of Privileges*: see Nader and Formisano, *The Book of Privileges Issued to Christopher Columbus by King Fernando and Queen Isabel*, pp. 92-93 (English) and 336-37 (Spanish); and Bartolomé de las Casas, *Las Casas on Columbus: Background and the Second and Fourth Voyages*, ed. Nigel Griffin (Turnhout: Brepols, 1999), pp. 89-90 (English) and 321 (Spanish).

[85] Regarding the ships on Juan de la Cosa's map, see Hugo O'Donnell y Duque de Estrada, "La carta de Juan de la Cosa: tradición y originalidad en sus aspectos decorativos," 75-87, at 80-81.

[86] The Cantino chart is in Modena, Biblioteca Estense Universitaria, C. G. A. 2, and is well reproduced in Kenneth Nebenzahl, *Atlas of Columbus and the Great Discoveries* (Chicago: Rand McNally, 1990), pp. 35-37; and better in Armando Cortesão and Avelino Teixeira da Mota, *Portugaliae monumenta cartographica* (Lisbon: Comissão Executiva das Comemorações do Quinto Centenário da Morte do Infante D. Henrique, 1960-62), vol. 1, plate 5, with discussion, transcriptions, and English translations of the map's legends on pp. 7-13. The map has also been reproduced in facsimile as *Carta del Cantino. Charta del navichare per le isole novament trovate in la parte de l'India* (Modena: Il Bulino, 2004), together with a volume of commentary by Ernesto Milano; a high-resolution digital image of the map has also been published on the CD-ROM titled *Antichi planisferi e portolani: Modena, Biblioteca Estense Univesitaria* (Modena: Il Bulino; and Milan: Y. Press, 2004).

[87] On policies to keep early modern maps secret, see J. B. Harley, "Silences and Secrecy: The Hidden Agenda of Cartography in Early Modern Europe," *Imago Mundi* 40 (1988), pp. 57-76; and Peter Barber, "'Procure as Many as You Can and Send Them Over': Cartographic Espionage and Cartographic Gifts in International Relations, 1460-1760," in Robyn Adams and Rosanna Cox, eds., *Diplomacy and Early Modern Culture* (London: Palgrave Macmillan, 2011), pp. 13-29.

[88] For discussion of images of New World parrots on maps, see Ferro et al., *Columbian Iconography*, pp. 528-35; and Renate Pieper, "Amerikanische Papageien als Symbol der Neuen Welt," in her *Die Vermittlung einer neuen Welt: Amerika im Nachrichtennetz des Habsburgischen Imperiums 1493-1598* (Mainz: P. von Zabern, 2000), pp. 245-71; a shorter version of her study was published in Spanish as "Papagayos americanos, mediadores culturales entre dos mundos" in Eddy Stols, Werner Thomas, and Johan Verberckmoes, eds., *Naturalia, mirabilia & monstrosa en los imperios Ibéricos (siglos xv-xix)* (Leuven: Leuven University Press, 2005), pp. 123-34.

[89] George E. Nunn, "The Identity of 'Florida' on the Cantino Map of 1502," in *The Geographical Conceptions of Columbus: A Critical Consideration of Four Problems* (New York: American Geographical Society, 1924), pp. 91-141; Donald L. McGuirk Jr., "The Depiction of Cuba on the Ruysch World Map," *Terrae Incognitae* 20 (1988): 89-97.

[90] The borders of the Cantino map were trimmed at some point in its history, probably in the mid-nineteenth century, and part of this western landmass was thus lost; a more complete version of this landmass may be seen on the closely related Caverio chart of c. 1504. The Caverio chart is in Paris, Bibliothèque nationale de France, Cartes et plans, SH archives 1. The chart is conveniently illustrated in Kenneth Nebenzahl, *Atlas of Columbus and the Great Discoveries* (Chicago: Rand McNally, 1990), pp. 41-43, and at a larger scale in the eleven-sheet, black-and-white facsimile that accompanies Edward L. Stevenson's study of the map, *Marine World Chart of Nicolo de Caneiro Januensis 1502 (circa)* (New York: American Geographical Society and the Hispanic Society of America, 1908). There is a color facsimile of the map that is smaller than the original: *Planisphere nautique sur velin du Genois Nicolao de Caverio* (Paris: Bibliothèque nationale, 1992).

[91] The curious and revealing name of this ocean has attracted little attention; one of the only substantive comments on it is by Duarte Leite, "O mais antigo mapa do Brasil," in Carlos Malheiros Dias, ed., *História da Colonização Portuguesa do Brasil* (Porto: Litografia nacional, 1921-1924), vol. 2, pp. 223-81, at 237.

[92] Neither the name *oceanus occiderorientalis* nor anything similar appears on the Caverio chart of c. 1504 (mentioned in note 90), which is in other respects very similar to the Cantino chart.

[93] The text and an English translation of Columbus's letter from Jamaica of July 7, 1503 is supplied in Christopher Columbus, *The Four Voyages of Columbus: A History in Eight Documents*, vol. 2, pp. 72-111; and Christopher Columbus, *Accounts and Letters of the Second, Third, and Fourth Voyages*, vol. 1, pp. 129-59.

[94] The sketch map is in Florence, Biblioteca Nazionale Centrale, Banco Rari 234, f. 60v. This map, together with those on ff. 56r and 57v in the same manuscript, were attributed to Bartholomew Columbus by Franz von Wieser, "Die Karte des Bartolomeo Columbo über die vierte Reise des Admirals," *Mitteilungen des Instituts für Österreichische Geschichtsforschung, Ergänzungsband* 4 (1893): 488-98; his article is summarized (with illustrations of the maps) by George C. Hurlbut, "Geographical Notes," *Journal of the American Geographical Society of New York* 26 (1894): 252-57. Also see John Bigelow, "The So-Called Bartholomew Columbus Map of 1506," *Geographical Review* 25.4 (1935): 643-56; and Roberto Almagià, "Intorno a quattro codici fiorentini e ad uno ferrarese dell'erudito veneziano Alessandro Zorzi," *La Bibliofilía* 38 (1936): 313-47, esp. 322-31.

[95] George E. Nunn, "The Three Maplets Attributed to Bartholomew Columbus," *Imago Mundi* 9 (1952): 12-22. A helpful transcription of the map is provided by Nicolás Wey Gómez, *The Tropics of Empire: Why Columbus Sailed South to the Indies* (Cambridge, Mass.: MIT Press, 2008), p. 213.

[96] See Nunn, "The Three Maplets," p. 21, comparing the names Nunn supplies in the column labeled "Plate 1" with those in the columns labeled "Informatione," "7th July Letter," "Las Casas," and "F. Columbus."

[97] Contarini's map is conveniently illustrated in Nebenzahl's *Atlas of Columbus*, pp. 45-47, and reproduced in facsimile with commentary in *A Map of the World, Designed by Gio. Matteo Contarini, Engraved by Fran. Roselli 1506* (London: Printed by Order of the Trustees, Sold at the British Museum, 1926).

[98] Waldseemüller's 1507 map has been published in facsimile in Joseph Fischer and Franz Ritter von Wieser, *Die älteste Karte mit dem Namen Amerika aus dem Jahre 1507 und die Carta marina aus dem Jahre 1516 des M. Waldseemüller (Ilacomilus)* (Innsbruck: Wagner'schen Universitäts-Buchhandlung, 1903; Amsterdam: Theatrum orbis terrarum, 1968), with a good but brief introduction; and now in John W. Hessler and Chet Van Duzer, *Seeing the World Anew: The Radical Vision of Martin Waldseemüller's 1507 & 1516 World Maps* (Delray Beach, Fla.: Levenger Press, 2012). An excellent high-resolution scan of the 1507 map is available on the Library of Congress website, at www.loc.gov/rr/geogmap/waldexh.html.

[99] For references on the Caverio chart, see note 90; for a demonstration that Waldseemüller used the Caverio chart in making his 1507 map, see Fischer and von Wieser, *Die älteste Karte mit dem Namen Amerika*, pp. 26-29.

[100] The translation of this passage in the *Cosmographiae introductio* is from Joseph Fischer and Franz von Wieser, *The Cosmographiae introductio of Martin Waldseemüller in Facsimile, Followed by the Four Voyages of Amerigo Vespucci, with their Translation into English* (New York: The United States Catholic Historical Society, 1907), p. 70. For discussion of the newly discovered lands as a fourth part of the world, see Carla Lois, "América quarta pars: ¿isla o continente? El debate conceptual sobre el estatus geográfico del Nuevo Mundo en el siglo XVI," *Fronteras de la historia* 13.2 (2008): 259-79.

[101] See G. C. Hurbult, "The Origin of the Name America," *Bulletin of the American Geographical Society* 18 (1886): 301-16; and Andrew M. Modelski, "Preliminary Chronology of the Naming of America on Maps," *Special Libraries Association, Geography and Map Division, Bulletin* 144 (June 1986): 40-42.

[102] On the Ruysch map, see John Boyd Thacher, *The Continent of America: Its Discovery and Its Baptism* (New York: William Evarts Benjamin, 1896), pp. 209-19; Bradford F. Swan, "The Ruysch Map of the World (1507-1508)," *Papers of the Bibliographical Society of America* 45 (1951): 219-36; Donald L. McGuirk Jr., "Ruysch World Map: Census and Commentary," *Imago Mundi* 41 (1989): 133-41; and Peter Meurer, "Der Maler und Kartograph Johann Ruysch," *Geschichte in Köln* 49 (2002): 85-104. Ruysch's map is well reproduced in Nebenzahl, *Atlas of Columbus*, pp. 48-49.

[103] On Taprobana as an *alter orbis*, see Pomponius Mela, *De situ orbis* 3.70 and Pliny, *Historia naturalis* 6.81; and on Britain, see Virgil, *Eclogae* 1.66 with Servius's comment, and Dio Cassius 49.50. Other citations are provided in the *Thesaurus Linguae Latinae* (Leipzig: Teubner, 1900-), s.v. "orbis," vol. 9.2, col. 918; there is also discussion in Veit Rosenberger, "Taprobane: Trauminsel oder der Beginn einer neuen Welt?," *Laverna* 7 (1996): 1-16.

[104] The legend on the western coast of South America on Ruysch's map is translated by Thacher, *The Continent of America*, p. 214; transcribed by Mauro Bini et al., *Alla scoperta del mondo: l'arte della cartografia da Tolomeo a Mercatore* (Modena: Il Bulino, 2001), p. 173; and transcribed and translated by Ferro et al., *Columbian Iconography*, p. 437.

[105] The legend about Sipango (Japan) and Hispaniola on Ruysch's map is translated by Thacher, *The Continent of America*, p. 215.

[106] Donald L. McGuirk Jr., "The Depiction of Cuba on the Ruysch World Map," *Terrae Incognitae* 20 (1988): 89-97.

[107] On Rosselli's maps, see Roberto Almagià, "On the Cartographic Work of Francesco Rosselli," *Imago Mundi* 8 (1951): 27-34; David Woodward, "Starting with the Map: The Rosselli Map of the World, ca. 1508," in *Plantejaments i objectius d'una història universal de la cartografia: Approaches and Challenges in a Worldwide History of Cartography: 11è curs: 21, 22, 23, 24 i 25 de febrer de 2000* (Barcelona: Institut Cartogràfic de Catalunya, 2001), pp. 71-90; and Chet Van Duzer, "A Newly Discovered Fourth Exemplar of Francesco Rosselli's Oval Planisphere of c. 1508," *Imago Mundi* 60.2 (2008): 195-201.

[108] George E. Nunn, *World Map of Francesco Roselli Drawn on an Oval Projection and Printed from a Woodcut Supplementing the Fifteenth Century Maps in the Second Edition of the Isolario of Bartolomeo dali Sonetti, Printed in Italy Anno Domini MDXXXII* (Philadelphia: Press of John T. Palmer Co., 1928), pp. 19-23.

[109] For discussion of a map on which placenames from Columbus's Fourth Voyage are located in southern Asia, see Chet Van Duzer, "Cartographic Invention: The Southern Continent on Vatican MS. Urb. Lat. 274, Folios 73v-74r (c. 1530)," *Imago Mundi* 59.2 (2007): 193-222; and Chet Van Duzer, "Un descubrimiento en la cartografía del Cuarto Viaje de Cristóbal Colón," *Boletín de la Real Sociedad Geográfica* 144 (2008): 275-80.

[110] Waldseemüller's *Carta marina* has been published in facsimile in Fischer and Ritter von Wieser, *Die älteste Karte mit dem Namen Amerika aus dem Jahre 1507 und die Carta marina aus dem Jahre 1516 des M. Waldseemüller (Ilacomilus)*, with a good but brief introduction; and now in Hessler and Van Duzer, *Seeing the World Anew: The Radical Vision of Martin Waldseemüller's 1507 & 1516 World Maps*.

[111] Chet Van Duzer, "Waldseemüller's World Maps of 1507 and 1516: Sources and Development of His Cartographical Thought," *The Portolan* 85 (2012): 8-20; and Chet Van Duzer, "The *Carta marina*, 1516," in Hessler and Van Duzer, *Seeing the World Anew: The Radical Vision of Martin Waldseemüller's 1507 & 1516 World Maps*, pp. 49-68.

[112] For a good discussion of the later development of the idea of the New World as a geographical entity, see David Beers Quinn, "New Geographical Horizons: Literature," in Fredi Chiappelli, Michael J. B. Allen, and Robert Louis Benson, eds., *First Images of America: The Impact of the New World on the Old* (Berkeley: University of California Press, 1976), vol. 2, pp. 635-58.

[113] John H. Parry, "Asia-in-the-West," *Terrae Incognitae* 8 (1976): 59-72; Folker Reichert, "Columbus und Marco Polo—Asien in Amerika. Zur Literaturgeschichte der Entdeckungen," *Zeitschrift für historische Forschung* 15 (1988): 1-63; and Marica Milanesi, "Arsarot oder Anian? Identität und Unterscheidung zwischen Asien und der Neuen Welt in der Kartographie des 16. Jahrhunderts (1500-1570)," in Adriano Prosperi and Wolfgang Reinhard, eds., *Die Neue Welt im Bewusstsein der Italiener und Deutschen des 16. Jahrhunderts* (Berlin: Duncker & Humblot, 1993), pp. 15-68.

Hessler, pp. 27 - 43

[1] Aldo Schiavone, *The Invention of Law in the West*, trans. Jeremy Carden and Anthony Shugar (Cambridge, Mass.: Harvard University Press, 2012).

[2] For more on the revival of Roman Law, see Charles M. Radding and Antonio Ciaralli, *The* Corpus Iuris Civilis *in the Middle Ages: Manuscripts and Transmission from the Sixth Century to the Juristic Revival* (Leiden: E. J. Brill, 2007).

[3] A good introduction to the full breadth of Roman law can be found in Alan Watson, *The Spirit of Roman Law* (Athens, Ga.: University of Georgia Press, 2008).

[4] For more on the later history of Roman law, see John W. Hessler, "Editing Justinian's Corpus: A Study of the Paul Kruger Archive," *Law Library Journal* 103 (2011): 459-72.

[5] Stephen Kuttner, "The Revival of Jurisprudence," in *Renaissance and Renewal in the Twelfth Century*, ed. Robert L. Benson and Giles Constable (Cambridge, Mass.: Harvard University Press, 1982), pp. 299-300.

[6] Ibid., p. 301.

[7] For more on the complicated history of the papal chancery, see C.R. Cheney, *The Study of the Medieval Papal Chancery* (Glasgow: Glasgow University Publications, 1966); and Lane Poole, *Lectures on the History of the Papal Chancery Down to the Time of Innocent III* (Cambridge, U.K.: Cambridge University Press, 1915).

[8] Walter Ullmann, *The Growth of Papal Government in the Middle Ages: A Study in the Ideological Relation of Clerical to Lay Power* (London: Methuen, 1962).

[9] John T. Vance, "The Old Spanish Code of 'Las Siete Partidas' in Mexico," *American Bar Association Journal* 17 (1928): 219-24.

[10] Mitchell Franklin, "The Place of Thomas Jefferson in the Expulsion of Spanish Medieval Law from Louisiana," *Tulane Law Review* 16 (1942): 319-38.

[11] Marie Madden, *Political Theory and Law in Medieval Spain* (Clark, N. J.: Law Book Exchange, 2005), pp. 75-81.

[12] Marcel A. Boisard, "On the Probable Influence of Islam on Western Public and International Law," *International Journal of Middle East Studies* 11 (1980): 429-50.

[13] Andrew R. Dyck, *A Commentary on Cicero, De Legibus* (Ann Arbor: University of Michigan Press, 2004), p. 35.

[14] Ioannis Lodovici Vivis Valentini, *Praefatio in Leges Ciceronis et Aedes Legum*, ed. Constantinus Matheeussen (Leipzig: Teubner, 1984), at *Praef. in Leg.*, 22-24.

[15] Georges Duby, *History Continues* (Chicago: University of Chicago Press, 1994).

[16] Ibid., pp. 17-18.

[17] For an introduction to the vast literature on charters and cartularies, see Richard Sharpe, "Charters, Deeds and Diplomatics," in *Medieval Latin: An Introduction and Bibliographic Guide* (Washington, D.C.: Catholic University Press of America, 1996). For more detailed information, see H. Bresslau, *Handbuch der Urkundenlehre fur Deutschland und Italien*, 2nd ed., 2 vols. (Berlin: W.D. Gruyter, 1912-1931).

[18] For more on the definition and range of the study of diplomatics, see Marc Bloch, *The Historian's Craft* (New York: Alfred A. Knopf, 1953), and Raymond Clemens and Timothy Graham, "Charters and Cartularies," in *Introduction to Manuscript Studies* (Ithaca, N.Y.: Cornell University Press, 2007), pp. 222-39.

[19] For more on the property charters and law in the Middle Ages, see Barbara H. Rosenwein, *To Be the Neighbor of Saint Peter: The Social Meaning of Cluny's Property*, 909-1049 (Ithaca, N.Y.: Cornell University Press, 1989).

[20] For more on forgery in the medieval period, see C.N.L. Brooke, "Approaches to Medieval Forgery," *Journal of the Society of Archivists* 3 (1965-1969): 377-86; and Giles Constable, "Forgery and Plagiarism in the Middle Ages," *Archiv fur Diplomatik* 29 (1983): 1-41.

[21] Laurent Morelle, "De l'original a la copie: Remarques sur l'evaluation des transcriptions dans les cartularies medievaux," in *Les cartularies: actes de la table ronde organisee par l'Ecole nationales des chartes et le G.D.R. 121 du C.N.R.S.*, ed. Olivier Guyotjeannin, *Mémoires et documents de l'Ecole des Chartes* 39 (Paris: Ecoles Nationale des Chartes, 1993), pp. 27-42.

[22] For a survey of the history of diplomatics, see C. Samaran, "Diplomatique," in *L'histoire et ses methods*, Encyclopédia de la Pléiade 11 (Paris: Gallimard, 1961), pp, 633-76.

[23] Jean Mabillon, *De re dipolmatica libri VI. in quibus quidquid ad veterum instrumentorum antiquitatem, materiam, scripuram & stilum, quidquid ad sigilla, monogrammata, subscriptiones ac notas chronologicas, quidquid inde ad antiquariam, historicam forensemque disciplinam pertinet, explicatur & illustratur* (Paris : Ludovici Billaine, 1681).

[24] Constance B. Bouchard, "Monastic Cartularies: Organizing Eternity," *in Charters, Cartularies, and Archives: The Preservation and Transmission of Documents in the Medieval West*, ed. Adam J. Kosto and Anders Winroth (Toronto: Pontifical Institute of Medieval Studies, 1999), pp. 22-32.

[25] Here I follow closely the presentation found in Raymond Clemens and Timothy Graham, *Introduction to Manuscript Studies* (Ithaca, N.Y.: Cornell University Press, 2007), p. 223.

[26] For the Santa Fe and Granada Capitulations, I am following, with my own modifications, the translation provided in Helen Nader and Luciano Formisano, *The Book of Privileges Issued to Christopher Columbus by King Fernando and Queen Isabel, 1492-1502* (Berkeley: University of California Press, 1996).

[27] For a detailed treatment of the negotiations and the writing of the Santa Fe Capitulations, see A. Rumeu de Armas, *Nueva luz sobre las capitulaciones de Sante Fe de 1492 concertadas entre los reyes catolicos y Cristobal Colon: Estudio instructional y diplomatico* (Madrid: CSIC, 1985).

[28] For a concise treatment of the practices and codes associated with Spanish medieval law and its evolution in the early modern period, see Nicolaas van Kleffens, *Hispanic Law Until the end of the Middle Ages; with a note on the continued validity after the fifteenth century of medieval Hispanic legislation in Spain, the Americas, Asia and Africa* (Edinburgh: Edinburgh University Press, 1968).

[29] All translations taken from Nader and Formisano, *The Book of Privileges Issued to Christopher Columbus by King Fernando and Queen Isabel*.

[30] Jacqueline Hollier and Peter Bakewell, *A History of Latin America to 1825* (New York: John Wiley, 2011), pp. 108-22.

[31] For more on the Taíno, see Irving Rouse, *The Taínos: Rise and Decline of the People Who Greeted Columbus* (New Haven: Yale University Press, 1992).

[32] Richard M. Poole, "What Became of the Taíno?" *Smithsonian Magazine*, October 2011.

[33] Jose Oliver, *Caciques and Cemi Idols* (Tuscaloosa. Ala.: University of Alabama Press, 2009).

34 Rouse, *The Taínos: Rise and Decline of the People Who Greeted Columbus.*

35 C. Gibson, *Tlaxcala in the Sixteenth Century* (New Haven: Yale University Press, 1952).

36 Nader and Formisano, *The Book of Privileges Issued to Christopher Columbus by King Fernando and Queen Isabel*, p. 47.

37 Geoffrey Barraclough, *Public Notaries and the Papal Curia* (London: Macmillan, 1934).

38 Harry Bresslau, "Papyrus und Pergament in der papstlichen Kanzlei bis zur Mitte des 11. Jahrhunderts: Ein Beitrag zur Lehre von den alteren Papsturkunden," *Mittheilungen des Instituts fur Osterreichische Geschichtsforschung* 9 (1988): 1-30.

39 For a survey of activities of the papal chancery, see Leonard E. Boyle, *A Survey of the Vatican Archives and of Its Medieval Holdings* (Toronto: University of Toronto Press, 1972).

40 Thomas Frenz, *Papsturkunden des Mittelalters und der Neuzeit* (Stuttgart: F. Steiner Verlag Wiesbaden, 1986).

41 For an interesting perspective on the history of the Washington Codex, see the article by former Librarian of Congress Herbert Putnam, "A Columbus Codex," *The Critic* 42 (1903): 244-51.

42 This is a rather complex issue and one that has not been settled by scholars. See Geoffrey Symcox, ed., *Italian Reports on America, 1493-1522* (Turnhout: Brepols, 2001), p. 10.

43 Luciano Formisano, "Philological Commentary on the Book of Privileges," in Nader and Formisano, *The Book of Privileges Issued to Christopher Columbus by King Fernando and Queen Isabel*, pp. 219-36.

De Simone, pages 145 - 152

1 Much of the information on the Washington Codex is based on an article by Herbert Putnam, the former Librarian of Congress, titled "A Columbus Codex," which appeared in the March 1903 edition of *The Critic.* In this article he outlines in great detail the history of the facts relating to the creation of the *Privileges,* the four copies that were produced and their provenance, and the gift of the Everett copy to the Library of Congress. He also makes some compelling statements about their authenticity and the methods used to come to his conclusions. Another critical reference work is Helen Nader and Luciano Formisano's *The Book of Privileges Issued to Christopher Columbus by King Fernando and Queen Isabel, 1492–1502* (Berkeley: University of California Press, 1996).

2 F. W. Meisnest, "The Lost Book of Privileges of Columbus Located and Identified," *Huntington Library Quarterly* 12 (1949): 401-06. With thanks to Chet Van Duzer for providing this citation.

3 Putnam, "A Columbus Codex," p. 248.

4 Ibid.

5 Henry Harrisse, *Bibliotheca Americana Vetustissima: A Description of Works Relating to America Published Between the years 1492 to 1551* (New York: Geo. P. Philes, 1866; additions, Paris: Librairie Tross, 1872). Future references to this work will be indicated as *BAV*.

6 Frederick W. Ashley, comp., *The Catalogue of the John Boyd Thacher Collection*. 3 vols. (Washington, D.C.: The Library of Congress, 1915, 1931).

7 Information on the life and work of Henry Harrisse can be found in three main sources: Frederick Goff, "Henry Harrisse: Americanist," *American Review of Bibliography* 3, no. 1 (1953): 3-10; Richard W. Stephenson, "The Henry Harrisse Collection of Publications, Papers, and Maps Pertaining to the Early Exploration of America," *Terrae Incognitae* 16 (1984): 37-55; and the unpublished finding aid by Rosemary Fry Plakas of the Library of Congress, "Henry Harrisse Collection, Rare Book and Special Collections Division," which contains a very useful chronology of Harrisse's life, provenance information, and a 52-page list with commentary on the contents of the collection. Plakas's guide to the collection is an indispensable tool to understanding the scope and potential of the Library's Harrisse collection. Additional information can be found in Randolph G. Adams, *Three Americanists: Henry Harrisse, Bibliographer; George Brinley, Book Collector; Thomas Jefferson, Librarian* (Philadelphia, 1939); in Henri Codier, "Henry Harrisse," in *Mélanges Américaines* (Paris, 1913); and in Henry Vignaud, *Henry Harrisse: Etude Bibliographique* (Paris, 1912).

8 See Plakas, "Henry Harrisse Collection, Rare Book and Special Collections Division," for a detailed inventory of the collection.

[9] Harrisse, *BAV,* pp. iii-v.

[10] Ibid., p. ix.

[11] Ibid., p. xlix.

[12] Plakas, "Henry Harrisse Collection, Rare Book and Special Collections Division," p. ii.

[13] Ibid., p. iv.

[14] The main source for biographical information on John Boyd Thacher is Frederick W. Ashley's "Introduction" prepared for the *Catalogue of the John Boyd Thacher Collection at the Library of Congress.* Ashley also provides a critical discussion of Thacher's study of Columbus, a discussion of the original documents that Thacher unearthed and used in his work, and an evaluation of the author's contribution to the study of the discovery of America. In 1951 Victor Hugo Paltsits wrote a short tribute to Thacher titled "The Honorable John Boyd Thacher, Man of Versatility" for *New York History,* and published one hundred copies for private distribution. Paltsits's essay focused on Thacher's upbringing, his life as a public official, his work on the Columbian Exposition, his historical writings, and his book and manuscript collection. As a young man Paltsits wrote catalogue descriptions for Thacher; much of his information is based on firsthand knowledge.

[15] John Boyd Thacher, *Christopher Columbus: His Life, His Work, His Remains, as revealed by Original Printed and Manuscript Records* (New York: G. P. Putnam, 1903-04).

[16] Ibid., p. vi.

[17] Ashley, *The Catalogue of the John Boyd Thacher Collection,* p. 13. This quote and the list of the original documents provided by Thacher first appeared in a review of Thacher's *Columbus* by Edward G. Bourne, published in the *American Historical Review* in 1904.

[18] Louis De Vorsey, *Keys to the Encounter: A Library of Congress Resource Guide to the Study of the Age of Discovery* (Washington, D.C.: The Library of Congress, 1992), p. 168.

[19] Ibid.

Biographies

Daniel De Simone was appointed Curator of the Lessing J. Rosenwald Collection of the Library of Congress in January 2000. He came to the Library after twenty-five years in the rare-book trade, principally as the owner of his own company. Mr. De Simone has organized a number of exhibitions and symposia, including *A Heavenly Craft: The Woodcut in Early Printed Books*, which was accompanied by an illustrated exhibition catalog that he edited of books from the Rosenwald Collection. He is the editor, with John W. Hessler, of *The Starry Messenger: 'From Doubt to Astonishment'* and has written numerous articles on the history of printing and the graphic arts. Mr. De Simone assumed a new role as Eric Weinmann Librarian at the Folger Shakespeare Library in January 2014. The Folger houses the world's largest Shakespeare collection.

John W. Hessler is Curator of the Jay I. Kislak Collection for the Archaeology and History of the Early Americas at the Library of Congress and Lecturer in the History of Archaeology and Exploration at Johns Hopkins University. He has written extensively on the history of science and cartography and is the author of *The Naming of America: Martin Waldseemüller's 1507 World Map and the Cosmographiae Introductio; Thoreau on Cape Cod: His Journeys and the Lost Maps; Seeing the World Anew: The Radical Vision of Martin Waldseemüller's 1507 & 1516 World Maps* (with Chet Van Duzer); *A Renaissance Globemaker's Toolbox: Johannes Schöner and the Revolution of Modern Science, 1475-1550;* and, with Daniel De Simone, the editor of *The Starry Messenger: 'From Doubt to Astonishment.'* Mr. Hessler is a Fellow of the Royal Geographical Society and a regular contributor to the mountaineering and exploration journal *Alpinist*. He is also the author of *Roman Law in Ruins: The Transmission and Reception of Roman Law from Manuscript to Print* (Franz-Steiner Verlag, forthcoming, 2015).

Chet Van Duzer is an Invited Research Scholar at the John Carter Brown Library in Providence, Rhode Island, and works on special projects in the Geography and Map Division at the Library of Congress. He has published extensively on medieval and Renaissance maps in journals such as *Imago Mundi*, *Terrae Incognitae*, and *Word & Image*. He is also the author of *Johann Schöner's Globe of 1515: Transcription and Study* (2010), the first detailed analysis of one of the earliest surviving terrestrial globes that includes the New World. Much of his work has involved the search for the sources of both texts and images on early maps. He is the author of *Seeing the World Anew: The Radical Vision of Martin Waldseemüller's 1507 & 1516 World Maps* (with John W. Hessler) and of *Sea Monsters on Medieval and Renaissance Maps*. He is currently completing a book on fifteenth-century manuscript maps that show what is supposed to happen to the world during the Apocalypse; his next project is the commentary for a facsimile of Pierre Desceliers's world map of 1550.

The Library of Congress endeavors to gather a record of human knowledge and to provide the broadest possible access to that information. Founded in 1800 for the use of members of the United States Congress, it has been open to the public since the 1870s, subsequently evolving into the "Nation's Library" and a vital resource for people around the world. Today it is the world's largest library, comprising more than 155 million items, with more added to the collections every day. Christopher Columbus's *Book of Privileges*, which has been in the Library's collections for more than a century, is one of the most valuable of the many treasures in the Library's vast collections.

The *Book of Privileges* evokes an age of great discoveries and attendant change. Many other materials held by the Library also shed light on that pivotal age. Among the more than 63 million items spanning several centuries that are in the Manuscript Division—which holds the papers of organizations and individuals both well-known and unsung—are, for example, the Harkness and Peter Force manuscript collections, which pertain to the early history of Europeans in the Americas.

Some materials collected by archivist and historian Peter Force (1790-1867) are also held in the Library's Rare Book and Special Collections Division, which traces its beginnings to Thomas Jefferson's wish to create a library for statesmen and for the people of the new nation. Jefferson's own books, which served as the foundation for the Library of Congress beginning in 1815, form the nucleus of the division. Today the division's collections amount to nearly 800,000 books, broadsides, pamphlets, theater playbills, title pages, prints, posters, photographs, and medieval and Renaissance manuscripts, with holdings that encompass nearly all eras and subjects.

The Jay I. Kislak Collection, housed within the Rare Book and Special Collections Division and the Geography and Map Division, includes nearly 3,000 rare books, maps, documents, paintings, prints, artifacts, and works of art related to early American history and the cultures of Florida, the Caribbean, and Mesoamerica. It is considered among the outstanding collections of its kind in the world.

Within the Hispanic Reading Room that the Library of Congress established in 1939 is the world's finest collection on the history and culture of Latin America, Iberia, and the Caribbean. The Reading Room serves as the primary access point for research relating to these geographical areas, their indigenous cultures, and peoples throughout the world historically influenced by Luso-Hispanic heritage. These include Latinos in the United States and peoples of Portuguese or Spanish heritage in Africa, Asia, and Oceania. The Archive of Hispanic Literature on Tape, a compilation of CD-ROMs that is part of the collection, provides a unique audio collection of authors reading passages from their own works.

Acknowledgments

The authors wish to thank Dr. James H. Billington, the thirteenth Librarian of Congress, whose support for scholarly projects like this one over the years has been unwavering. We would also like to acknowledge the hard work of the staff of the Library of Congress's Publishing Office, including its acting managing editor Margaret E. Wagner, along with Peter Devereaux and Aimee Hess Nash. Nothing like this could happen without their dedication, support, and attention to detail. Several members of the Library of Congress's Conservation Division helped to make available the Washington Codex and graciously gave their time and advice on its condition and make-up, in particular Elmer Eusman, Chief of the Conservation Division, and Maria Nugent, Head of the Book Conservation Section.

As with any facsimile, much of the work takes place with those who scan and process the images of the original documents. The authors would like to thank Domenic Sergi and Ronnie Hawkins for their patience and expertise working with this most difficult and rare of documents. Special thanks go to Mark Dimunation, Chief of the Rare Book and Special Collections Division of the Library of Congress, whose enthusiasm for this project pushed it forward and helped bring it to completion. Thanks also to Mark Manivong in this same division.

All three of us thank Mim Harrison, the editor of Levenger Press, for urging us to undertake this project, and Danielle Furci and Alfred Guerra, whose design and color correction enhance our work in wondrous ways.

In addition, Chet Van Duzer would like to thank the staff of the Geography and Map Division and the Rare Book and Special Collections Division of the Library of Congress for their help, particularly Eric Frazier in the Rare Book and Special Collections Division; as well as those colleagues who read drafts of the "Geography" commentary and offered valuable suggestions: Carol Delaney, Gregory McIntosh, Geoffrey Symcox, and Consuelo Varela.

From John Hessler go thanks, first and foremost, to Roberta I. Shaffer, the former Law Librarian of Congress and the current Associate Librarian for Library Services, whose support for a Kluge Fellowship on Roman law and several other projects helped pave the way for his interest in the legal foundations of the *Book of Privileges*. He also thanks Professor Roberto Unger of Harvard University, whose lectures and book, *What Should Legal Analysis Become?*, enkindled interest in the history of law. Dr. Unger's attempt to look at legal structures as sites of institutional imagination is a powerful tool that can be used on these most difficult of historical documents. His thanks also go to the librarians and archivists at the *École Nationale des Chartes* in Paris, whose gentle guidance in researching the difficult language of early medieval land charters was valuable preparation for the challenges of Columbus's cartulary. Thanks to Professor Aldo Schiavone from the University of Florence, whose ideas have made many realize that the history of Roman law and its transmission through the Renaissance is a history that is yet to be written. Finally, he would like to express his gratitude to Professor Okko Behrends, whose lectures on Roman law, like Cicero's *Orations*, first suggested to him that history begins with legal structures, no matter what their form.

The coat of arms featured as a drop cap throughout the book is that of Columbus. The first and second quadrants are the royal symbols of Castille and León, the castle and the lion. The islands depicted in the third quadrant represent Columbus's discoveries. Columbus borrowed the coat of arms of the Admiral of Castille for the fourth quadrant. From Henry Harrisse's personal copy of his 1893 edition of Columbus's *Book of Privileges*, which he had printed on vellum. Rare Book and Special Collections Division, Library of Congress.

Uncommon Books for Thoughtful Readers

Levenger Press is the publishing arm of

LEVENGER®

 Levengerpress.com   800.544.0880

To write your review of this book or any Levenger Press title,
please visit Levenger.com and type the book title into the Search box.

"What I began by reading, I must finish by acting."
Henry David Thoreau